PEARSON
COMMON CORE
Literature

Common Core Companion Workbook

GRADE 7

PEARSON

HOBOKEN, NEW JERSEY • BOSTON, MASSACHUSETTS
CHANDLER, ARIZONA • GLENVIEW, ILLINOIS

PEARSON

ISBN-13: 978-0-13-327108-9
ISBN-10: 0-13-327108-0
4 5 6 7 8 9 10 11 12 13 V039 18 17 16 15 14

Table of Contents

The instruction and activities in this book are organized around the Common Core State Standards for English and Language Arts.

Reading Standards for Literature 1

Literature 1: Cite several pieces of textual evidence to support analysis of what the text says explicitly as well as inferences drawn from the text.

Instruction and Model **2**
Citing Textual Evidence: Supporting an Analysis of Explicit Statements 3
Making Inferences: Supporting an Inference 9

Literature 2: Determine a theme or central idea of a text and analyze its development over the course of the text; provide an objective summary of the text.

Instruction and Model **15**
Summarizing a Literary Work 16
Determining the Theme or Central Idea of a Work 22

Literature 3: Analyze how particular elements of a story or drama interact (e.g., how setting shapes the characters or plot).

Instruction and Model **28**
Analyzing Story Elements: Setting and Character 29
Analyzing Story Elements: Plot and Character 35

Literature 4: Determine the meaning of words and phrases as they are used in a text, including figurative and connotative meanings; analyze the impact of rhymes and other repetitions of sounds (e.g., alliteration) on a specific verse or stanza of a poem or section of a story or drama.

Instruction and Model **41**
Understanding Figurative and Connotative Language 42
Analyzing Sound Devices 48

Literature 5: Analyze how a drama's or poem's form or structure (e.g., soliloquy, sonnet) contributes to its meaning.

Instruction and Model **54**
Analyzing Form 55
Analyzing Structure 61

Literature 6: Analyze how an author develops and contrasts the points of view of different characters or narrators in a text.

Instruction and Model **67**
Analyzing Point of View 68

Literature 7: Compare and contrast a written story, drama, or poem to its audio, filmed, staged, or multimedia version, analyzing the effects of techniques unique to each medium (e.g., lighting, sound, color, or camera focus and angles in a film).

Instruction and Model **74**
Comparing and Contrasting Different Formats 75

Literature 8: (Not applicable to literature)

Literature 9: Compare and contrast a fictional portrayal of a time, place, or character and a historical account of the same period as a means of understanding how authors of fiction use or alter history.

Instruction and Model **81**
Comparing and Contrasting Two Texts 82

Literature 10: By the end of the year, read and comprehend literature, including stories, dramas, and poems, in the grades 6–8 text complexity band proficiently, with scaffolding as needed at the high end of the range.

Instruction and Model **88**
Comprehending Complex Texts 89

Reading Standards for Informational Texts 95

Informational Text 1: Cite several pieces of textual evidence to support analysis of what the text says explicitly as well as inferences drawn from the text.

Instruction and Model **96**
Identifying Textual Evidence 97
Citing Textual Evidence: Supporting an Inference 103

Informational Text 2: Determine two or more central ideas in a text and analyze their development over the course of the text; provide an objective summary of the text.

Instruction and Model **109**
Summarizing Key Supporting Details 110
Determining Central Ideas 116

Informational Text 3: Analyze the interactions between individuals, events, and ideas in a text (e.g., how ideas influence individuals or events, or how individuals influence ideas or events).

Instruction and Model **122**
Analyzing Interactions 123

Informational Text 4: Determine the meaning of words and phrases as they are used in a text, including figurative, connotative, and technical meanings; analyze the impact of a specific word choice on meaning and tone.

Instruction and Model **129**

Understanding Connotations, Figurative Language, and Technical Terms 130

Analyzing Word Choice 136

Informational Text 5: Analyze the structure an author uses to organize a text, including how the major sections contribute to the whole and to the development of the ideas.

Instruction and Model **142**

Analyzing Text Structure 143

Informational Text 6: Determine an author's point of view or purpose in a text and analyze how the author distinguishes his or her position from that of others.

Instruction and Model **149**

Determining Point of View and Purpose 150

Analyzing Author's Position 156

Informational Text 7: Compare and contrast a text to an audio, video, or multimedia version of the text, analyzing each medium's portrayal of the subject (e.g., how the delivery of a speech affects the impact of the words).

Instruction and Model **162**

Comparing and Contrasting Versions 163

Informational Text 8: Trace and evaluate the argument and specific claims in a text, assessing whether the reasoning is sound and the evidence is relevant and sufficient to support the claims.

Instruction and Model **169**

Evaluating an Argument 170

Informational Text 9: Analyze how two or more authors writing about the same topic shape their presentations of key information by emphasizing different evidence or advancing different interpretations of facts.

Instruction and Model **176**

Analyzing a Authors' Approaches 177

Informational Text 10: By the end of the year, read and comprehend literary nonfiction in the grades 6–8 text complexity band proficiently, with scaffolding as needed at the high end of the range.

Instruction and Model **183**

Comprehending Complex Texts 184

Writing Standards 190

Writing 1: Write arguments to support claims with clear reasons and relevant evidence.

- Introduce claim(s), acknowledge alternate or opposing claims, and organize the reasons and evidence logically.
- Support claim(s) with logical reasoning and relevant evidence, using accurate, credible sources and demonstrating an understanding of the topic or text.
- Use words, phrases, and clauses to create cohesion and clarify the relationships among claim(s), reasons, and evidence.
- Establish and maintain a formal style.
- Provide a concluding statement or section that follows from and supports the argument presented.

Writing Workshop: Argument 191
Prewriting/Planning Strategies 192
Supporting a Claim 193
Drafting Strategies 194
Developing and Evaluating Your Claim 195
Style and Tone 196
Conclusion 197
Revising Strategies 198
Revising 199
Editing and Proofreading 200
Publishing and Presenting 201

Writing 2: Write informative/explanatory texts to examine a topic and convey ideas, concepts, and information through the selection, organization, and analysis of relevant content.

- Introduce a topic clearly, previewing what is to follow; organize ideas, concepts, and information, using strategies such as definition, classification, comparison/contrast, and cause/effect; include formatting (e.g., headings), graphics (e.g., charts, tables), and multimedia when useful to aiding comprehension.
- Develop the topic with relevant facts, definitions, concrete details, quotations, or other information and examples.
- Use appropriate transitions to create cohesion and clarify the relationships among ideas and concepts.
- Use precise language and domain-specific vocabulary to inform about or explain the topic.
- Establish and maintain a formal style.
- Provide a concluding statement or section that follows from and supports the information or explanation presented

Writing Workshop: Comparison-and-Contrast Essay 202
Prewriting/Planning Strategies 203
Prewriting/Planning Strategies 204
Drafting Strategies 205
Develop Your Comparison-and-Contrast Essay 206

Style 207
Conclusion 208
Revising 209
Revising Strategies 210
Revising 211
Editing and Proofreading 212
Publishing and Presenting 213

Writing 3: Write narratives to develop real or imagined experiences or events using effective technique, relevant descriptive details, and well-structured event sequences.

- Engage and orient the reader by establishing a context and point of view and introducing a narrator and/or characters; organize an event sequence that unfolds naturally and logically
- Use narrative techniques, such as dialogue, pacing, and description, to develop experiences, events, and/or characters.
- Use a variety of transition words, phrases, and clauses to convey sequence and signal shifts from one time frame or setting to another.
- Use precise words and phrases, relevant descriptive details, and sensory language to capture the action and convey experiences and events.
- Provide a conclusion that follows from and reflects on the narrated experiences or events.

Writing Workshop: Short Story 214
Prewriting/Planning Strategies 215
Understand Your Main Character 216
Drafting Strategies 217
Narrative Techniques 218
Organize Your Narrative 219
Conclusion 220
Revising Strategies 221
Revising 222
Editing and Proofreading 223
Publishing and Presenting 224

Writing 4: Produce clear and coherent writing in which the development, organization, and style are appropriate to task, purpose, and audience.

Instruction and Model 225
Writing to a Specific Task, Purpose, and Audience 226

Writing 5: With some guidance and support from peers and adults, develop and strengthen writing as needed by planning, revising, editing, rewriting, or trying a new approach, focusing on how well purpose and audience have been addressed.

Instruction and Model 232
Evaluating Writing with Peers 233
Revising and Editing 239

Writing 6: Use technology, including the Internet, to produce and publish writing and link to and cite sources as well as to interact and collaborate with others, including linking to and citing sources.

Instruction and Model **245**
Using Technology 246
Collaborating with Others 252

Writing 7: Conduct short research projects to answer a question, drawing on several sources and generating additional related, focused questions for further research and investigation.

Instruction and Model **258**
Researching to Answer a Question 259
Synthesizing Information from Different Sources 262

Writing 8: Gather relevant information from multiple print and digital sources, using search terms effectively; assess the credibility and accuracy of each source; and quote or paraphrase the data and conclusions of others while avoiding plagiarism and following a standard format for citation.

Writing Workshop: Research Report **265**
Prewriting/Planning Strategies 266
Ask Questions About Your Topic 267
Evaluating Sources 268
Record Source Information 269
Take Notes 270
Drafting Strategies 271
Crediting Sources 273
Creating a Bibliography 273
Revising Strategies 274
Revising to Correct Use of Pronoun Case 275
Editing and Proofreading 276
Publishing and Presenting 277

Writing 9: Draw evidence from literary or informational texts to support analysis, reflection, and research.

- Apply grade 7 Reading standards to literature (e.g., "Compare and contrast a fictional portrayal of a time, place, or character and a historical account of the same period as a means of understanding how authors of fiction use or alter history").
- Apply grade 7 Reading standards to literary nonfiction (e.g., "Trace and evaluate the argument and specific claims in a text, assessing whether the reasoning is sound and the evidence is relevant and sufficient to support the claims").

Instruction and Model **279**
Comparing and Contrasting 280
Instruction and Model **283**
Evaluating an Argument 284

Writing 10: Write routinely over extended time frames (time for research, reflection, and revision) and shorter time frames (a single sitting or a day or two) for a range of discipline-specific tasks, purposes, and audiences.

Instruction and Model **287**
Writing a Friendly Letter 288
Instruction and Model **289**
Writing a Description 290
Instruction and Model **293**
Writing a Character Sketch 294
Instruction and Model **295**
Writing a How-to Essay 296

Speaking and Listening Standards 297

Speaking and Listening 1: Engage effectively in a range of collaborative discussions (one-on-one, in groups, and teacher-led) with diverse partners on grade 7 topics, texts, and issues, building on others' ideas and expressing their own clearly.

- Come to discussions prepared, having read or researched material under study; explicitly draw on that preparation by referring to evidence on the topic, text, or issue to probe and reflect on ideas under discussion.
- Follow rules for collegial discussions, track progress toward specific goals and deadlines, and define individual roles as needed.
- Pose questions that elicit elaboration and respond to others' questions and comments with relevant observations and ideas that bring the discussion back on topic as needed.
- Acknowledge new information expressed by others and, when warranted, modify their own views.

Speaking and Listening Workshop: Present a Critique of a Literary Work **298**
Organize Your Oral Presentation 299
Organize Your Critique 300
Visuals and Multimedia 301
Presentation Techniques 302
Discuss and Evaluate 303
Self-Assessment 304

Speaking and Listening 2: Analyze the main ideas and supporting details presented in diverse media and formats (e.g., visually, quantitatively, orally) and explain how the ideas clarify a topic, text, or issue under study.

Instruction **305**
Analyzing Information from Different Media 306

Speaking and Listening 3: Delineate a speaker's argument and specific claims, evaluating the soundness of the reasoning and the relevance and sufficiency of the evidence.

Instruction **309**
Understanding a Speaker's Argument 310
Evaluating Evidence and Reasoning 313

Speaking and Listening 4: Present claims and findings, emphasizing salient points in a focused, coherent manner with pertinent descriptions, facts, details, and examples; use appropriate eye contact, adequate volume, and clear pronunciation.

Instruction **316**
Organizing Information as a Speaker 317
Presenting a Speech Effectively 320

Speaking and Listening 5: Include multimedia components and visual displays in presentations to clarify claims and findings and emphasize salient points.

Instruction **323**
Using Multimedia and Visuals 324

Speaking and Listening 6: Adapt speech to a variety of contexts and tasks, demonstrating command of formal English when indicated or appropriate.

Instruction **325**
Adapting Speech to an Audience 326
Using Appropriate Language 329

Language Standards 332

Language 1: Demonstrate command of the conventions of standard English grammar and usage when writing or speaking.

- Explain the function of phrases and clauses in general and their function in specific sentences.
- Choose among simple, compound, complex, and compound-complex sentences to signal differing relationships among ideas.
- Place phrases and clauses within a sentence, recognizing and correcting misplaced and dangling modifiers.

Using Phrases and Clauses **333**
Practice Exercises 334
Using Sentences **335**
Practice Exercises 336
Avoiding Misplaced and Dangling Modifiers **337**
Practice Exercises 338

Language 2: Demonstrate command of the conventions of standard English capitalization, punctuation, and spelling when writing.

Using Commas **339**
Practice Exercises 340
Checking Spelling **341**
Practice Exercises 342

Language 3: Use knowledge of language and its conventions when writing, speaking, reading, or listening.

- Choose language that expresses ideas precisely and concisely, recognizing and eliminating wordiness and redundancy.

Using Language Precisely **343**
Practice Exercises 344

Language 4: Determine or clarify the meaning of unknown and multiple-meaning words and phrases based on grade 7 reading and content, choosing flexibly from a range of strategies.

- Use context (e.g., the overall meaning of a sentence or paragraph; a word's position or function in a sentence) as a clue to the meaning of a word or phrase.
- Use common, grade-appropriate Greek or Latin affixes and roots as clues to the meaning of a word (e.g., *belligerent, bellicose, rebel*).
- Consult general and specialized reference materials (e.g., dictionaries, glossaries, thesauruses), both print and digital, to find the pronunciation of a word or determine or clarify its precise meaning or its part of speech.
- Verify the preliminary determination of the meaning of a word or phrase (e.g., by checking the inferred meaning in context or in a dictionary).

Using Context Clues **345**
Practice Exercises 346
Understanding Greek or Latin Affixes and Roots **347**
Practice Exercises 348
Using Reference Materials **349**
Practice Exercises 350
Verifying Word Meanings from Context or a Dictionary **351**
Practice Exercises 352

Language 5: Demonstrate understanding of figurative language, word relationships, and nuances in word meanings.

- Interpret figures of speech (e.g., literary, biblical, and mythological allusions) in context.
- Use the relationship between particular words (e.g., synonym/antonym, analogy) to better understand each of the words.
- Distinguish among the connotations (associations) of words with similar denotations (definitions) (e.g., *refined, respectful, polite, diplomatic, condescending*).

Interpreting Figures of Speech **353**
Practice Exercises 354
Understanding the Relationship Between Words **355**
Practice Exercises 356
Understanding Connotations and Denotations **357**
Practice Exercises 358

Language 6: Acquire and use accurately grade-appropriate general academic and domain-specific words and phrases; gather vocabulary knowledge when considering a word or phrase important to comprehension or expression.

Understanding Academic Vocabulary and Domain-specific Words **359**
Practice Exercises 360

Performance Tasks 361

Performance Task 1: Support Analysis of Story or a Poem........................ 362
Use Multimedia Components in a Presentation...... 363

Performance Task 2: Determine the Theme of a Story or Poem.............. 364
Discuss Responses to a Literary Text......................... 365

Performance Task 3: Analyze How Elements of a Drama Interact 366
Present Claims About a Story or Drama Effectively 367

Performance Task 4: Analyze the Figurative Meanings of Words and the Impact of Repeated Sounds 368
Discuss Responses to a Story or Drama 369

Performance Task 5: Analyze How a Poem's Structure Adds to Its Meaning 370
Adapt Speech When Performing and Analyzing a Poem.. 371

Performance Task 6: Analyze an Author's Development of Point of View 372
Discuss Points of View in a Literary Text................. 373

Performance Task 7: Compare and Contrast a Short Story and Its Filmed Version 374
Adapt Speech When Comparing a Story and a Film... 375

Performance Task 8: Compare and Contrast Historical Fiction and Historical Nonfiction 376
Bring to life a Period of History.............................. 377

Performance Task 9: Read and Comprehend Literature 378
Present Claims About a Drama............................... 379

Performance Task 10: Support an Analysis of a News Article.................. 380
Discuss an Informational Text................................ 381

Performance Task 11: Determine the Central Idea of an Essay 382
Present Claims About an Essay 383

Performance Task 12: Analyze the Interactions Among People, Events, and Ideas 384
Use Multimedia Components in a Presentation 385

Performance Task 13: Analyze Connotations and Technical Terms 386
Discuss How Connotations and Technical Terms Affect Meaning and Tone 387

Performance Task 14: Analyze How a Section Fits into an Article 388
Present the Findings from an Article 389

Performance Task 15: Determine an Author's Point of View 390
Use Multimedia in Analyzing Author's Viewpoint 391

Performance Task 16: Compare and Contrast Versions of a Speech 392
Deliver and Analyze Persuasive Speeches 393

Performance Task 17: Assess the Claims in a Persuasive Essay 394
Evaluate the Claims of a Politician 395

Performance Task 18: Analyze How Authors Shape the Same Information Differently 396
Present Claims Comparing Two Editorials 397

Performance Task 19: Read and Contrast Two History Books 398
Use Multimedia Components in a Presentation 399

About the *Common Core Companion*

The Common Core Companion student workbook provides instruction and practice in the Common Core State Standards. The standards are designed to help all students become college and career ready by the end of grade 12. Here is a closer look at this workbook:

Reading Standards

Reading Standards for Literature and Informational Texts are supported with instruction, examples, and multiple copies of worksheets that you can use over the course of the year. These key standards are revisited in the Performance Tasks section of your workbook.

Writing Standards

Full writing workshops are provided for Writing standards 1, 2, 3, and 8. Writing standards 4, 5, 6, 7, 9, and 10 are supported with direct instruction and worksheets that provide targeted practice. In addition, writing standards are revisited in Speaking and Listening activities and in Performance Tasks.

Speaking and Listening Standards

Detailed instruction and practice are provided for each Speaking and Listening standard. Additional opportunities to master these standards are provided in the Performance Tasks.

Language Standards

Explicit instruction and detailed examples support each Language standard. In addition, practice worksheets and graphic organizers provide additional opportunities for students to master these standards.

Performance Tasks

Using the examples in the Common Core framework as a guide, we provide opportunities for you to test your ability to master each reading standard, along with tips for success and rubrics to help you evaluate your work.

Reading Standards for Literature

Literature 1

1. Cite several pieces of textual evidence to support analysis of what the text says explicitly as well as inferences drawn from the text.

Explanation

When you analyze a text, think about different parts of it and how they relate to each other. Your analysis leads you to ideas about what the text means. However, you must support your analysis with evidence from the text. Even when you analyze **explicit** details, or direct statements, in a text, you must support what you are saying. You may also **make inferences**, or reach conclusions, about what a text hints at but does not say directly.

Examples

- Explicit details provide basic information for readers and are directly stated. "The storm raged outside, but the family was safe inside" is an explicit detail.
- Inferences are assumptions readers make based on details in the text, as well as their own experience and knowledge. For example, in a story about two brothers, the author might provide this dialogue:

  "All right, where is it?" asked John as he stormed into Tom's room.

  "Where is what?" replied Tom, who couldn't control his glance under the bed.

  The textual evidence of John's anger and Tom's glance under his bed support these inferences: Tom has taken something belonging to John, that this isn't the first time, and that Tom has hidden it under the bed.
- Textual evidence is information used to support an analysis of a text. You could support an analysis that the brothers don't get along by using explicit details and inferences you've drawn from their conversation.

Academic Vocabulary

explicit details information that is directly stated in a text

inference a logical guess based on details in the text, and on personal experience

Apply the Standard

Use the worksheets that follow to help you apply the standard as you read. Several copies of each worksheet have been provided for you to use with different literature selections.

- Citing Textual Evidence: Supporting an Analysis of Explicit Statements
- Citing Textual Evidence: Supporting an Inference

Name ______________________ Date ____________ Selection ________________

Citing Textual Evidence: Supporting an Analysis of Explicit Statements

Analyze a literary work to identify four important things it says explicitly. Enter those statements in the left column of the chart, below. Then, in the right column, cite textual evidence to support and explain your choices.

Explicit Statement from the Text	Textual Evidence: Why the Statement is Important
1.	**a.** **b.** **c.**
2.	**a.** **b.** **c.**

Name ______________________ Date ____________ Selection ________________

Citing Textual Evidence: Supporting an Analysis of Explicit Statements

Analyze a literary work to identify four important things it says explicitly. Enter those statements in the left column of the chart, below. Then, in the right column, cite textual evidence to support and explain your choices.

Explicit Statement from the Text	Textual Evidence: Why the Statement is Important
1.	**a.** **b.** **c.**
2.	**a.** **b.** **c.**

Name ______________________ Date ____________ Selection ________________

Citing Textual Evidence: Supporting an Analysis of Explicit Statements

Analyze a literary work to identify four important things it says explicitly. Enter those statements in the left column of the chart, below. Then, in the right column, cite textual evidence to support and explain your choices.

Explicit Statement from the Text	Textual Evidence: Why the Statement is Important
1.	**a.** **b.** **c.**
2.	**a.** **b.** **c.**

Name ______________________ Date ______________ Selection ____________________

Citing Textual Evidence: Supporting an Analysis of Explicit Statements

Analyze a literary work to identify four important things it says explicitly. Enter those statements in the left column of the chart, below. Then, in the right column, cite textual evidence to support and explain your choices.

Explicit Statement from the Text	Textual Evidence: Why the Statement is Important
1.	**a.** **b.** **c.**
2.	**a.** **b.** **c.**

D

Name ______________________ Date ____________ Selection ________________

Citing Textual Evidence: Supporting an Analysis of Explicit Statements

Analyze a literary work to identify four important things it says explicitly. Enter those statements in the left column of the chart, below. Then, in the right column, cite textual evidence to support and explain your choices.

Explicit Statement from the Text	Textual Evidence: Why the Statement is Important
1.	**a.** **b.** **c.**
2.	**a.** **b.** **c.**

Name ______________________ Date ______________ Selection ____________________

Citing Textual Evidence: Supporting an Analysis of Explicit Statements

Analyze a literary work to identify four important things it says explicitly. Enter those statements in the left column of the chart, below. Then, in the right column, cite textual evidence to support and explain your choices.

Explicit Statement from the Text	Textual Evidence: Why the Statement is Important
1.	**a.** **b.** **c.**
2.	**a.** **b.** **c.**

Name ______________________ Date ______________ Selection ____________________

Citing Textual Evidence: Supporting an Inference

Use the left column of this chart to make three inferences from the text. Then, in the right column, support each inference with textual evidence.

Inference from the Text	Textual Evidence Supporting the Inference
1.	
2.	
3.	

Name ______________________ Date ____________ Selection ________________

Citing Textual Evidence: Supporting an Inference

Use the left column of this chart to make three inferences from the text. Then, in the right column, support each inference with textual evidence.

Inference from the Text	Textual Evidence Supporting the Inference
1.	
2.	
3.	

Name ______________________ Date ____________ Selection ________________

Citing Textual Evidence: Supporting an Inference

Use the left column of this chart to make three inferences from the text. Then, in the right column, support each inference with textual evidence.

Inference from the Text	Textual Evidence Supporting the Inference
1.	
2.	
3.	

Name ______________________ Date ______________ Selection ____________________

Citing Textual Evidence: Supporting an Inference

Use the left column of this chart to make three inferences from the text. Then, in the right column, support each inference with textual evidence.

Inference from the Text	Textual Evidence Supporting the Inference
1.	
2.	
3.	

Name ______________________ Date ____________ Selection ________________

Citing Textual Evidence: Supporting an Inference

Use the left column of this chart to make three inferences from the text. Then, in the right column, support each inference with textual evidence.

Inference from the Text	Textual Evidence Supporting the Inference
1.	
2.	
3.	

Name ______________________ Date ____________ Selection ________________

Citing Textual Evidence: Supporting an Inference

Use the left column of this chart to make three inferences from the text. Then, in the right column, support each inference with textual evidence.

Inference from the Text	Textual Evidence Supporting the Inference
1.	
2.	
3.	

Literature 2

2. Determine a theme or central idea of a text and analyze its development over the course of the text; provide an objective summary of the text.

Explanation

A theme is an idea about life that an author explores in a literary work.

An author does not necessarily state the theme of a story directly. It often develops gradually over the course of the text, and the reader has to figure it out by studying the story details that develop the theme. As you read, look at what the characters say and do, where the story takes place, and objects in the story that seem important.

A good first step when thinking about theme is to **summarize** the text by restating, in your own words, the most important things it says or describes. A summary is an objective restatement of the information; it does not include your own personal opinions or ideas.

Examples

- **Summary** This summary identifies the main characters, setting, and important details of a story.

  School is out, and Lou is looking forward to playing baseball with his friends. His plans change when his mother gets a call that Lou's aunt is sick and needs someone to care for her. Lou and his mom have to leave the city and spend the summer with his aunt in a small, rural town. Lou is bored and lonely there. But his aunt's dog is also lonely and eager to play. At first Lou rejects the dog's advances, but he softens over time, and by the end of the summer, they are inseparable. Lou hates the thought of leaving the dog behind. Lou's Aunt can no longer care for her dog and asks Lou to give him a home.

- **Theme** A main theme in the story above is *friendship can be found in surprising places.* Details in the story, such as Lou leaving his friends and the city for a small town and Lou's unexpected friendship with the dog are clues to this theme.

Academic Vocabulary

theme the central message or insight into life that a literary work explores

summary a brief restatement of the important details in a work

Apply the Standard

Use the worksheets that follow to help you apply the standard as you read. Several copies of each worksheet have been provided for you to use with different literature selections.

- Summarizing a Literary Work
- Determining the Theme or Central Idea of a Work

Name ______________________ Date ____________ Selection ________________

Summarizing a Literary Work

Use the organizer to list the most important details in the text. Then use that information to write an objective summary of the text. Remember to leave out personal opinions and judgments.

Main Characters
Setting
Key Events, Descriptions, or Details **1.** **2.** **3.** **4.** **5.**

Summary ....

....

....

....

....

Name ______________________ Date ____________ Selection ________________

Summarizing a Literary Work

Use the organizer to list the most important details in the text. Then use that information to write an objective summary of the text. Remember to leave out personal opinions and judgments.

Main Characters
Setting
Key Events, Descriptions, or Details **1.** **2.** **3.** **4.** **5.**

Summary ....

....

....

....

....

Name ______________________ Date ____________ Selection ________________

Summarizing a Literary Work

Use the organizer to list the most important details in the text. Then use that information to write an objective summary of the text. Remember to leave out personal opinions and judgments.

Main Characters
Setting
Key Events, Descriptions, or Details **1.** **2.** **3.** **4.** **5.**

Summary ....

....

....

....

....

Name ______________________ Date ____________ Selection ________________

Summarizing a Literary Work

Use the organizer to list the most important details in the text. Then use that information to write an objective summary of the text. Remember to leave out personal opinions and judgments.

Main Characters
Setting
Key Events, Descriptions, or Details **1.** **2.** **3.** **4.** **5.**

Summary ....

....

....

....

....

Name ______________________ Date ____________ Selection ________________

Summarizing a Literary Work

Use the organizer to list the most important details in the text. Then use that information to write an objective summary of the text. Remember to leave out personal opinions and judgments.

Main Characters
Setting
Key Events, Descriptions, or Details **1.** **2.** **3.** **4.** **5.**

Summary ....

....

....

....

....

Name ______________________ Date ____________ Selection ________________

Summarizing a Literary Work

Use the organizer to list the most important details in the text. Then use that information to write an objective summary of the text. Remember to leave out personal opinions and judgments.

Main Characters
Setting
Key Events, Descriptions, or Details **1.** **2.** **3.** **4.** **5.**

Summary ....

....

....

....

....

Name ______________________ Date ____________ Selection __________________

Determining the Theme or Central Idea of a Work

Use the organizer below to state the theme of a story you have read. List details about the setting and the characters that convey the theme. Explain how each detail you list helps develop the theme.

Theme:

Details about the Setting:

Details about the Characters:

Name ______________________ Date ____________ Selection ________________

Determining the Theme or Central Idea of a Work

Use the organizer below to state the theme of a story you have read. List details about the setting and the characters that convey the theme. Explain how each detail you list helps develop the theme.

Theme:

Details about the Setting:

Details about the Characters:

Name ______________________ Date ____________ Selection ________________

Determining the Theme or Central Idea of a Work

Use the organizer below to state the theme of a story you have read. List details about the setting and the characters that convey the theme. Explain how each detail you list helps develop the theme.

Theme:

Details about the Setting:

Details about the Characters:

Name ______________________ Date ____________ Selection ________________

Determining the Theme or Central Idea of a Work

Use the organizer below to state the theme of a story you have read. List details about the setting and the characters that convey the theme. Explain how each detail you list helps develop the theme.

Theme:

Details about the Setting:	**Details about the Characters:**

Name ______________________ Date ____________ Selection ________________

Determining the Theme or Central Idea of a Work

Use the organizer below to state the theme of a story you have read. List details about the setting and the characters that convey the theme. Explain how each detail you list helps develop the theme.

Theme:

Details about the Setting:

Details about the Characters:

Name ______________________ Date ______________ Selection ______________________

Determining the Theme or Central Idea of a Work

Use the organizer below to state the theme of a story you have read. List details about the setting and the characters that convey the theme. Explain how each detail you list helps develop the theme.

Theme:

Details about the Setting:

Details about the Characters:

Literature 3

3. Analyze how particular elements of a story or drama interact (e.g., how setting shapes the characters or plot).

Explanation

When you analyze a text, you think about different parts of it and how they relate to each other. Your analysis leads you to ideas about what the text means. To understand the story, you must explore how different elements of the story or drama interact and shape each other as the story progresses. The **plot** of a literary work is the related series of events that moves the action forward. The **setting** is the time and location of the story. A **character** is a person or animal that takes part in the action. A character's motives and traits influence what that character does and how he or she interacts with others. Similarly, the sequence of plot events may influence how the characters behave. The setting may also affect the characters or plot.

In a drama, or play, the **dialogue** (conversation between characters) affects various elements of the work. For example, dialogue advances the plot and influences the **conflict**, or struggle the main character faces. It also helps develop characters. By carefully reading dialogue, you can see how characters react to one another and how they change over the course of the story. Noticing how characters change will help you determine the story's theme.

Examples

- In *A Christmas Carol*, by Charles Dickens, the graveyard setting shapes the character of Scrooge. The graveyard makes him reflect on death and helps him realize the seriousness of the ghost's prediction about his future. Scrooge understands the prediction for the sad truth that it is.

- Character and plot also affect Scrooge. The third spirit—a character who visits Scrooge—shows Scrooge his own grave. The spirit lets Scrooge see and hear how others view him as a miser and an unkind human being. As a result of the spirit and this plot event, Scrooge decides to change. He will no longer be a miser, and he will no longer be hated. This transformation affects the story's theme.

Academic Vocabulary

plot the series of events that move a story forward

setting time and location of the action in a work

character a person or animal who takes part in the action

Apply the Standard

Use the worksheets that follow to help you apply the standard as you read. Several copies of each worksheet have been provided for you to use with different literature selections.

- Analyzing Story Elements: Setting and Character
- Analyzing Story Elements: Plot and Character

Name ______________________ Date ____________ Selection ________________

Analyzing Story Elements: Setting and Character

Use the organizer below to analyze how setting interacts with characters in a story or drama. In the left column, enter elements from the setting. Then, in the middle column, list the character from the story or drama. Explain how the setting and the character interact in the column on the right.

Setting	Character	How the Character Reacts

Name ______________________ Date ______________ Selection ____________________

Analyzing Story Elements: Setting and Character

Use the organizer below to analyze how setting interacts with characters in a story or drama. In the left column, enter elements from the setting. Then, in the middle column, list the character from the story or drama. Explain how the setting and the character interact in the column on the right.

Setting	Character	How the Character Reacts

Name ______________________ Date ______________ Selection ____________________

Analyzing Story Elements: Setting and Character

Use the organizer below to analyze how setting interacts with characters in a story or drama. In the left column, enter elements from the setting. Then, in the middle column, list the character from the story or drama. Explain how the setting and the character interact in the column on the right.

Setting	Character	How the Character Reacts

Name ______________________ Date ______________ Selection ____________________

Analyzing Story Elements: Setting and Character

Use the organizer below to analyze how setting interacts with characters in a story or drama. In the left column, enter elements from the setting. Then, in the middle column, list the character from the story or drama. Explain how the setting and the character interact in the column on the right.

Setting	Character	How the Character Reacts

Name ______________________ Date ______________ Selection ____________________

Analyzing Story Elements: Setting and Character

Use the organizer below to analyze how setting interacts with characters in a story or drama. In the left column, enter elements from the setting. Then, in the middle column, list the character from the story or drama. Explain how the setting and the character interact in the column on the right.

Setting	Character	How the Character Reacts

Name ______________________ Date ______________ Selection ____________________

Analyzing Story Elements: Setting and Character

Use the organizer below to analyze how setting interacts with characters in a story or drama. In the left column, enter elements from the setting. Then, in the middle column, list the character from the story or drama. Explain how the setting and the character interact in the column on the right.

Setting	Character	How the Character Reacts

Name ______________________ Date ____________ Selection ________________

Analyzing Story Elements: Plot and Character

Use the organizer to analyze how plot events interact with characters in a story or drama. In the left column, enter elements of the plot. Then, in the middle column, list the character affected. Then, in the right column, explain how the character reacts to the changes in the plot.

Plot Event	Character	How the Character Reacts
Event 1:		
Event 2:		
Event 3:		

A

Name ______________________ Date ______________ Selection ____________________

Analyzing Story Elements: Plot and Character

Use the organizer to analyze how plot events interact with characters in a story or drama. In the left column, enter elements of the plot. Then, in the middle column, list the character affected. Then, in the right column, explain how the character reacts to the changes in the plot.

Plot Event	Character	How the Character Reacts
Event 1:		
Event 2:		
Event 3:		

Name ______________________ Date ____________ Selection ________________

Analyzing Story Elements: Plot and Character

Use the organizer to analyze how plot events interact with characters in a story or drama. In the left column, enter elements of the plot. Then, in the middle column, list the character affected. Then, in the right column, explain how the character reacts to the changes in the plot.

Plot Event	Character	How the Character Reacts
Event 1:		
Event 2:		
Event 3:		

Name ______________________ Date ____________ Selection __________________

Analyzing Story Elements: Plot and Character

Use the organizer to analyze how plot events interact with characters in a story or drama. In the left column, enter elements of the plot. Then, in the middle column, list the character affected. Then, in the right column, explain how the character reacts to the changes in the plot.

Plot Event	Character	How the Character Reacts
Event 1:		
Event 2:		
Event 3:		

Name ______________________ Date ____________ Selection ________________

Analyzing Story Elements: Plot and Character

Use the organizer to analyze how plot events interact with characters in a story or drama. In the left column, enter elements of the plot. Then, in the middle column, list the character affected. Then, in the right column, explain how the character reacts to the changes in the plot.

Plot Event	Character	How the Character Reacts
Event 1:		
Event 2:		
Event 3:		

Name ______________________ Date ______________ Selection ____________________

Analyzing Story Elements: Plot and Character

Use the organizer to analyze how plot events interact with characters in a story or drama. In the left column, enter elements of the plot. Then, in the middle column, list the character affected. Then, in the right column, explain how the character reacts to the changes in the plot.

Plot Event	Character	How the Character Reacts
Event 1:		
Event 2:		
Event 3:		

Literature 4

4. Determine the meaning of words and phrases as they are used in a text, including figurative and connotative meanings; analyze the impact of rhymes and other repetitions of sounds (e.g., alliteration) on a specific verse or stanza of a poem or section of a story or drama.

Explanation

Good writers choose their words carefully. They choose language that expresses exactly what they want to say and conveys to the reader how they feel about their subject. The overall attitude, or feeling, that a writer expresses about a subject is called **tone.**

To determine the meaning and tone of a literary text, you need to analyze the words and phrases the author uses, paying special attention to connotations and figurative language. **Connotations** are the negative or positive ideas associated with a word. **Figurative language** is language that is used imaginatively, rather than literally. It includes figures of speech that make unexpected comparisons, such as similes (comparisons using the words *like* or *as*) and metaphors (comparisons that describe one thing as if it were another). Writers use figurative language to state ideas in vivid and imaginative ways.

Examples

- **Figurative language** The comparison "The band played like a storm" means they put so much energy into playing that their music felt like a storm.
- **Connotative meaning** Both *confident* and *arrogant* mean "self-assured," but *arrogant* creates a very different impression than *confident.*
- **Alliteration** In "Nearly soundless, the snake slithered silently through the grasses," the use of the letter *s* emphasizes the snake's quietness.
- **Repetition** "Bang, bang, bang went the drum," creates the sound and rhythm of a drumbeat.

Academic Vocabulary

figurative language language that is not meant to be taken literally, including similes and metaphors

connotative meaning positive and negative feelings associated with a word

Apply the Standard

Use the worksheets that follow to help you apply the standard as you read. Several copies of each worksheet have been provided for you to use with different literature selections.

- Understanding Figurative and Connotative Language
- Analyzing Sound Devices

Name ______________________ Date ______________ Assignment ______________

Understanding Figurative and Connotative Language

Use the organizer to help you determine the figurative and connotative meanings of words and phrases you encounter in your reading. In the first column, record the word or phrase. Write its figurative meaning in the next column. Then, note if a word's connotation is positive, negative, or neutral.

Word or Phrase	Figurative Meaning	Connotative Meaning
1.		❑ positive ❑ negative ❑ neutral
2.		❑ positive ❑ negative ❑ neutral
3.		❑ positive ❑ negative ❑ neutral
4.		❑ positive ❑ negative ❑ neutral
5.		❑ positive ❑ negative ❑ neutral

Name ______________________ Date ______________ Assignment ______________

Understanding Figurative and Connotative Language

Use the organizer to help you determine the figurative and connotative meanings of words and phrases you encounter in your reading. In the first column, record the word or phrase. Write its figurative meaning in the next column. Then, note if a word's connotation is positive, negative, or neutral.

Word or Phrase	Figurative Meaning	Connotative Meaning
1.		❑ positive ❑ negative ❑ neutral
2.		❑ positive ❑ negative ❑ neutral
3.		❑ positive ❑ negative ❑ neutral
4.		❑ positive ❑ negative ❑ neutral
5.		❑ positive ❑ negative ❑ neutral

Name ______________________ Date ____________ Assignment ______________

Understanding Figurative and Connotative Language

Use the organizer to help you determine the figurative and connotative meanings of words and phrases you encounter in your reading. In the first column, record the word or phrase. Write its figurative meaning in the next column. Then, note if a word's connotation is positive, negative, or neutral.

Word or Phrase	Figurative Meaning	Connotative Meaning
1.		❑ positive ❑ negative ❑ neutral
2.		❑ positive ❑ negative ❑ neutral
3.		❑ positive ❑ negative ❑ neutral
4.		❑ positive ❑ negative ❑ neutral
5.		❑ positive ❑ negative ❑ neutral

Name ______________________ Date ____________ Assignment ______________

Understanding Figurative and Connotative Language

Use the organizer to help you determine the figurative and connotative meanings of words and phrases you encounter in your reading. In the first column, record the word or phrase. Write its figurative meaning in the next column. Then, note if a word's connotation is positive, negative, or neutral.

Word or Phrase	Figurative Meaning	Connotative Meaning
1.		❑ positive ❑ negative ❑ neutral
2.		❑ positive ❑ negative ❑ neutral
3.		❑ positive ❑ negative ❑ neutral
4.		❑ positive ❑ negative ❑ neutral
5.		❑ positive ❑ negative ❑ neutral

Name ______________________ Date ____________ Assignment ______________

Understanding Figurative and Connotative Language

Use the organizer to help you determine the figurative and connotative meanings of words and phrases you encounter in your reading. In the first column, record the word or phrase. Write its figurative meaning in the next column. Then, note if a word's connotation is positive, negative, or neutral.

Word or Phrase	Figurative Meaning	Connotative Meaning
1.		❑ positive ❑ negative ❑ neutral
2.		❑ positive ❑ negative ❑ neutral
3.		❑ positive ❑ negative ❑ neutral
4.		❑ positive ❑ negative ❑ neutral
5.		❑ positive ❑ negative ❑ neutral

Name ______________________ Date ____________ Assignment ______________

Understanding Figurative and Connotative Language

Use the organizer to help you determine the figurative and connotative meanings of words and phrases you encounter in your reading. In the first column, record the word or phrase. Write its figurative meaning in the next column. Then, note if a word's connotation is positive, negative, or neutral.

Word or Phrase	Figurative Meaning	Connotative Meaning
1.		❑ positive ❑ negative ❑ neutral
2.		❑ positive ❑ negative ❑ neutral
3.		❑ positive ❑ negative ❑ neutral
4.		❑ positive ❑ negative ❑ neutral
5.		❑ positive ❑ negative ❑ neutral

Name ______________________ Date ____________ Assignment ______________

Analyzing Sound Devices

Use the organizer to help you analyze the impact of sound devices in poetry, stories, or dramas you have read.

Sound Device		Effect on poem, story, or drama
Examples of Rhyme:	→	
Examples of Alliteration:	→	
Examples of Repetition:	→	

Name ______________________ Date ______________ Assignment ________________

Analyzing Sound Devices

Use the organizer to help you analyze the impact of sound devices in poetry, stories, or dramas you have read.

Sound Device		Effect on poem, story, or drama
Examples of Rhyme:	→	
Examples of Alliteration:	→	
Examples of Repetition:	→	

Name ______________ Date ______________ Assignment ______________

Analyzing Sound Devices

Use the organizer to help you analyze the impact of sound devices in poetry, stories, or dramas you have read.

Sound Device		Effect on poem, story, or drama
Examples of Rhyme:	→	
Examples of Alliteration:	→	
Examples of Repetition:	→	

Name ______________________ Date ______________ Assignment ________________

Analyzing Sound Devices

Use the organizer to help you analyze the impact of sound devices in poetry, stories, or dramas you have read.

Sound Device		Effect on poem, story, or drama
Examples of Rhyme:	→	
Examples of Alliteration:	→	
Examples of Repetition:	→	

Name ______________________ Date ____________ Assignment ______________

Analyzing Sound Devices

Use the organizer to help you analyze the impact of sound devices in poetry, stories, or dramas you have read.

Sound Device		Effect on poem, story, or drama
Examples of Rhyme:	→	
Examples of Alliteration:	→	
Examples of Repetition:	→	

Name ______________________ Date ____________ Assignment ______________

Analyzing Sound Devices

Use the organizer to help you analyze the impact of sound devices in poetry, stories, or dramas you have read.

Sound Device		Effect on poem, story, or drama
Examples of Rhyme:	→	
Examples of Alliteration:	→	
Examples of Repetition:	→	

Literature 5

5. Analyze how a drama's or poem's form or structure (e.g., soliloquy, sonnet) contributes to its meaning.

Explanation

Literary form refers to the general type or category of a work. In drama, two of the major forms are tragedy and comedy. Poetic forms include book-length epics, fourteen-line sonnets, and three-line haiku.

The **structure** of a work is the way it is built from various elements. The main elements of dramatic structure are acts, scenes, and dialogue. Elements of poetic structure include lines, stanzas, rhyme scheme, rhythm, and meter.

Examples

- **Form: haiku** The form of a haiku is suited to its meaning, as shown here:

  Ragged lines of birds,
  sandhill cranes flying southward,
  leave autumn behind.

  The poem conveys an image of autumn that suggests change. The first two lines present an image of migrating birds associated with the season. The final line is a response to that image.

- **Structure: dialogue** In a play, the words that characters speak convey the conflicts that give the play meaning, such as in the following excerpt from William Gillette's *Sherlock Holmes*:

  MORIARTY: . . . if you do not drop this case at once your life is not worth that! *(snap of finger)*
  HOLMES: I shall be pleased to drop it—at ten o'clock tomorrow night.
  MORIARTY: Why then?
  HOLMES: Because at that hour, Moriarty, your life will not be worth that! *(snap of finger)* You will be under arrest!

Academic Vocabulary

Literary form type or category of a literary work

structure make-up of a literary work, consisting of various elements

Apply the Standard

Use the worksheets that follow to help you apply the standard as you read. Several copies of each worksheet have been provided for you to use with different literature selections.

- Analyzing Form
- Analyzing Structure

Name ______________________ Date ____________ Selection ________________

Analyzing Form

Use the organizer, below, to analyze the form of poems and plays you have read and to explain how the form contributes to the work's meaning.

Title of Work and Form (such as haiku or comedy)	How It Contributes to Meaning

Name ______________________ Date ____________ Selection ________________

Analyzing Form

Use the organizer, below, to analyze the form of poems and plays you have read and to explain how the form contributes to the work's meaning.

Title of Work and Form (such as haiku or comedy)	How It Contributes to Meaning

Name ______________________ Date ____________ Selection ________________

Analyzing Form

Use the organizer, below, to analyze the form of poems and plays you have read and to explain how the form contributes to the work's meaning.

Title of Work and Form (such as haiku or comedy)	How It Contributes to Meaning

Name ______________________ Date ______________ Selection ____________________

Analyzing Form

Use the organizer, below, to analyze the form of poems and plays you have read and to explain how the form contributes to the work's meaning.

Title of Work and Form (such as haiku or comedy)	How It Contributes to Meaning

Name ______________________ Date ______________ Selection ____________________

Analyzing Form

Use the organizer, below, to analyze the form of poems and plays you have read and to explain how the form contributes to the work's meaning.

Title of Work and Form (such as haiku or comedy)	How It Contributes to Meaning

Name ______________________ Date ____________ Selection ________________

Analyzing Form

Use the organizer, below, to analyze the form of poems and plays you have read and to explain how the form contributes to the work's meaning.

Title of Work and Form (such as haiku or comedy)	How It Contributes to Meaning

Name ______________________ Date ______________ Selection ____________________

Analyzing Structure

Use the organizer, below, to analyze the structure of poems and plays you have read and to explain how structural elements add to a work's meaning.

Title of Work and Structural Element (such as a poetic line or a passage of dialogue)	How It Contributes to Meaning

Name _______________ Date _______________ Selection _______________

Analyzing Structure

Use the organizer, below, to analyze the structure of poems and plays you have read and to explain how structural elements add to a work's meaning.

Title of Work and Structural Element (such as a poetic line or a passage of dialogue)	How It Contributes to Meaning

Name ______________________ Date ____________ Selection ________________

Analyzing Structure

Use the organizer, below, to analyze the structure of poems and plays you have read and to explain how structural elements add to a work's meaning.

Title of Work and Structural Element (such as a poetic line or a passage of dialogue)	How It Contributes to Meaning

Name ______________________ Date ____________ Selection ________________

Analyzing Structure

Use the organizer, below, to analyze the structure of poems and plays you have read and to explain how structural elements add to a work's meaning.

Title of Work and Structural Element (such as a poetic line or a passage of dialogue)	How It Contributes to Meaning

Name ______________________ Date ____________ Selection ________________

Analyzing Structure

Use the organizer, below, to analyze the structure of poems and plays you have read and to explain how structural elements add to a work's meaning.

Title of Work and Structural Element (such as a poetic line or a passage of dialogue)	How It Contributes to Meaning

Name ______________________ Date ____________ Selection ________________

Analyzing Structure

Use the organizer, below, to analyze the structure of poems and plays you have read and to explain how structural elements add to a work's meaning.

Title of Work and Structural Element (such as a poetic line or a passage of dialogue)	How It Contributes to Meaning

Literature 6

6. Analyze how an author develops and contrasts the points of view of different characters or narrators in a text.

Explanation

Authors develop the viewpoints of the narrator and characters in their stories through the details they give about these characters. By telling what a character says, does, and thinks, as well as what others say about this person, the author reveals important information about the character's traits and motivations. You can contrast the viewpoints of different characters by paying attention to the varying kinds of information provided about each of them.

Dialogue, or conversation between characters, is one element writers use to establish characters' differing points of view. What characters say reveals their attitudes, interests, and values. The characters' word choices and speech patterns give clues about their personalities. Dialogue can show how two characters see things very differently.

Examples

- Stories about sisters or brothers who have conflicts with one another often include contrasting points of view. For example, older sister Sylvia is a budding artist and younger sister Christina is an athlete. Conflict occurs when these two share a room. Their different viewpoints affect everything from which posters to put on the walls to where to place the beds. The author develops the sisters' different qualities through details in each character's speech, thoughts, and actions. The girls' points of view are also revealed by what each character says about the other.
- Stories of friendship between people from different cultures provide a chance to examine contrasting points of view. For example, the dialogue between an American boy and an exchange student from Lithuania might reveal that each boy has had different experiences and values different things.

Academic Vocabulary

point of view is the perspective from which a story is told

dialogue conversation between characters

Apply the Standard

Use the worksheet that follows to help you apply the standard as you read. Several copies have been provided for you to use with different literature selections.

- Analyzing Point of View

Name ________________ Date ____________ Assignment ____________

Analyzing Point of View

Use the organizer to analyze the points of view of different characters in a selection.

Character 1:	**Character 2:**
Detail 1	Detail 1
Detail 2	Detail 2
Detail 3	Detail 3
Point of View:	**Point of View:**

Name ______________________ Date ____________ Assignment ______________

Analyzing Point of View

Use the organizer to analyze the points of view of different characters in a selection.

Character 1:	Character 2:
Detail 1	Detail 1
Detail 2	Detail 2
Detail 2	Detail 2
Point of View:	**Point of View:**

Name ______________________ Date ______________ Assignment ______________

Analyzing Point of View

Use the organizer to analyze the points of view of different characters in a selection.

Character 1:	**Character 2:**
Detail 1	Detail 1
Detail 2	Detail 2
Detail 3	Detail 3
Point of View:	**Point of View:**

C

For use with Literature 6

Name ______________________ Date ____________ Assignment ______________

Analyzing Point of View

Use the organizer to analyze the points of view of different characters in a selection.

Character 1:	**Character 2:**
Detail 1	Detail 1
Detail 2	Detail 2
Detail 3	Detail 3
Point of View:	**Point of View:**

Name ______________________ Date ____________ Assignment ______________

Analyzing Point of View

Use the organizer to analyze the points of view of different characters in a selection.

Character 1:	**Character 2:**
Detail 1	Detail 1
Detail 2	Detail 2
Detail 3	Detail 3
Point of View:	**Point of View:**

Name ______________________ Date ____________ Assignment ______________

Analyzing Point of View

Use the organizer to analyze the points of view of different characters in a selection.

Character 1:	**Character 2:**
Detail 1	Detail 1
Detail 2	Detail 2
Detail 3	Detail 3
Point of View:	**Point of View:**

Literature 7

7. Compare and contrast a written story, drama, or poem to its audio, filmed, staged, or multimedia version, analyzing the effects of techniques unique to each medium (e.g., lighting, sound, color or camera focus and angles in a film).

Explanation

Many works of literature appear in other media **formats,** including audio recording, film, live performance on stage, or multimedia presentation. These formats have the advantage of using various **techniques** that are not possible in written text, such as lighting, sound, color, camera focus, or camera angles. The techniques used to create each format contribute to your experience as you listen to or watch a presentation. When you compare your experience of reading a text to the alternative formats, pay attention to how the techniques influence your experience and understanding of the text.

Examples

- **Sound** is often used to emphasize what is happening in a story, to build suspense or excitement, or reflect a mood.
- **Lighting** is also used to express mood. For example, a shadowy scene can create a sense of menace.
- **Color** can heighten drama or be part of characterization. For example, filmmakers often dress a character in bright colors to call attention to him or her.
- **Camera angles** give the viewer a point of view. For example, a camera at a high angle looks down, making a character appear small. A low angle looks up at a character and makes him or her look powerful.
- **Camera focus** affects both characters and the setting. A close-up gives you a view of a character's facial expression. A long shot provides a wide view of a scene. The camera focus can establish where things are by showing the distance between characters.

Academic Vocabulary

format the way something is presented

technique the procedure used in a task

Apply the Standard

Use the worksheet that follows to help you apply the standard as you read literature selections. Several copies of the worksheet have been provided for you.

- Comparing and Contrasting Different Formats

Name ______________________ Date ____________ Selection ________________

Comparing and Contrasting Different Formats

Use the organizer to help you compare and contrast a written text with an alternate format. First, analyze the effect of the techniques used in the alternate format. Then you will compare the written format with the alternate format.

Name of Text: ....

Alternate format (audio, film, stage version, or multimedia): ....

Technique	Effect of Technique
sound	
lighting	
color	
camera angles	
camera focus	

In which ways are the written format and the alternate format alike?

....

....

In which ways are they different?

....

....

Which format do you prefer? Why?

....

....

Name ______________________ Date ____________ Selection ________________

Comparing and Contrasting Different Formats

Use the organizer to help you compare and contrast a written text with an alternate format. First, analyze the effect of the techniques used in the alternate format. Then you will compare the written format with the alternate format.

Name of Text: ....

Alternate format (audio, film, stage version, or multimedia): ....

Technique	Effect of Technique
sound	
lighting	
color	
camera angles	
camera focus	

In which ways are the written format and the alternate format alike?

....

....

In which ways are they different?

....

....

Which format do you prefer? Why?

....

....

Name ______________________ Date ____________ Selection ________________

Comparing and Contrasting Different Formats

Use the organizer to help you compare and contrast a written text with an alternate format. First, analyze the effect of the techniques used in the alternate format. Then you will compare the written format with the alternate format.

Name of Text: ....

Alternate format (audio, film, stage version, or multimedia): ....

Technique	Effect of Technique
sound	
lighting	
color	
camera angles	
camera focus	

In which ways are the written format and the alternate format alike?

....

....

In which ways are they different?

....

....

Which format do you prefer? Why?

....

....

Name ________________ Date ____________ Selection ________________

Comparing and Contrasting Different Formats

Use the organizer to help you compare and contrast a written text with an alternate format. First, analyze the effect of the techniques used in the alternate format. Then you will compare the written format with the alternate format.

Name of Text: ....

Alternate format (audio, film, stage version, or multimedia): ....

Technique	Effect of Technique
sound	
lighting	
color	
camera angles	
camera focus	

In which ways are the written format and the alternate format alike?

....

....

In which ways are they different?

....

....

Which format do you prefer? Why?

....

....

Name ______________________ Date ____________ Selection __________________

Comparing and Contrasting Different Formats

Use the organizer to help you compare and contrast a written text with an alternate format. First, analyze the effect of the techniques used in the alternate format. Then you will compare the written format with the alternate format.

Name of Text: ....

Alternate format (audio, film, stage version, or multimedia): ....

Technique	Effect of Technique
sound	
lighting	
color	
camera angles	
camera focus	

In which ways are the written format and the alternate format alike?

....

....

In which ways are they different?

....

....

Which format do you prefer? Why?

....

....

Name ________________ Date ____________ Selection ________________

Comparing and Contrasting Different Formats

Use the organizer to help you compare and contrast a written text with an alternate format. First, analyze the effect of the techniques used in the alternate format. Then you will compare the written format with the alternate format.

Name of Text: ....

Alternate format (audio, film, stage version, or multimedia): ....

Technique	Effect of Technique
sound	
lighting	
color	
camera angles	
camera focus	

In which ways are the written format and the alternate format alike?

....

....

In which ways are they different?

....

....

Which format do you prefer? Why?

....

....

Literature 9

9. Compare and contrast a fictional portrayal of a time, place, or character and a historical account of the same period as a means of understanding how authors of fiction use or alter history.

Explanation

There are two broad categories of writing: **fiction** and **nonfiction**. Fiction tells an imaginary story and is generally written to entertain. Fiction includes such forms as novels and short stories. Nonfiction tells about real people, places, and events. It is often written to convey factual information. Types of nonfiction include articles, essays, and biographies.

Legends blend fact and fiction. A **legend** is a traditional story about the past. Most legends center on people of heroic accomplishments, but they usually have some basis in historical facts. Every culture has its own legends to immortalize famous people, and the various stories reflect the cultures that created them.

Examples

- **Historical Account.** "Tenochtitlan, Inside the Aztec Capital," is a factual and historical account of how the Aztecs designed their city to prevent crop damage and protect against flooding. The information in the essay was researched and documented to ensure its accuracy. The essay blends description, eyewitness accounts, maps, photographs, and art to give readers a sense of what it took to build the city. Individual sections report on farming techniques, family structure, differences between the rich and the poor, and other topics.
- **Fictional Portrayal.** "Popocatepetl and Ixtlaccihuatl" is a modern retelling of a legend that blends fact and fiction to explain how two mountains near Tenochtitlan were formed. It draws upon historical facts to convey the magnificence of Tenochtitlan. Reflecting the gulf between rich and poor mentioned in the historical account of Tenochtitlan, the imaginary emperor in the legend refused to allow his daughter to marry the man she loved. The ill-fated lovers died and were buried under two large stones. According to legend, those stones grew into the two white-capped mountains near present-day Mexico City. Geological facts are changed to suit the story.

Academic Vocabulary

fiction prose writing that tells an imaginary story

nonfiction writing that tells about real people, places, and events in a factual manner

legend a traditional story about the past

Apply the Standard

Use the worksheet that follows to help you apply the standard as you read. Several copies of the worksheet have been provided for you to use with different literature selections.

- Comparing and Contrasting Two Texts

Name ______________________ Date ______________ Selection ____________________

Comparing and Contrasting Two Texts

First enter important facts from a historical account; then explain briefly how the facts are used or changed in a legend on the same subject.

Facts from a Historical Account	How Facts Are Used or Changed in a Legend

Name _______________ Date _______________ Selection _______________

Comparing and Contrasting Two Texts

First enter important facts from a historical account; then explain briefly how the facts are used or changed in a legend on the same subject.

Facts from a Historical Account	How Facts Are Used or Changed in a Legend

Name ______________________ Date ____________ Selection ________________

Comparing and Contrasting Two Texts

First enter important facts from a historical account; then explain briefly how the facts are used or changed in a legend on the same subject.

Facts from a Historical Account	How Facts Are Used or Changed in a Legend

Name ____________________ Date ____________ Selection ________________

Comparing and Contrasting Two Texts

First enter important facts from a historical account; then explain briefly how the facts are used or changed in a legend on the same subject.

Facts from a Historical Account	How Facts Are Used or Changed in a Legend

Name ______________________ Date ______________ Selection ____________________

Comparing and Contrasting Two Texts

First enter important facts from a historical account; then explain briefly how the facts are used or changed in a legend on the same subject.

Facts from a Historical Account	How Facts Are Used or Changed in a Legend

Name ______________________ Date ______________ Selection ____________________

Comparing and Contrasting Two Texts

First enter important facts from a historical account; then explain briefly how the facts are used or changed in a legend on the same subject.

Facts from a Historical Account	How Facts Are Used or Changed in a Legend

Literature 10

10. By the end of the year, read and comprehend literature, including stories, dramas, and poems, in the grades 6–8 text complexity band proficiently, with scaffolding as needed at the high end of the range.

Explanation

Some works of literature have more **complexity** than others. Complexity is the difficulty level of a work of any kind. Some stories, dramas, and poems are less complex than others—they have familiar subjects, use directly stated ideas and themes, and have a simple style that uses conversational vocabulary and short sentences. Others literary selections, however, are more complex because they introduce unfamiliar concepts, have implied ideas and themes, and include advanced vocabulary, figurative language, and long sentences.

You will read literary works in different genres, including stories, dramas, and poems. You will also be expected to **comprehend,** or understand the meaning and importance of, more complex texts than you have read before. To comprehend complex texts, use reading strategies such as the ones below.

Examples

- **Monitor** your comprehension as you read by stopping periodically to ask yourself questions about what you have read. For example, in Ernest Hemingway's story "A Day's Wait," stop to ask yourself why the boy does not want anybody to stay in the room with him. Then **reread** or read ahead to find out why he feels this way.
- In the same story, use **context clues** to understand the boy's confusion between 102 degrees and 44 degrees on two different scales of measurement. You can figure out that the boy heard that 44 degrees is dangerous, but that the scale used was Centigrade, not the Fahrenheit scale that the doctor used. His father clears up the confusion by explaining that it is like miles and kilometers, meaning that two different scales of measurement are being used.
- **Summarize** sections of the story. You will notice that in each summary, the boy is staring at the foot of his bed and seems to be holding himself tightly. These summaries will help you understand the mood of the boy and the intensity of his feelings of worry about being sick.

Academic Vocabulary

complexity the degree to which a story, poem, drama, or other work is difficult to understand

comprehend understand the meaning and importance of something

Apply the Standard

Use the worksheet that follows to help you apply the standard as you read literature selections. Several copies of the worksheet have been provided for you.

- Comprehending Complex Texts

Name ______________________ Date ____________ Selection ________________

Comprehending Complex Texts

Explain what makes the story, poem, drama, or other selection you are reading complex. Then explain how the strategy on the left in the chart helps you comprehend the selection.

What makes this selection complex?

....

....

Strategy	How the Strategy Helped Me Comprehend the Selection
monitoring comprehension	
using context	
summarizing	
Rereading	

A

Name ______________________ Date ______________ Selection ______________________

Comprehending Complex Texts

Explain what makes the story, poem, drama, or other selection you are reading complex. Then explain how the strategy on the left in the chart helps you comprehend the selection.

What makes this selection complex?

....

....

Strategy	How the Strategy Helped Me Comprehend the Selection
monitoring comprehension	
using context	
summarizing	
Rereading	

Name ______________________ Date ____________ Selection ________________

Comprehending Complex Texts

Explain what makes the story, poem, drama, or other selection you are reading complex. Then explain how the strategy on the left in the chart helps you comprehend the selection.

What makes this selection complex?

....

....

Strategy	How the Strategy Helped Me Comprehend the Selection
monitoring comprehension	
using context	
summarizing	
Rereading	

Name ______________________ Date ______________ Selection ______________________

Comprehending Complex Texts

Explain what makes the story, poem, drama, or other selection you are reading complex. Then explain how the strategy on the left in the chart helps you comprehend the selection.

What makes this selection complex?

....

....

Strategy	How the Strategy Helped Me Comprehend the Selection
monitoring comprehension	
using context	
summarizing	
Rereading	

Name ______________________ Date ______________ Selection ____________________

Comprehending Complex Texts

Explain what makes the story, poem, drama, or other selection you are reading complex. Then explain how the strategy on the left in the chart helps you comprehend the selection.

What makes this selection complex?

....

....

Strategy	How the Strategy Helped Me Comprehend the Selection
monitoring comprehension	
using context	
summarizing	
Rereading	

Name ______________________ Date ____________ Selection ________________

Comprehending Complex Texts

Explain what makes the story, poem, drama, or other selection you are reading complex. Then explain how the strategy on the left in the chart helps you comprehend the selection.

What makes this selection complex?

....

....

Strategy	How the Strategy Helped Me Comprehend the Selection
monitoring comprehension	
using context	
summarizing	
Rereading	

F

Reading Standards for Informational Texts

Informational Text 1

1. Cite several pieces of textual evidence to support analysis of what the text says explicitly as well as inferences drawn from the text.

Explanation

When you read informational texts, you think about different parts of it and how they relate to each other. Your analysis leads you to ideas about what the text means. However, you must support your ideas with evidence from the text. Even when you analyze explicit details, or direct statements, in a text, you must support what you are saying.

You may also **make inferences**, or reach conclusions, about what a text hints at but does not say directly. It is important to support an inference with evidence from the text that will convince others your inference is correct.

Examples

- **Explicit details** provide basic information for readers and are directly stated. For example, "Dwight D Eisenhower was the 34th president of the United States" and "He served as president from 1953–1961" are explicit details.
- **Inferences** are logical guesses readers make based on details in the text and their own personal experience and knowledge. For example, the author might also say the following about President Eisenhower: "As a five-star general, Eisenhower led the Allied forces against Germany during World War II and became the first commander of NATO. As president, he worked with China to negotiate the end to the Korean war." Although the text doesn't explicitly say it, you can infer that Eisenhower was a successful leader and respected for his leadership.
- **Textual evidence** consists of examples from the text used to support a response or analysis. For example, you could support an opinion that Eisenhower had a successful military career by citing the evidence that he was a five-star general and led the Allied forces during World War II.

Academic Vocabulary

explicit details information that is directly stated in the text

inference logical guess based on details in the text as well as personal experience

textual evidence words or phrases that support an analysis

Apply the Standard

Use the worksheets that follow to help you apply the standard as you read. Several copies of each worksheet have been provided for you to use with different informational texts.

- Identifying Textual Evidence
- Citing Textual Evidence: Supporting an Inference

Name ______________________ Date ______________ Assignment ________________

Identifying Textual Evidence

Analyze an informational text to identify four important things it says explicitly. Enter those statements in the left column of the chart, below. Then, in the right column, cite textual evidence to support and explain your choices. Cite 3 or more pieces of text evidence for each analysis.

What the Text States Explicitly	Textual Evidence: Why the Statement Is Important
1.	**a.** **b.** **c.**
2.	**a.** **b.** **c.**

Name _______________ Date _______________ Assignment _______________

Identifying Textual Evidence

Analyze an informational text to identify four important things it says explicitly. Enter those statements in the left column of the chart, below. Then, in the right column, cite textual evidence to support and explain your choices. Cite 3 or more pieces of text evidence for each analysis.

What the Text States Explicitly	Textual Evidence: Why the Statement Is Important
1.	**a.** **b.** **c.**
2.	**a.** **b.** **c.**

Name ______________________ Date ____________ Assignment ________________

Identifying Textual Evidence

Analyze an informational text to identify four important things it says explicitly. Enter those statements in the left column of the chart, below. Then, in the right column, cite textual evidence to support and explain your choices. Cite 3 or more pieces of text evidence for each analysis.

What the Text States Explicitly	Textual Evidence: Why the Statement Is Important
1.	**a.** **b.** **c.**
2.	**a.** **b.** **c.**

Name ______________________ Date ______________ Assignment ____________________

Identifying Textual Evidence

Analyze an informational text to identify four important things it says explicitly. Enter those statements in the left column of the chart, below. Then, in the right column, cite textual evidence to support and explain your choices. Cite 3 or more pieces of text evidence for each analysis.

What the Text States Explicitly	Textual Evidence: Why the Statement Is Important
1.	**a.** **b.** **c.**
2.	**a.** **b.** **c.**

Name ______________________ Date ______________ Assignment ________________

Identifying Textual Evidence

Analyze an informational text to identify four important things it says explicitly. Enter those statements in the left column of the chart, below. Then, in the right column, cite textual evidence to support and explain your choices. Cite 3 or more pieces of text evidence for each analysis.

What the Text States Explicitly	Textual Evidence: Why the Statement Is Important
1.	**a.** **b.** **c.**
2.	**a.** **b.** **c.**

Name ______________________ Date ______________ Assignment ________________

Identifying Textual Evidence

Analyze an informational text to identify four important things it says explicitly. Enter those statements in the left column of the chart, below. Then, in the right column, cite textual evidence to support and explain your choices. Cite 3 or more pieces of text evidence for each analysis.

What the Text States Explicitly	Textual Evidence: Why the Statement Is Important
1.	**a.** **b.** **c.**
2.	**a.** **b.** **c.**

Name ______________________ Date ____________ Assignment ________________

Citing Textual Evidence: Supporting an Inference

Use this chart to make inferences from the text. Combine details you have gathered from the text with your own knowledge or experience to make inferences.

Details from the Text	Inferences from Text
1.	
2.	
3.	
4.	

Name ______________________ Date ____________ Assignment ________________

Citing Textual Evidence: Supporting an Inference

Use this chart to make inferences from the text. Combine details you have gathered from the text with your own knowledge or experience to make inferences.

Details from the Text	Inferences from Text
1.	
2.	
3.	
4.	

Name ______________________ Date ____________ Assignment ________________

Citing Textual Evidence: Supporting an Inference

Use this chart to make inferences from the text. Combine details you have gathered from the text with your own knowledge or experience to make inferences.

Details from the Text	Inferences from Text
1.	
2.	
3.	
4.	

Name ______________________ Date ____________ Assignment ________________

Citing Textual Evidence: Supporting an Inference

Use this chart to make inferences from the text. Combine details you have gathered from the text with your own knowledge or experience to make inferences.

Details from the Text	Inferences from Text
1.	
2.	
3.	
4.	

Informational Text 2

2. Determine two or more central ideas in a text and analyze their development over the course of the text; provide an objective summary of the text.

Explanation

The **central idea** is the most important point of a piece of writing. It is what the author is trying to say to readers. Sometimes the central idea is stated directly, but usually the reader has to figure it out by studying the supporting details in the text. Supporting details are pieces of information—such as examples, facts, reasons, or descriptions–that convey the central idea. Keep track of these details as you read. Ask yourself: Why did the author include this detail? How does this detail help me understand the central idea of the text?

A good way to clarify the central idea of a text is to **summarize** it. A summary is a brief restatement in your own words of the key ideas in the text. A summary includes only the most important details, and it presents the information objectively, without personal opinions or judgments. When writing a summary, state the main point of the text in the first sentence and give the other key details to support it in the sentences that follow.

Examples

- **Summarize** Here is a summary of an article about national parks in the United States.

  National parks provide a habitat for unique plants, animals, and ecosystems. Yellowstone Park, for example, contains geysers, forests, grasslands, and free-roaming bison, elk, bear, eagles, and other wildlife. Grey wolves, once endangered, have been reintroduced in the parks. Everglades Park in Florida is home to endangered sea turtles, crocodiles, and frogs.

  National parks are also used for human recreation. Visitors to the Grand Canyon can camp, hike, canoe, and even take a helicopter or mule ride to the bottom of the canyon. Those interested in geology can see evidence of Earth's age on the canyon walls. In Alaska's Denali National Park, visitors enjoy dog-sledding, mountaineering, and skiing.

- **Central Idea** Note that the central idea in each paragraph is developed through facts and examples. The central ideas can also be combined into a single statement: *The U.S. national parks are important ecological and recreational resources.*

Academic Vocabulary

central idea the main idea or central message of a text

summary a statement of the central idea and important details in a work

Apply the Standard

Use the worksheets that follow to help you apply the standard as you read. Several copies of each worksheet have been provided for you to use with different informational texts.

- Summarizing Key Supporting Details
- Determining Central Ideas

Name ______________________ Date ______________ Assignment ______________

Summarizing Key Supporting Details

Use the organizer to summarize a text. First present the central idea; then record the most important details. Use your own words, and write in full sentences.

Central Idea ....

1. Detail ....

2. Detail ....

3. Detail ....

4. Detail ....

Name ______________________ Date ____________ Assignment ________________

Summarizing Key Supporting Details

Use the organizer to summarize a text. First present the central idea; then record the most important details. Use your own words, and write in full sentences.

Central Idea ....

1. Detail ....

2. Detail ....

3. Detail ....

4. Detail ....

Name ______________________ Date ______________ Assignment ______________

Summarizing Key Supporting Details

Use the organizer to summarize a text. First present the central idea; then record the most important details. Use your own words, and write in full sentences.

Central Idea ....

1. Detail ....

2. Detail ....

3. Detail ....

4. Detail ....

Name ______________________ Date ____________ Assignment ________________

Summarizing Key Supporting Details

Use the organizer to summarize a text. First present the central idea; then record the most important details. Use your own words, and write in full sentences.

Central Idea ....

....

....

....

....

1. Detail ....

....

....

....

....

2. Detail ....

....

....

....

....

3. Detail ....

....

....

....

....

4. Detail ....

....

....

....

....

Name ______________________ Date ______________ Assignment ______________

Summarizing Key Supporting Details

Use the organizer to summarize a text. First present the central idea; then record the most important details. Use your own words, and write in full sentences.

Central Idea ....

1. Detail ....

2. Detail ....

3. Detail ....

4. Detail ....

E

Name ______________________ Date ______________ Assignment ________________

Summarizing Key Supporting Details

Use the organizer to summarize a text. First present the central idea; then record the most important details. Use your own words, and write in full sentences.

Central Idea ....

....

....

....

....

1. Detail ....

....

....

....

....

2. Detail ....

....

....

....

....

3. Detail ....

....

....

....

....

4. Detail ....

....

....

....

....

Name ______________________ Date ______________ Assignment __________________

Determining Central Ideas

Group important details under two or more central ideas in a text you have read.

Central Idea 1

Detail a:
Detail b:
Detail c:
Detail d:

Central Idea 2

Detail a:
Detail b:
Detail c:
Detail d:

Name ______________________ Date ____________ Assignment ________________

Determining Central Ideas

Group important details under two or more central ideas in a text you have read.

Central Idea 1

Detail a:
Detail b:
Detail c:
Detail d:

Central Idea 2

Detail a:
Detail b:
Detail c:
Detail d:

Name ______________________ Date ____________ Assignment ________________

Determining Central Ideas

Group important details under two or more central ideas in a text you have read.

Central Idea 1

Detail a:
Detail b:
Detail c:
Detail d:

Central Idea 2

Detail a:
Detail b:
Detail c:
Detail d:

Name ______________________ Date ____________ Assignment ________________

Determining Central Ideas

Group important details under two or more central ideas in a text you have read.

Central Idea 1

Detail a:
Detail b:
Detail c:
Detail d:

Central Idea 2

Detail a:
Detail b:
Detail c:
Detail d:

Name _______________ Date _______________ Assignment _______________

Determining Central Ideas

Group important details under two or more central ideas in a text you have read.

Central Idea 1

Detail a:
Detail b:
Detail c:
Detail d:

Central Idea 2

Detail a:
Detail b:
Detail c:
Detail d:

Name ______________________ Date ______________ Assignment ________________

Determining Central Ideas

Group important details under two or more central ideas in a text you have read.

Central Idea 1

Detail a:
Detail b:
Detail c:
Detail d:

Central Idea 2

Detail a:
Detail b:
Detail c:
Detail d:

Informational Text 3

3. Analyze the interactions between individuals, events, and ideas in a text (e.g., how ideas influence individuals or events, or how individuals influence ideas or events).

Explanation

The way in which individuals interact with the events of a text can be a powerful way for a writer to engage readers. Informational text often contains cause-effect relationships between individuals, events, and ideas. An individual in an article may influence what happens (an event) or how an idea develops. Sometimes an idea that already exists affects an individual's actions or thoughts. An event might also cause or affect another event, or it may affect an individual or an idea.

To analyze these **interactions**, focus on a single individual, event, or idea and notice what happens as a result. This type of analysis will help you understand the content of an informational text.

Examples

- In a biography of the Dutch painter Vincent van Gogh, the endlessly hot sun in the south of France seems to drive the artist mad. This is an example of an event (sun shining) affecting an individual (the artist).
- Another artist, Paul Gauguin, joins Van Gogh, but their artistic ideas differ and they soon quarrel. This is an example of an individual interacting with another individual.
- Van Gogh eventually cuts off part of one of his ears, a result of his madness. Biographers have found other, specific causes for this shocking event as well. This is an example of a chain of cause and effect.
- Van Gogh's bold style of applying brilliantly colored paint so thickly that it stands out on the canvas affected countless other artists' work. This is an example of an idea affecting many individuals.

Academic Vocabulary

interaction a cause and an effect

Apply the Standard

Use the worksheet that follows to help you apply the standard as you read. Several copies of the worksheet have been provided for you to use with different informational texts.

- Analyzing Interactions

Name ______________________ Date ____________ Assignment ______________

Analyzing Interactions

Use the organizer to analyze how individuals, events, and ideas interact in informational text.

Cause-Effect Interactions

Cause	Effect
Individual:	Interacts with:
Event:	Interacts with:
Idea:	Interacts with:

Name ____________________ Date ______________ Assignment ______________

Analyzing Interactions

Use the organizer to analyze how individuals, events, and ideas interact in informational text.

Cause-Effect Interactions

Cause	Effect
Individual:	Interacts with:
Event:	Interacts with:
Idea:	Interacts with:

Name ______________________ Date ____________ Assignment ______________

Analyzing Interactions

Use the organizer to analyze how individuals, events, and ideas interact in informational text.

Cause-Effect Interactions

Cause	Effect
Individual:	Interacts with:
Event:	Interacts with:
Idea:	Interacts with:

Name ______________________ Date ____________ Assignment ________________

Analyzing Interactions

Use the organizer to analyze how individuals, events, and ideas interact in informational text.

Cause-Effect Interactions

Cause	Effect
Individual:	Interacts with:
Event:	Interacts with:
Idea:	Interacts with:

Name ______________________ Date ____________ Assignment ________________

Analyzing Interactions

Use the organizer to analyze how individuals, events, and ideas interact in informational text.

Cause-Effect Interactions

Cause	**Effect**
Individual:	Interacts with:
Event:	Interacts with:
Idea:	Interacts with:

Name ________________ Date ____________ Assignment ________________

Analyzing Interactions

Use the organizer to analyze how individuals, events, and ideas interact in informational text.

Cause-Effect Interactions

Cause	**Effect**
Individual:	Interacts with:
Event:	Interacts with:
Idea:	Interacts with:

F

For use with Informational Text 3

Informational Text 4

4. Determine the meaning of words and phrases as they are used in a text, including figurative, connotative, and technical meanings; analyze the impact of a specific word choice on meaning and tone.

Explanation

Unlike fictional works, informational texts must be clear and accurate. In many other subjects, writers use technical terms to explain a concept. In some cases, you might already be familiar with a word but not its technical meaning. Figuring out **technical meanings** is an important part of reading informational text. Authors of informational text may also use **figurative language** to express ideas in a fresh way. Good writers are aware of the **connotative meanings,** or the emotions and feelings that are associated with the words they use.

Authors choose their words carefully because they know that their choices affect the meaning and tone of their writing. **Tone** is the author's attitude toward a subject or character. As you read informational texts, analyze how the author's word choices influence the text's meaning and tone.

Examples

- The **figurative meaning** of words goes beyond the literal, word-for-word meaning. "The hot car became a sauna" and "A blanket of fog covered the coastline" are examples of figurative language.
- **Connotative meanings** refer to the feelings that words have. These associations can be positive or negative. The words *fragrance* and *odor* both describe a smell, but each word has a different connotation. Which smell would you rather detect in your home?
- Authors use **technical meanings** when discussing specific subjects. The words *equator, longitude,* and *latitude* are examples of technical terms you might find in social studies texts.
- The author's attitude, or **tone,** can often be described by adjectives, such as *serious, humorous, formal,* and *informal.* Authors choose their words carefully to suggest a specific tone in their writing.

Academic Vocabulary

figurative language words or phrases that are used imaginatively, not literally

connotative meaning feelings and emotions associated with a word or phrase

technical meanings word meanings specifically related to a subject

Apply the Standard

Use the worksheets that follow to help you apply the standard as you read. Several copies of each worksheet have been provided for you to use with different informational texts.

- Understanding Connotations, Figurative Language, and Technical Terms
- Analyzing Word Choice

Name _______________ Date _______________ Assignment _______________

Understanding Connotations, Figurative Language, and Technical Terms

Use the organizer below to help you determine the figurative, connotative, or technical meaning of words and phrases you encounter in reading informational texts. Use the first column to record 3–4 words and phrases that stand out or are memorable. Write their meanings in the second column. Use a dictionary, if necessary, to identify the meanings of technical terms.

Word or Phrase	**Figurative, Connotative, or Technical Meaning**
1.	
2.	
3.	
4.	

A

Name ______________________ Date ______________ Assignment ____________________

Understanding Connotations, Figurative Language, and Technical Terms

Use the organizer below to help you determine the figurative, connotative, or technical meaning of words and phrases you encounter in reading informational texts. Use the first column to record 3–4 words and phrases that stand out or are memorable. Write their meanings in the second column. Use a dictionary, if necessary, to identify the meanings of technical terms.

Word or Phrase	Figurative, Connotative, or Technical Meaning
1.	
2.	
3.	
4.	

Name ______________________ Date ____________ Assignment ________________

Understanding Connotations, Figurative Language, and Technical Terms

Use the organizer below to help you determine the figurative, connotative, or technical meaning of words and phrases you encounter in reading informational texts. Use the first column to record 3–4 words and phrases that stand out or are memorable. Write their meanings in the second column. Use a dictionary, if necessary, to identify the meanings of technical terms.

Word or Phrase	Figurative, Connotative, or Technical Meaning
1.	
2.	
3.	
4.	

Name ______________________ Date ____________ Assignment ________________

Understanding Connotations, Figurative Language, and Technical Terms

Use the organizer below to help you determine the figurative, connotative, or technical meaning of words and phrases you encounter in reading informational texts. Use the first column to record 3–4 words and phrases that stand out or are memorable. Write their meanings in the second column. Use a dictionary, if necessary, to identify the meanings of technical terms.

Word or Phrase	**Figurative, Connotative, or Technical Meaning**
1.	
2.	
3.	
4.	

Name ______________________ Date ______________ Assignment ______________

Understanding Connotations, Figurative Language, and Technical Terms

Use the organizer below to help you determine the figurative, connotative, or technical meaning of words and phrases you encounter in reading informational texts. Use the first column to record 3–4 words and phrases that stand out or are memorable. Write their meanings in the second column. Use a dictionary, if necessary, to identify the meanings of technical terms.

Word or Phrase	Figurative, Connotative, or Technical Meaning
1.	
2.	
3.	
4.	

Name ______________________ Date ______________ Assignment ________________

Understanding Connotations, Figurative Language, and Technical Terms

Use the organizer below to help you determine the figurative, connotative, or technical meaning of words and phrases you encounter in reading informational texts. Use the first column to record 3–4 words and phrases that stand out or are memorable. Write their meanings in the second column. Use a dictionary, if necessary, to identify the meanings of technical terms.

Word or Phrase	**Figurative, Connotative, or Technical Meaning**
1.	
2.	
3.	
4.	

Name ______________________ Date ____________ Assignment ________________

Analyzing Word Choice

Use the organizer below to help you analyze the effect of specific word choices on tone and meaning. Choose an informational text you are studying. In the left-hand column, write 3 or 4 words or phrases from the text that seem particularly vivid, descriptive, or effective. In the right-hand column, describe the effect the choices have on the author's tone and the meaning of the piece.

Word Choices	Effect on Tone or Meaning
→	
→	
→	
→	

Name ______________________ Date ____________ Assignment ________________

Analyzing Word Choice

Use the organizer below to help you analyze the effect of specific word choices on tone and meaning. Choose an informational text you are studying. In the left-hand column, write 3 or 4 words or phrases from the text that seem particularly vivid, descriptive, or effective. In the right-hand column, describe the effect the choices have on the author's tone and the meaning of the piece.

Word Choices	**Effect on Tone or Meaning**
→	
→	
→	
→	

Name ______________________ Date ____________ Assignment ________________

Analyzing Word Choice

Use the organizer below to help you analyze the effect of specific word choices on tone and meaning. Choose an informational text you are studying. In the left-hand column, write 3 or 4 words or phrases from the text that seem particularly vivid, descriptive, or effective. In the right-hand column, describe the effect the choices have on the author's tone and the meaning of the piece.

Word Choices	Effect on Tone or Meaning
→	
→	
→	
→	

Name ______________________ Date ____________ Assignment ________________

Analyzing Word Choice

Use the organizer below to help you analyze the effect of specific word choices on tone and meaning. Choose an informational text you are studying. In the left-hand column, write 3 or 4 words or phrases from the text that seem particularly vivid, descriptive, or effective. In the right-hand column, describe the effect the choices have on the author's tone and the meaning of the piece.

Word Choices	Effect on Tone or Meaning
→	
→	
→	
→	

Name ______________________ Date ____________ Assignment ________________

Analyzing Word Choice

Use the organizer below to help you analyze the effect of specific word choices on tone and meaning. Choose an informational text you are studying. In the left-hand column, write 3 or 4 words or phrases from the text that seem particularly vivid, descriptive, or effective. In the right-hand column, describe the effect the choices have on the author's tone and the meaning of the piece.

Word Choices	Effect on Tone or Meaning
→	
→	
→	
→	

Name ______________________________ Date ________________ Assignment ____________________

Analyzing Word Choice

Use the organizer below to help you analyze the effect of specific word choices on tone and meaning. Choose an informational text you are studying. In the left-hand column, write 3 or 4 words or phrases from the text that seem particularly vivid, descriptive, or effective. In the right-hand column, describe the effect the choices have on the author's tone and the meaning of the piece.

Word Choices	Effect on Tone or Meaning
→	
→	
→	
→	

Informational Text 5

5. Analyze the structure an author uses to organize a text, including how the major sections contribute to the whole and to the development of the ideas.

Explanation

The pattern of sentences, paragraphs, and chapters forms the structure of an informational text. By analyzing this structure, you can determine if the ideas flow logically and if the text achieves its purpose. To get an overview of how an informational text is structured and how the parts fit into the whole, look at the **text features,** which include titles, **subheadings,** lists, sidebars, and **graphic aids.**

To organize information or to highlight important ideas in a text, authors sometimes use boldface type, bullets, or boxes. Titles and subheadings point out the main topic of a text before the body text, and lists and sidebars give more information on topics. If authors want to represent information visually, they may use a chart or another **graphic aid.**

Examples

- The title of an encyclopedia entry, "Indian Grey Mongoose," indicates its general topic. The entry contains a map that shows where the mongoose lives and a chart with basic facts about the animal's size, diet, and lifespan. Subheadings such as Habitat, Behavior, and Feeding Habits break up the text into smaller sections that provide specific details about the mongoose. For example, the Behavior section explains when the mongoose sleeps, when it is active, how it moves, and how it finds and kills its prey. Each section develops the topic and contributes to the whole.

- A handbook on venomous snakes contains two major sections. The first is a guide to recognizing venomous snakes. It includes graphic aids such as photographs and anatomical drawings, as well as text. Each type of snake is discussed in a separate paragraph, which opens with the name of the snake in boldface letters. The second major section of the handbook explains how to treat a snakebite. The text in the second section is a list of bulleted points.

Academic Vocabulary

graphic aids maps, photographs, graphs, and other visual elements that give additional information about a topic

subheading a headline, often boldfaced, that signals the beginning of a new topic within a text

text features design elements that organize information in a text and highlight key ideas

Apply the Standard

Use the worksheet that follows to help you apply the standard as you read. Several copies have been provided for you to use with different informational texts.

- Analyzing Text Structure

Name ______________________ Date ____________ Assignment ______________

Analyzing Text Structure

Use the organizer below to identify the text features in an informational text and to describe their purposes. Then, answer the question.

Text Feature	Purpose
1.	
2.	
3.	
4.	
5.	

How do the different sections of the text contribute to the development of its main idea?

....

....

....

....

....

....

Name ______________________ Date ______________ Assignment ________________

Analyzing Text Structure

Use the organizer below to identify the text features in an informational text and to describe their purposes. Then, answer the question.

Text Feature	Purpose
1.	
2.	
3.	
4.	
5.	

How do the different sections of the text contribute to the development of its main idea?

....

....

....

....

....

....

Name ______________________ Date ____________ Assignment ______________

Analyzing Text Structure

Use the organizer below to identify the text features in an informational text and to describe their purposes. Then, answer the question.

Text Feature	Purpose
1.	
2.	
3.	
4.	
5.	

How do the different sections of the text contribute to the development of its main idea?

....

....

....

....

....

....

C

For use with Informational Text 5

Name ______________________ Date ____________ Assignment ______________

Analyzing Text Structure

Use the organizer below to identify the text features in an informational text and to describe their purposes. Then, answer the question.

Text Feature	Purpose
1.	
2.	
3.	
4.	
5.	

How do the different sections of the text contribute to the development of its main idea?

....

....

....

....

....

....

Name ______________________ Date ____________ Assignment ______________

Analyzing Text Structure

Use the organizer below to identify the text features in an informational text and to describe their purposes. Then, answer the question.

Text Feature	Purpose
1.	
2.	
3.	
4.	
5.	

How do the different sections of the text contribute to the development of its main idea?

....

....

....

....

....

....

Name ______________________ Date ______________ Assignment ______________

Analyzing Text Structure

Use the organizer below to identify the text features in an informational text and to describe their purposes. Then, answer the question.

Text Feature	Purpose
1.	
2.	
3.	
4.	
5.	

How do the different sections of the text contribute to the development of its main idea?

....

....

....

....

....

....

Informational Text 6

6. Determine an author's point of view or purpose in a text and analyze how the author distinguishes his or her position from that of others.

Explanation

An author's **point of view** is the perspective from which he or she writes. The author's beliefs and background shape this point of view. Nonfiction authors write with a **purpose** in mind, such as *to inform, to persuade, to entertain,* or *to reflect.* Authors can have more than one purpose, as when an author informs readers in order to persuade them of something. You can determine the author's point of view and purpose or purposes by noticing the details in the work.

Often a point of view is the author's opinion on an issue. Nonfiction authors sometimes distinguish their position from the ideas of others by presenting responses to arguments. These responses to opposing arguments are known as **counterarguments.** The author may state an opposing argument in order to respond to it with his or her own view.

Examples

- An editorial writer presents his point of view through the opinions he expresses in his columns. He lives in a big city, which contributes to his point of view about running big cities, his topic for today. He includes opposing arguments to make his own ideas stand out. For example, he quotes an argument that a big city cannot be run as efficiently as a small city because it has bigger problems. He counters that big cities have more resources.
- Another nonfiction writer seeks to persuade readers to recycle more of their waste products. Her magazine articles are filled with facts backing up her appeals to readers to help save the planet. She includes the common concern that recycling costs too much money and provides the counterargument that recycling will actually save precious resources, which will save money in the long run.

Academic Vocabulary

point of view an author's perspective; sometimes an opinion on a specific topic

purpose the main reason an author writes a work

counterargument an argument made to respond to another argument

Apply the Standard

Use the worksheets that follow to help you apply the standard as you read. Several copies of each worksheet have been provided for you to use with different informational texts.

- Determining Point of View and Purpose
- Analyzing an Author's Position

Name ______________________ Date ____________ Assignment ______________

Determining Point of View and Purpose

Complete the organizer to determine the author's point of view and purpose in an informational text. First, write the title and topic of the selection. Then, in the left column, identify the author's point of view and purpose for writing. In the right column, provide details from the text that helped you determine the point of view and purpose.

Title of the Text:

Topic of the Text:

Author's Point of View:	**Details from the Text:**
Author's Purpose(s): ❑ to inform ❑ to persuade ❑ to entertain ❑ to reflect	

Name ______________________ Date ____________ Assignment ______________

Determining Point of View and Purpose

Complete the organizer to determine the author's point of view and purpose in an informational text. First, write the title and topic of the selection. Then, in the left column, identify the author's point of view and purpose for writing. In the right column, provide details from the text that helped you determine the point of view and purpose.

Title of the Text:

Topic of the Text:

Author's Point of View:	**Details from the Text:**
Author's Purpose(s): ❑ to inform ❑ to persuade ❑ to entertain ❑ to reflect	

Name ______________________ Date ______________ Assignment ________________

Determining Point of View and Purpose

Complete the organizer to determine the author's point of view and purpose in an informational text. First, write the title and topic of the selection. Then, in the left column, identify the author's point of view and purpose for writing. In the right column, provide details from the text that helped you determine the point of view and purpose.

Title of the Text:

Topic of the Text:

Author's Point of View:	**Details from the Text:**
Author's Purpose(s): ❑ to inform ❑ to persuade ❑ to entertain ❑ to reflect	

Name ______________________ Date ____________ Assignment ______________

Determining Point of View and Purpose

Complete the organizer to determine the author's point of view and purpose in an informational text. First, write the title and topic of the selection. Then, in the left column, identify the author's point of view and purpose for writing. In the right column, provide details from the text that helped you determine the point of view and purpose.

Title of the Text:

Topic of the Text:

Author's Point of View:	**Details from the Text:**
Author's Purpose(s): ❑ to inform ❑ to persuade ❑ to entertain ❑ to reflect	

Name ______________________ Date ____________ Assignment ______________

Determining Point of View and Purpose

Complete the organizer to determine the author's point of view and purpose in an informational text. First, write the title and topic of the selection. Then, in the left column, identify the author's point of view and purpose for writing. In the right column, provide details from the text that helped you determine the point of view and purpose.

Title of the Text:

Topic of the Text:

Author's Point of View:	**Details from the Text:**
Author's Purpose(s): ❑ to inform ❑ to persuade ❑ to entertain ❑ to reflect	

Name ______________________ Date ____________ Assignment ______________

Determining Point of View and Purpose

Complete the organizer to determine the author's point of view and purpose in an informational text. First, write the title and topic of the selection. Then, in the left column, identify the author's point of view and purpose for writing. In the right column, provide details from the text that helped you determine the point of view and purpose.

Title of the Text:

Topic of the Text:

Author's Point of View:	**Details from the Text:**
Author's Purpose(s): ❑ to inform ❑ to persuade ❑ to entertain ❑ to reflect	

Name ______________________ Date ______________ Assignment ________________

Analyzing an Author's Position

Use the organizer to analyze the author's position in an informational text.

Title:

Author:

Author's Position:

↓

Details that support the author's position:

↓

Arguments against the author's position:

↓

Author's counterarguments:

Name ______________________ Date ______________ Assignment ________________

Analyzing an Author's Position

Use the organizer to analyze the author's position in an informational text.

Title: Author: Author's Position:

↓

Details that support the author's position:

↓

Arguments against the author's position:

↓

Author's counterarguments:

Name ______________________ Date ______________ Assignment ______________

Analyzing an Author's Position

Use the organizer to analyze the author's position in an informational text.

Title: Author: Author's Position:

↓

Details that support the author's position:

↓

Arguments against the author's position:

↓

Author's counterarguments:

Name ______________________ Date ____________ Assignment ______________

Analyzing an Author's Position

Use the organizer to analyze the author's position in an informational text.

Title: Author: Author's Position:

↓

Details that support the author's position:

↓

Arguments against the author's position:

↓

Author's counterarguments:

Name ______________________ Date ____________ Assignment ______________

Analyzing an Author's Position

Use the organizer to analyze the author's position in an informational text.

Title:

Author:

Author's Position:

↓

Details that support the author's position:

↓

Arguments against the author's position:

↓

Author's counterarguments:

Name ______________________ Date ____________ Assignment ______________

Analyzing an Author's Position

Use the organizer to analyze the author's position in an informational text.

Title:

Author:

Author's Position:

↓

Details that support the author's position:

↓

Arguments against the author's position:

↓

Author's counterarguments:

Informational Text 7

7. Compare and contrast a text to an audio, video, or multimedia version of the text, analyzing each medium's portrayal of the subject (e.g., how the delivery of a speech affects the impact of the words)

Explanation

When reading informational texts, you develop your own interpretation based on your understanding of the material. Some informational texts also appear in an audio, video, or multimedia version. When you listen to an **audio** version of a text, you can often feel the passion or concern of the speaker in his or her tone of voice or through the emphasis the speaker places on certain words or phrases. If you watch a **video** or **multimedia** version of the same text, you may be able to see the speaker's facial expressions and gestures. Comparing and contrasting different versions of a text in different media can help you gain a better understanding of the most important ideas.

Examples

- When you read a text, pay attention to words, phrases, and sentences that provide important information or that catch your interest. Think about the author's purpose. What information does the author want you to know?
- When you listen to an audio version of a text, notice the words, phrases, and sentences the speaker emphasizes. Does the speaker give any special emphasis to the elements you identified? Think about the speaker's pace or rhythm. How did the speaker's reading affect your understanding and enjoyment of the text?
- In a video or multimedia version of a text, certain information and details are emphasized through the speaker's delivery, music, sound effects, or graphics. How does the speaker's delivery affect the impact of the words?

Academic Vocabulary

audio recording of sound

multimedia a format for presenting information that combines media (text, graphics, sound, video)

video recording of visual and audio components

Apply the Standard

Use the worksheet that follows to help you apply the standard as you read informational texts. Several copies of the worksheet have been provided for you.

- Comparing and Contrasting Versions

Name ______________________ Date ______________ Assignment ________________

Comparing and Contrasting Versions

Use the organizer below to compare and contrast different versions of the same text. In the center of the diagram, describe information or details that are emphasized in both versions. In the outer circles, describe information or details that are unique to each version. Then answer the questions.

Title of Text: ....

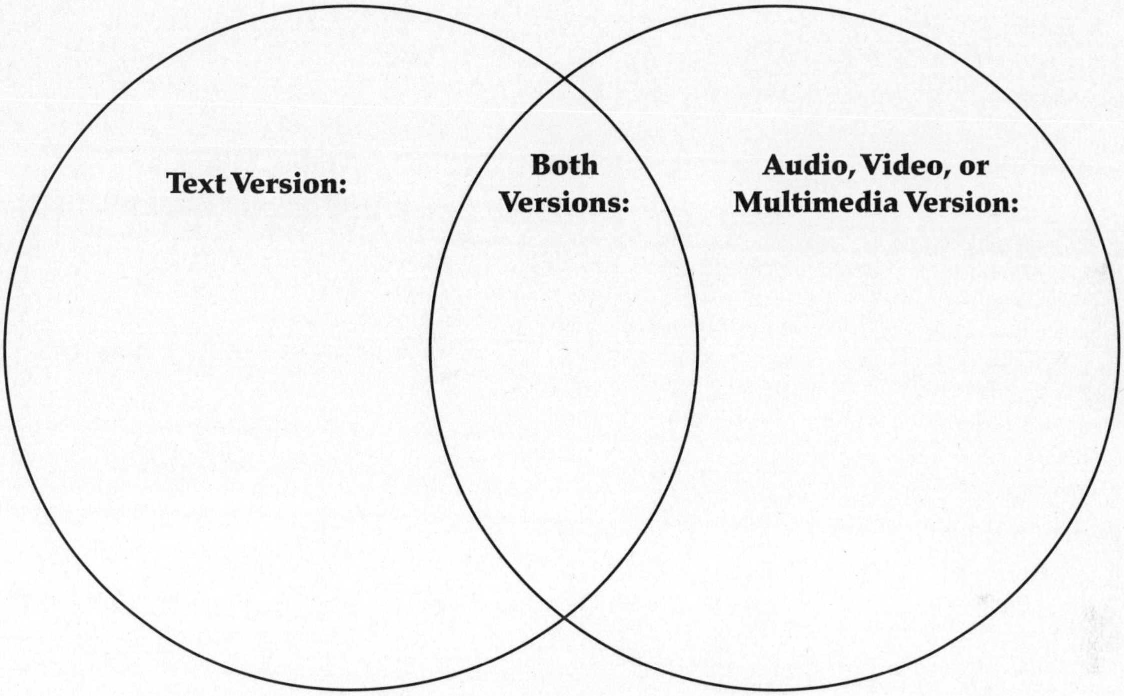

How did each version add to your understanding?

....

....

....

Which version did you prefer? Why?

....

....

....

Name ______________________ Date ____________ Assignment ______________

Comparing and Contrasting Versions

Use the organizer below to compare and contrast different versions of the same text. In the center of the diagram, describe information or details that are emphasized in both versions. In the outer circles, describe information or details that are unique to each version. Then answer the questions.

Title of Text: ....

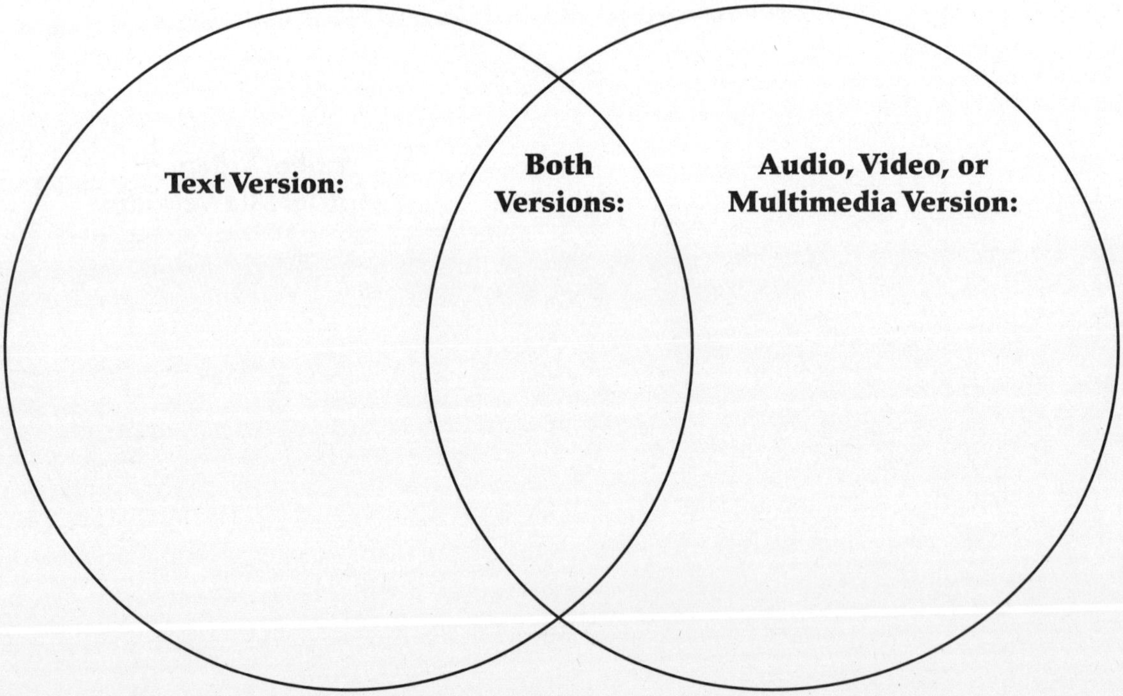

How did each version add to your understanding?

....

....

....

Which version did you prefer? Why?

....

....

....

Name ______________________ Date ____________ Assignment ______________

Comparing and Contrasting Versions

Use the organizer below to compare and contrast different versions of the same text. In the center of the diagram, describe information or details that are emphasized in both versions. In the outer circles, describe information or details that are unique to each version. Then answer the questions.

Title of Text: ....

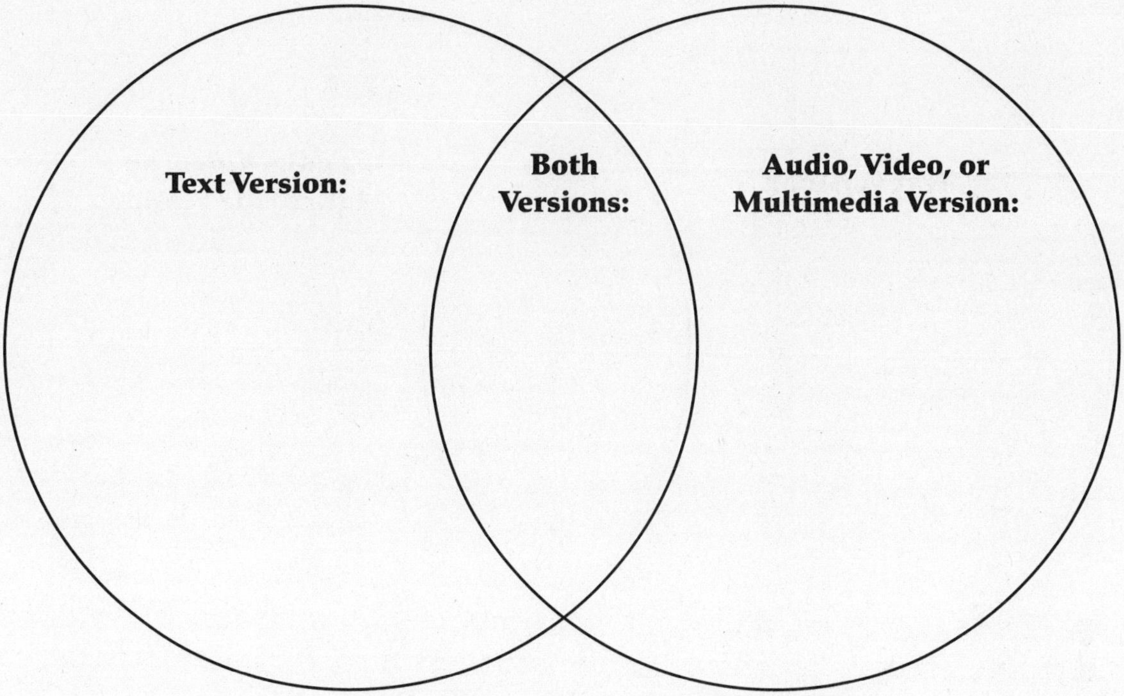

How did each version add to your understanding?

....

....

....

Which version did you prefer? Why?

....

....

....

C

For use with Informational Text 7

Name ______________________ Date ____________ Assignment ________________

Comparing and Contrasting Versions

Use the organizer below to compare and contrast different versions of the same text. In the center of the diagram, describe information or details that are emphasized in both versions. In the outer circles, describe information or details that are unique to each version. Then answer the questions.

Title of Text: ....

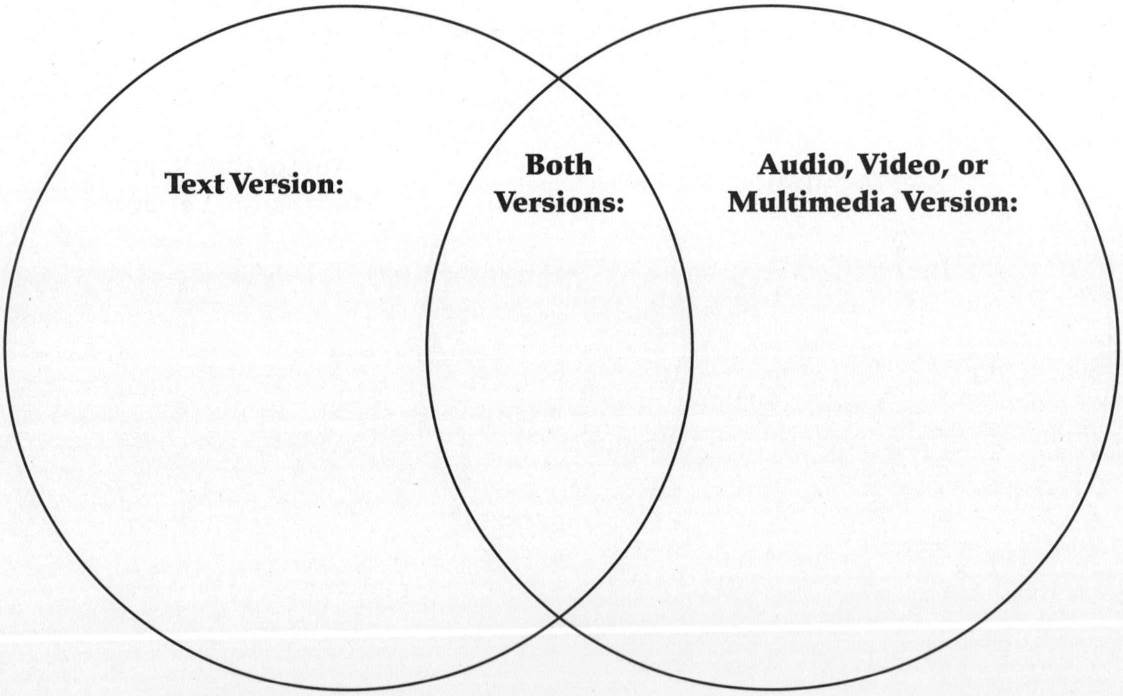

How did each version add to your understanding?

....

....

....

Which version did you prefer? Why?

....

....

....

Name ______________________ Date ____________ Assignment ______________

Comparing and Contrasting Versions

Use the organizer below to compare and contrast different versions of the same text. In the center of the diagram, describe information or details that are emphasized in both versions. In the outer circles, describe information or details that are unique to each version. Then answer the questions.

Title of Text: ....

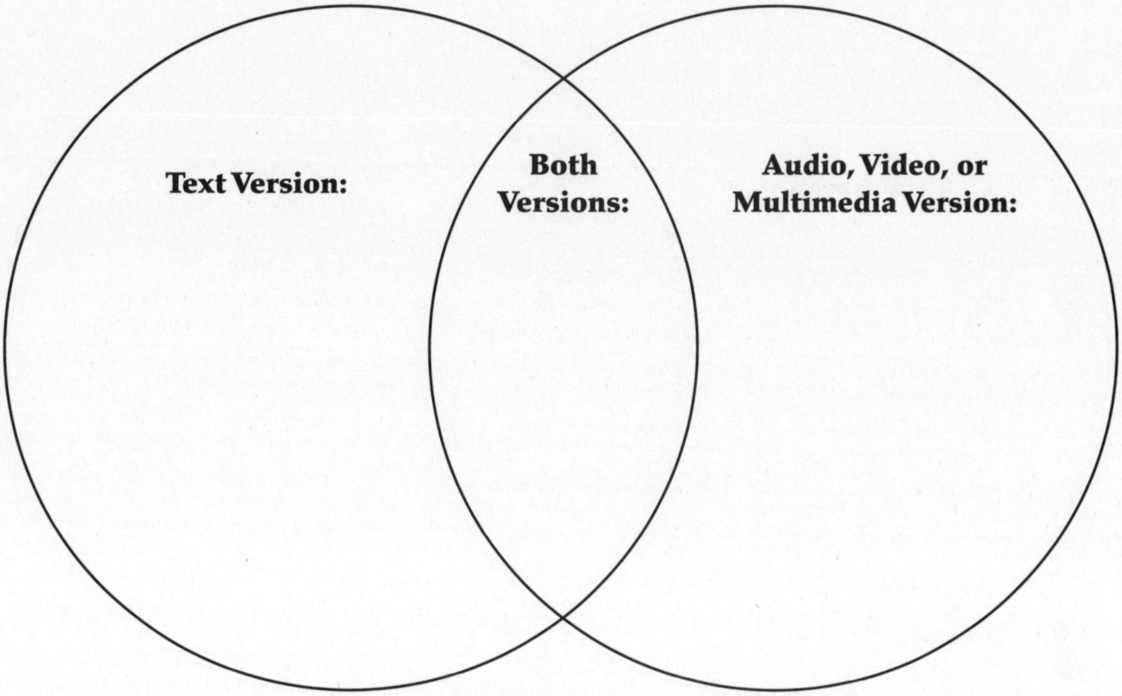

How did each version add to your understanding?

....

....

....

Which version did you prefer? Why?

....

....

....

Name ______________________ Date ______________ Assignment ________________

Comparing and Contrasting Versions

Use the organizer below to compare and contrast different versions of the same text. In the center of the diagram, describe information or details that are emphasized in both versions. In the outer circles, describe information or details that are unique to each version. Then answer the questions.

Title of Text: ....

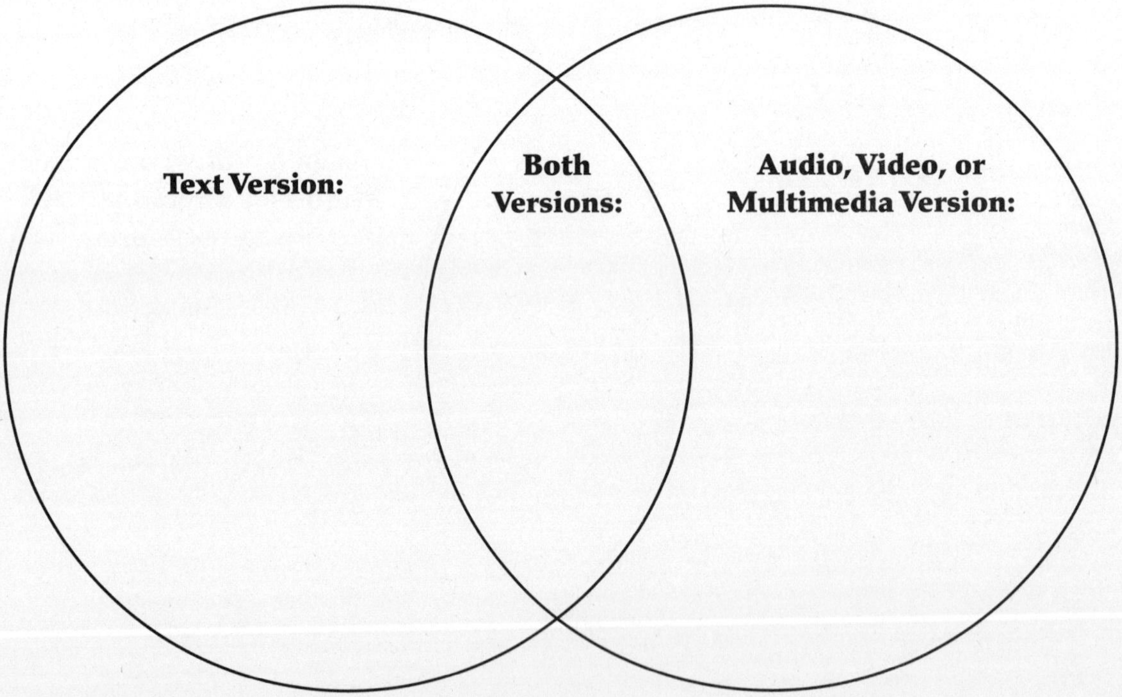

How did each version add to your understanding?

....

....

....

Which version did you prefer? Why?

....

....

....

Informational Text 8

8. Trace and evaluate the argument and specific claims in a text, assessing whether the reasoning is sound and the evidence is relevant and sufficient to support the claims.

Explanation

An author's **argument** contains a **claim,** or a statement about what an author believes to be true. The author supports a claim by giving **reasons** why the claim must be true. The author also supplies **evidence,** which is information that supports the reasons.

Evidence can consist of facts, examples, or statistics. When you read a persuasive argument, you should evaluate the author's argument by judging the reasoning and the evidence. Ask yourself whether the reasoning is sound—does it make sense? Judge whether the evidence is relevant to the argument—does it relate to the specific claim? Is it about the same specific idea? You should judge also whether the evidence is sufficient—are there enough facts to support the claim? One example might not be enough.

Examples

- A veterinarian has written a lengthy essay about her belief that zoos are cruel to wild animals. She provides facts about the natural habitats of most zoo animals versus the habitats provided by most big-city zoos. Further, she gives statistics about the number of zoos in cities of different sizes throughout the United States, listing the number of zoos that provide a natural environment versus cages, which she claims are cruel. Her reasoning seems sound, and her evidence is relevant to animals' living conditions.

- A former teacher who is now a full-time parent has written an editorial to encourage others to home-school their children. He explains that parents who home-school their children use approved textbook materials and follow guidelines for curriculum so that their children receive a good education. As evidence of the success of their education, he points out that his children have consistently achieved high scores on nationally standardized tests, as have his friends' children who are home schooled. Although his reasoning is sound, his evidence is not sufficient to draw the conclusion that everyone should use home schooling.

Academic Vocabulary

argument writing that expresses a position on an issue and supports it with evidence

claim the statement of an argument

evidence information that supports an author's reasons

Apply the Standard

Use the worksheet that follows to help you apply the standard as you read. Several copies of the worksheet have been provided for you to use with different informational text selections.

- Evaluate an Argument

Name ______________________ Date ______________ Assignment ______________

Evaluate an Argument

Use the organizer to evaluate an argument.

Argument: Claim

Reason | **Reason** | **Reason**

Evidence | **Evidence** | **Evidence**

A

For use with Informational Text 8

Name ______________________ Date ____________ Assignment ______________

Evaluate an Argument

Use the organizer to evaluate an argument.

Argument: Claim

Reason | **Reason** | **Reason**

Evidence | **Evidence** | **Evidence**

Name ______________________ Date ______________ Assignment ________________

Evaluate an Argument

Use the organizer to evaluate an argument.

Argument: Claim

Reason

Reason

Reason

Evidence

Evidence

Evidence

C

For use with Informational Text 8

Name ______________________ Date ____________ Assignment ______________

Evaluate an Argument

Use the organizer to evaluate an argument.

Argument: Claim

Reason

Reason

Reason

Evidence

Evidence

Evidence

Name ______________________ Date ______________ Assignment ________________

Evaluate an Argument

Use the organizer to evaluate an argument.

Argument: Claim

Reason

Reason

Reason

Evidence

Evidence

Evidence

Name ______________________ Date ____________ Assignment ______________

Evaluate an Argument

Use the organizer to evaluate an argument.

Argument: Claim

Reason

Reason

Reason

Evidence

Evidence

Evidence

Informational Text 9

9. Analyze how two or more authors writing about the same topic shape their presentations of key information by emphasizing different evidence or advancing different interpretations of facts.

Explanation

In persuasive writing, authors present **evidence** to support their point of view on an issue. Evidence consists of facts, statistics, and examples—information that can be proved or verified. As a careful reader, you should assess the evidence in a text to determine if it is adequate, accurate, and reliable. Look for bias. **Bias** is a leaning toward a certain position. Writers can exhibit bias not only in the words they choose but also in the way they present key information. They may emphasize evidence that supports their point of view, or they may interpret facts in a way that agrees with their thinking.

Examples

- **Emphasizing Different Evidence.** Writers with different points of view on an issue may emphasize different evidence. For example, a writer who favors jogging as a form of exercise might downplay or discredit evidence of its dangers. He or she would not discuss the risks of falls or injuries. Instead, the writer might present evidence of the many benefits of jogging, including cardiac fitness and weight control. Conversely, a writer who doesn't like jogging as a form of aerobic exercise might present statistics on injuries to knees, shins, and feet caused by jogging while ignoring the many medical studies that document the benefits of jogging as an all-around aerobic workout.
- **Interpreting Facts Differently.** Writers with different points of view on an issue may interpret facts differently. For example, a writer may sees space exploration as a noble scientific venture that benefits all people. He or she will interpret a report on a space mission's failure as a disappointment for everyone and as a reason to improve and expand the program. A writer who thinks that the money spent on space exploration would be better spent on social programs may interpret the same facts about a failed space mission to mean that government should shut down its space programs.

Academic Vocabulary

bias a leaning toward a certain position

evidence information that supports a claim

Apply the Standard

Use the worksheet that follows to help you apply the standard as you read. Several copies of the worksheet have been provided for you to use with different informational texts.

- Analyzing Authors' Approaches

Name ______________ Date ______________ Assignment ______________

Analyzing Authors' Approaches

Use the organizer below to analyze how two authors with different points of view approach the same subject. Consider the evidence presented and the way in which facts are interpreted.

	Evidence Presented	Interpretation of Facts
Point of View		
Evidence Presented		
Interpretation of Facts		

Name ______________________ Date ____________ Assignment ____________

Analyzing Authors' Approaches

Use the organizer below to analyze how two authors with different points of view approach the same subject. Consider the evidence presented and the way in which facts are interpreted.

	Evidence Presented	Interpretation of Facts
Point of View		
Evidence Presented		
Interpretation of Facts		

Name ______________________ Date ____________ Assignment ______________

Analyzing Authors' Approaches

Use the organizer below to analyze how two authors with different points of view approach the same subject. Consider the evidence presented and the way in which facts are interpreted.

	Evidence Presented	**Interpretation of Facts**
Point of View		
Evidence Presented		
Interpretation of Facts		

Name ______________________ Date ______________ Assignment ________________

Analyzing Authors' Approaches

Use the organizer below to analyze how two authors with different points of view approach the same subject. Consider the evidence presented and the way in which facts are interpreted.

	Evidence Presented	Interpretation of Facts
Point of View		
Evidence Presented		
Interpretation of Facts		

D

For use with Informational Text 9

Name ______________________ Date ______________ Assignment ________________

Analyzing Authors' Approaches

Use the organizer below to analyze how two authors with different points of view approach the same subject. Consider the evidence presented and the way in which facts are interpreted.

	Evidence Presented	Interpretation of Facts
Point of View		
Evidence Presented		
Interpretation of Facts		

Name ______________________ Date ______________ Assignment ________________

Analyzing Authors' Approaches

Use the organizer below to analyze how two authors with different points of view approach the same subject. Consider the evidence presented and the way in which facts are interpreted.

	Evidence Presented	Interpretation of Facts
Point of View		
Evidence Presented		
Interpretation of Facts		

Informational Text 10

10. By the end of the year, read and comprehend literary nonfiction in the grades 6–8 text complexity band proficiently, with scaffolding as needed at the high end of the range.

Explanation

The **complexity** of a work refers to how difficult it is to understand. Works of literary nonfiction can vary greatly in their complexity. For example, essays and editorials can use familiar subjects that are easy to understand. However, they can also use unfamiliar subjects and present concepts that are difficult to understand. Some works use a simple style with ordinary vocabulary and short sentences; others use advanced vocabulary featuring figurative language and long sentences.

You will be expected to **comprehend**, or understand the meaning and importance of, more complex texts as you read more works of literary nonfiction. To comprehend complex texts, use reading strategies, such as monitoring comprehension, paraphrasing, summarizing, using context, connecting, and visualizing, some of which are described here.

Examples

- **Monitor** your comprehension by asking yourself questions about what you have just read. Do this whenever something happens that you might not have understood. For example, in Judith Ortiz Cofer's essay "Volar: To Fly," how does she look into the landlord's home, and what happens there? Why does she choose to do what she did? Reread the section until you understand what has happened. If necessary, go back a little and reread the start of that section; then read ahead to see if you understood it correctly.

- In the same essay, you can also use **context** to understand her vocabulary. She speaks of the alley behind her apartment as being "dismal." The context clues to the meaning of *dismal* include "littered," "narrow," and "never cleaned." From these clues, you understand that the alley was not pleasant.

- **Paraphrase** sections that you may not completely understand. The ending of the essay shows the author's parents discussing something at the kitchen table; her mother seems especially wistful and longing. Why does her mother say, "Oh, if only I could fly"? Restate the discussion in your own words and you will understand why her mother wants to fly.

Academic Vocabulary

complexity the degree to which a work is difficult to understand

comprehend understand the meaning and importance of something

Apply the Standard

Use the worksheet that follows to help you apply the standard as you read. Several copies of the worksheet have been provided for you to use with different informational text selections.

- Comprehending Complex Texts

Name ______________________ Date ____________ Assignment ______________

Comprehending Complex Texts

Explain what makes the literary nonfiction selection you are reading complex. Then explain how the strategy on the left in the chart helps you comprehend the selection.

What makes this selection complex?

....

....

Strategy	How the Strategy Helped Me Comprehend the Selection
monitoring comprehension	
using context	
paraphrasing	

A

Name ______________________ Date ____________ Assignment ______________

Comprehending Complex Texts

Explain what makes the literary nonfiction selection you are reading complex. Then explain how the strategy on the left in the chart helps you comprehend the selection.

What makes this selection complex?

....

....

Strategy	How the Strategy Helped Me Comprehend the Selection
monitoring comprehension	
using context	
paraphrasing	

Name ______________________ Date ______________ Assignment ______________

Comprehending Complex Texts

Explain what makes the literary nonfiction selection you are reading complex. Then explain how the strategy on the left in the chart helps you comprehend the selection.

What makes this selection complex?

....

....

Strategy	How the Strategy Helped Me Comprehend the Selection
monitoring comprehension	
using context	
paraphrasing	

Name ______________________ Date ______________ Assignment ________________

Comprehending Complex Texts

Explain what makes the literary nonfiction selection you are reading complex. Then explain how the strategy on the left in the chart helps you comprehend the selection.

What makes this selection complex?

....

....

Strategy	How the Strategy Helped Me Comprehend the Selection
monitoring comprehension	
using context	
paraphrasing	

D

For use with Informational Text 10

Name ______________________ Date ______________ Assignment ________________

Comprehending Complex Texts

Explain what makes the literary nonfiction selection you are reading complex. Then explain how the strategy on the left in the chart helps you comprehend the selection.

What makes this selection complex?

....

....

Strategy	How the Strategy Helped Me Comprehend the Selection
monitoring comprehension	
using context	
paraphrasing	

Name _______________ Date _______________ Assignment _______________

Comprehending Complex Texts

Explain what makes the literary nonfiction selection you are reading complex. Then explain how the strategy on the left in the chart helps you comprehend the selection.

What makes this selection complex?

....

....

Strategy	How the Strategy Helped Me Comprehend the Selection
monitoring comprehension	
using context	
paraphrasing	

Writing Standards

Writing 1

1. Write arguments to support claims with clear reasons and relevant evidence.

Writing Workshop: Argument

When you write an argument, you make a claim and then offer details to support your claim. For example, an essay about a longer school day might state the claim that the current six-and-a-half-hour school day should not be extended. The reasons and evidence used to elaborate that claim are the core of that argument. If the reasons are logical and the evidence is specific, detailed, and relevant, then the argument will be sound. If the reasons are illogical and the evidence is inaccurate, then the argument cannot be sound.

Assignment

Write an argumentative essay about an issue that concerns people in your community or school. Include these elements:

✓ a claim, or clear opinion statement that presents your position on an issue

✓ logical reasons and accurate evidence that support your position

✓ the use of reliable sources to give your argument credibility

✓ evidence to address opposing points of view

✓ clear and effective organization

✓ the use of transitions and conjunctions to clarify the relationship between ideas

✓ a formal style and objective tone

✓ correct use of language convention

Additional Standards

Writing

1. Write arguments to support claims with clear reasons and relevant evidence.

1.a. Introduce claim(s), acknowledge alternate or opposing claims, and organize the reasons and evidence logically.

1.b. Support claim(s) with logical reasoning and relevant evidence, using accurate, credible sources and demonstrating an understanding of the topic or text.

1.c. Use words, phrases, and clauses to create cohesion and clarify the relationships among claim(s), reasons, and evidence.

1.d. Establish and maintain a formal style.

1.e. Provide a concluding statement or section that follows from and supports the argument presented.

2.d. Use precise language and domain-specific vocabulary to inform about or explain the topic.

4. Produce clear and coherent writing in which the development, organization, and style are appropriate to task, purpose, and audience.

6. Use technology, including the Internet, to produce and publish writing and link to and cite sources as well as to interact and collaborate with others, including linking to and citing sources.

Language

1. Demonstrate command of the conventions of standard English grammar and usage when writing or speaking.

3.b. Maintain consistency in style and tone.

Name ______________________ Date ____________ Assignment ______________

Prewriting/Planning Strategies

Choose a topic. Find a topic for your essay. Engage in a group roundtable discussion about problems in your school or community. Raise as many different issues as possible. Take notes about topics that spark your interest and that arouse lively discussion. Choose one of these issues for your essay topic.

You can also make a quick list to explore a variety of issues. In the first column, list issues that interest you. In the second column, write a word to describe each issue. In the third column, give a specific example for each descriptive word you wrote. In the last column, describe at least one opposing point of view. Choose the issue that you feel most strongly about as the topic for your essay. Make sure it has an opposing side.

Issues and Ideas	Descriptive Word	Examples	What is at least one opposing side?
Example: *School Uniforms*	*unattractive*	*brown pleated skirts, tan shirts*	*They can lower clothing budget.*

Narrow your topic. To write an effective essay, your topic should be focused and manageable. Evaluate your chosen topic to be sure that it is specific enough to be covered effectively in a short essay. For example, you could never cover the topic "protecting the environment" in an essay. There are too many ideas related to this topic. Instead, you could narrow the topic and make it more focused. For example, you could write about the importance of not littering on school grounds.

Name ______________________ Date ____________ Assignment ______________

Supporting a Claim

Consider all sides of an issue. Collect evidence, such as facts, examples, and expert opinions, from accurate and credible sources. Focus on current publications and try to find a minimum of two sources for each fact. Consult books written by experts on your topic. When doing research on the Internet, look at sites sponsored by the government (".gov") or an educational institution (".edu"). These sites are usually more reliable than sites written by individuals or special interest groups. Gather evidence to address questions and opposing points of view. Once you have completed your chart, review the evidence to make sure it is specific and relevant.

- If any source you list is not **clear** and **specific,** look for more facts and details to clarify and strengthen your ideas.
- If any evidence contradicts another piece of evidence, delete it, or put a question mark next to it until you can confirm which evidence is **accurate.**
- If any idea is not **relevant,** or directly related to your topic, delete it.

Reasons and Evidence That Support My Claim	Sources Used
Reasons and Evidence That Address Counterarguments	

Name ______________________ Date ____________ Assignment ________________

Drafting Strategies

Create a structure for your draft. Make an organizational plan for your essay that is both logical and persuasive.

- Use the graphic organizer below to construct a sound argument. Begin by writing a thesis statement that identifies the issue and clearly states your position.
- Review the reasons and evidence you have gathered to support your claim. Rank reasons in order of importance, starting with number 1 for least important. List reasons in this order in the organizer. Choose one counterargument to address.

Claim **Thesis Statement:**	
Supporting Reason #1 (least important):	**Evidence** **A.** **B.**
Supporting Reason #2:	**Evidence** **A.** **B.**
Supporting Reason #3 (most important):	**Evidence** **A.** **B.**
Counterargument:	**Evidence** **A.** **B.**

Name ______________________ Date ____________ Assignment ______________

Developing and evaluating your claim. Keep your task, purpose, and audience in mind as you draft your essay.

1. Write an introduction that includes a strong thesis statement. State your claim, or position, on the topic in clear, memorable terms. Use words and phrases that your audience will understand.
2. As you draft your claim, continue to make your position clear. Use precise, lively language to emphasize well-supported points and build support for your position. Make your audience want to keep reading.
3. Use your notes as a guide. Include transitions to create a cohesive argument and to make the relationships among your claims, reasons, and evidence clear.
4. Present counterarguments fairly and reasonably. Give factual evidence that shows why an opposing point of view should not be supported.
5. Conclude with a strong statement that summarizes your argument and gives readers something new to think about.

My Claim	Evaluating the Claim, Reasons, and Evidence
	❑ Is the claim clearly stated? ❑ Is there any doubt which side of the issue my argument supports? ❑ Are the reasons logical and serious? ❑ Is all the evidence specific, accurate, and relevant? ❑ Does the argument consider the audience's age and knowledge?
Counterarguments	
	❑ Have I addressed a counterargument fairly and reasonably? ❑ Have I used sufficient evidence to prove the counterargument is weak or incorrect?

For use with Writing 1

Style and Tone

Establish and maintain a formal style. Use a formal, objective style and tone when you write your argument. An informal, subjective style expresses personal feelings and opinions that many readers will not share and may even find offensive. On the other hand, a formal and objective style appeals to a widely shared sense of what is right and fair. It encourages readers to give your ideas serious consideration.

Examples:

Claim: Old Oak Park should not be destroyed so that a new office complex can be built.

Not a Formal, Objective Style: I can't believe that people are being so stupid.

Formal, Objective Style: The mayor and city council members have not considered how residents on the east side will be affected by this decision.

Not a Formal, Objective Tone: Okay, it's true that some of you have been out of work like forever!

Formal: The office complex will provide new job opportunities for residents.

Clarify the relationships among ideas. A cohesive argument is easy to follow and understand because all the ideas relate to one another clearly and logically. You can create cohesion in several ways:

- Make connections between claims, reasons, and pieces of evidence. Use conjunctions such as *and, but, or, so, yet, although, because,* and *whenever* to combine clauses to form compound and complex sentences.
- Vary sentence beginnings to link ideas between sentences and paragraphs. For example, begin sentences with prepositions, such as *despite, concerning, regardless of,* and *in addition to.*
- Use transitional words, phrases, and clauses, such as *consequently, for this reason,* and *however,* to clarify connections between ideas and sentences.

Use precise, neutral language. Precise, neutral language will convey your ideas without being overly emotional or insensitive to the feelings of others. Choose language that stirs readers' emotions while still appealing to their sense of reason. Avoid words that are vague or that convey sarcasm, contempt, delight, impatience or other personal attitudes.

Examples:

Vague: a *lot of* residents

Too personal: some *ignorant* officials

Neutral and precise: *seventy-five percent* of *informed* residents

Name ______________________ Date ______________ Assignment ________________

Conclusion

Provide a strong conclusion. Your written argument should end with a strong conclusion that progresses logically from and supports the argument presented in the body of the essay. Use the following strategies to write a strong conclusion.

- Begin with a summary statement of the claim: *The recycling center is a valuable asset to the community and should not be relocated.*
- Then review the main points of the argument: *The facts show that more than 45 percent of town residents use the recycling center on a weekly basis. More than 80 percent use it at least once a month. Many residents admit that they are less likely to recycle on a regular basis if it means that they will have to drive 40 miles to the closest recycling center.*
- End by restating the claim in a memorable way. Give readers something important to think about. *Moving the recycling center to Rockville creates an unnecessary hardship for people in our community who care about the survival of our planet.*

My Conclusion	Evaluating My Conclusion
	❑ Does it begin with a restatement of my claim?
	❑ Does it review the main points of my argument?
	❑ Does it end with a memorable statement that gives readers something new or more to think about?

Name ______________________ Date ____________ Assignment ______________

Revising Strategies

Put a checkmark beside each question as you revise.

	Questions to Ask as You Revise
Writing Task	❑ Have I written an essay that argues for my position on an issue? ❑ Does my topic have at least two sides? ❑ Does my essay have a clear and effective beginning, middle, and end?
Purpose	❑ Does my introduction contain a thesis statement that clearly states my claim or position? ❑ Do I give reasons and specific, relevant evidence to support my claim? ❑ Are the reasons clear and logical? ❑ Do I have enough facts, quotations, expert opinions, examples, and other evidence to support my claim? ❑ Do I use only relevant evidence to strengthen my argument? ❑ Does my conclusion follow logically from ideas presented in my argument?
Audience	❑ Do I use precise language and details that are appropriate for the age and knowledge level of my readers? ❑ Is my argument cohesive? ❑ Do I use transitions to clarify relationships between ideas? ❑ Do I address questions and concerns my readers might have about my topic? ❑ Does my argument appeal to reason and not just to emotion? ❑ Do I vary sentence structure to add interest to my ideas? ❑ Will my audience be persuaded to agree with my position?

For use with Writing 1

Revising

Revise to emphasize connections. As you revise, check to see that you have used a variety of sentence lengths. You can add interest to your writing and emphasize the relationships between ideas by combining short, choppy sentences into new, longer sentences. Before you combine sentences, check that the ideas are closely related.

Similar Ideas: The chorus puts on six concerts a year. The concerts raise much-needed funds for the school.

Combined: The chorus puts on six concerts a year, <u>which</u> raise much-needed funds for the school.

Opposing Ideas: The music program depends on volunteer instructors. There are always more volunteers than required.

Combined: The music program depends on volunteer instructors, <u>but</u> there are always more volunteers than required.

Revising fragments. Be sure that your new sentences are complete. A complete sentence contains a single **independent clause** with a subject and a verb, and it expresses a complete thought. A **fragment** is a group of words that is often missing a subject, a verb, or both. A fragment does not express a complete thought.

Fragment: The chorus is open to all students. Although they must sign up early.

Corrected: The chorus is open to all students, although they must sign up early.

Revising run-on sentences. When combining ideas, avoid creating run-on sentences. A **run-on sentence** happens when two or more independent clauses are joined without proper punctuation. There are several ways to correct run-on sentences.

Run-on: Last year, the chorus sang at the children's hospital, the chorus also gave a concert at the Senior Center.

Corrected: Last year, the chorus sang at the children's hospital. The chorus also gave a concert at the Senior Center. *(Create two complete sentences.)*

Corrected: Last year, the chorus sang at the children's hospital, and it also gave a concert at the Senior Center. *(Use a conjunction and comma to connect ideas.)*

Corrected: Last year, the chorus sang at the children's hospital; it also gave a concert at the Senior Center. *(Use a semicolon to connect ideas.)*

Revision Checklist

- ❑ Do I combine closely related ideas into interesting sentences?
- ❑ Are all my sentences complete?
- ❑ Do I avoid fragments and run-on sentences?

Editing and Proofreading

Review your draft to correct errors in capitalization, spelling, and punctuation.

Focus on Capitalization: Review your draft carefully to find and correct capitalization errors. Make sure each sentence begins with a capital letter. If your argumentative essay names places, people, or official groups and organizations, be sure that you have capitalized the proper name correctly.

Incorrect capitalization	Correct capitalization
The rose lamont senior center	The Rose Lamont Senior Center

Focus on Spelling: An argumentative essay that includes spelling errors suggests that you do not care about your writing, your readers, or your topic. Check the spelling of each word. Look for words that you frequently misspell and make sure that they are correct. If you have typed your draft on a computer, use the spell-check feature to double-check for errors. Keep in mind that spell-checkers will not find words that are typed correctly but spell the wrong word—for example, if you typed *write* instead of *right*. Proofread carefully, even after you run spell-check.

Focus on Punctuation: End Punctuation Proofread your writing to find and correct punctuation errors. Pay particular attention to different sentence types. Be sure you use the correct end mark for each kind of sentence.

Rule: Use a period at the end of a statement: *School uniforms can help create equality.*

Rule: Use a question mark at the end of a question: *Should students have to worry that their clothes are not stylish enough?*

Rule: Use an exclamation mark at the end of a statement that indicates strong feeling: *School corridors are not fashion runways!*

Rule: Use a dash to offset important information or to add emphasis: *School uniforms will not resolve all the problems we face—they are not magical—but they can shift the focus from what we are wearing back to what we are learning.*

Revision Checklist

- ❑ Have you reviewed your essay for words, titles, or names that should be capitalized?
- ❑ Have you read each sentence and checked that all of the words are spelled correctly?
- ❑ Do all your sentences begin with a capital letter and end with the correct punctuation mark?

Name ______________________ Date ____________ Assignment ______________

Publishing and Presenting

Consider one of the ways shown below to present your writing:

Deliver a speech. Use your argumentative essay as a basis for a speech that you give to classmates. Allow time to practice before you give your speech. Print out a copy and highlight important details that you want to emphasize. Rehearse with a peer, and pay particular attention to your pace and volume. Make eye contact with your listener and pause after important points for dramatic effect. Ask your peer for feedback and advice on how to deliver your speech more persuasively.

Submit a newspaper article. Many newspapers have both print and online editions. Local newspapers will often publish well-written, objective essays if the arguments will appeal to the newspaper's audience. Submit your essay by mail to the newspaper, or follow the newspaper's Web site directions for submitting it online.

Rubric for Self-Assessment

Find evidence in your writing to address each category. Then use the rating scale to grade your work.

Evaluating Your Argument	not very					very
Focus: How clearly is your position stated?	1	2	3	4	5	6
Organization: How cohesive and logical is your argument?	1	2	3	4	5	6
Support/Elaboration: How specific, accurate, relevant, and persuasive is your evidence?	1	2	3	4	5	6
Style: How well have you maintained a formal, objective style throughout your argument?	1	2	3	4	5	6
Conventions: How free of errors in grammar, usage, spelling, and punctuation is your argument?	1	2	3	4	5	6

Writing 2

2. Write informative/explanatory texts to examine a topic and convey ideas, concepts, and information through the selection, organization, and analysis of relevant content.

Writing Workshop: Comparison-and-Contrast Essay

A comparison-and-contrast essay examines the similarities and differences between two or more related subjects. A well-constructed comparison-and-contrast essay can change the way people look at something and even influence their choices. For example, an essay that compares brands of bicycles can help you decide which bicycle is best for you. An essay that compares candidates in an election might surprise readers, changing how they view each candidate and influencing how they vote.

Assignment

Write a comparison-and-contrast essay that helps readers make a decision or see things in a fresh way. Include these elements:

✓ a topic, involving two or more related subjects that are neither nearly identical nor extremely different

✓ an attention-grabbing introduction that includes a thesis

✓ a clear, consistent organizational pattern that highlights points of comparison

✓ facts, descriptions, and examples that illustrate similarities and differences between the subjects

✓ a strong conclusion that follows from and supports the comparison and contrast

✓ a formal style

✓ correct use of language conventions

Additional Standards

Writing

2. Write informative/ explanatory texts to examine a topic and convey ideas, concepts, and information through the selection, organization and analysis of relevant content.

2.a. Introduce a topic clearly, previewing what is to follow; organize idea, concepts, and information, using strategies such as definition, classification, comparison/ contrast, and cause/ effect; include formatting (e.g., headings), graphics (e.g., charts, tables), and multimedia when useful to aiding comprehension.

2.b. Develop the topic with relevant facts, definitions, concrete details, quotations, or other information and examples.

2.c. Use appropriate transitions to create cohesion and clarify the relationships among ideas and concepts.

2.d. Use precise language and domain-specific vocabulary to inform about or explain the topic.

2.e. Establish and maintain a formal style.

2.f. Provide a concluding statement or section that follows from and supports the information or explanation presented.

4. Produce clear and coherent writing in which the development, organization, and style are appropriate to task, purpose, and audience.

6. Use technology, including the Internet, to produce and publish writing and link to and cite sources as well as to interact and collaborate with others, including linking to and citing sources.

Language

2. Demonstrate command of the conventions of standard English capitalization, punctuation, and spelling when writing.

6. Acquire and use accurately grade-appropriate general academic and domain-specific words and phrases; gather vocabulary knowledge when considering a word or phrase important to comprehension or expression.

Name ______________________ Date ____________ Assignment ______________

Prewriting/Planning Strategies

Choose a topic. Draw a line down the center of a piece of paper and write the word *BUT* on the line. Then on the left side of the page, list pairs of items with something in common, such as two brands of athletic shoes. On the right, write the differences between each pair of items. Choose your topic from the pairs that you list.

You can also use the chart below to list choices you've made, such as products you chose to buy, or books or music you picked. In the second column, write a word or phrase that describes your choice. In the third column, write an alternate choice that you could have picked. For example, you might list a plaid flannel shirt with snaps you bought for cold weather. The shirt might be comfortable but not warm enough, and your alternate choice might be a zippered jacket. Keep listing choices and alternatives until you find a pair that interests you. Make sure there are enough points of comparison for your essay.

Choices:	Descriptive Word or Phrase	Alternate Choice

Narrow your topic. Some topics are too broad to compare in a brief essay. For example, you could write volumes comparing and contrasting all the features of movies and books. To make a broad topic more manageable, divide it into smaller subtopics. Then focus your essay on one of these subtopics, such as the movie version of a specific book.

Broad Topic	→	Subtopic 1	→	Subtopic 2	→	Subtopic 3
Subject a:		Subject a:		Subject a:		Subject a:
Subject b:		Subject b:		Subject b:		Subject b:

Name ______________________ Date ______________ Assignment ________________

Prewriting/Planning Strategies

Gather details. Use the diagram below to gather facts, definitions, descriptions, quotations, and examples related to your two subjects. Use the middle section where the ovals overlap to record details that show how the subjects are alike. Record details that show how each subject is different in the outside sections. Look for interesting points of comparison that will engage your audience and may also surprise them. Try to include an equal number of points for each subject so that your comparison and contrast essay will be balanced.

Subject 1. ....

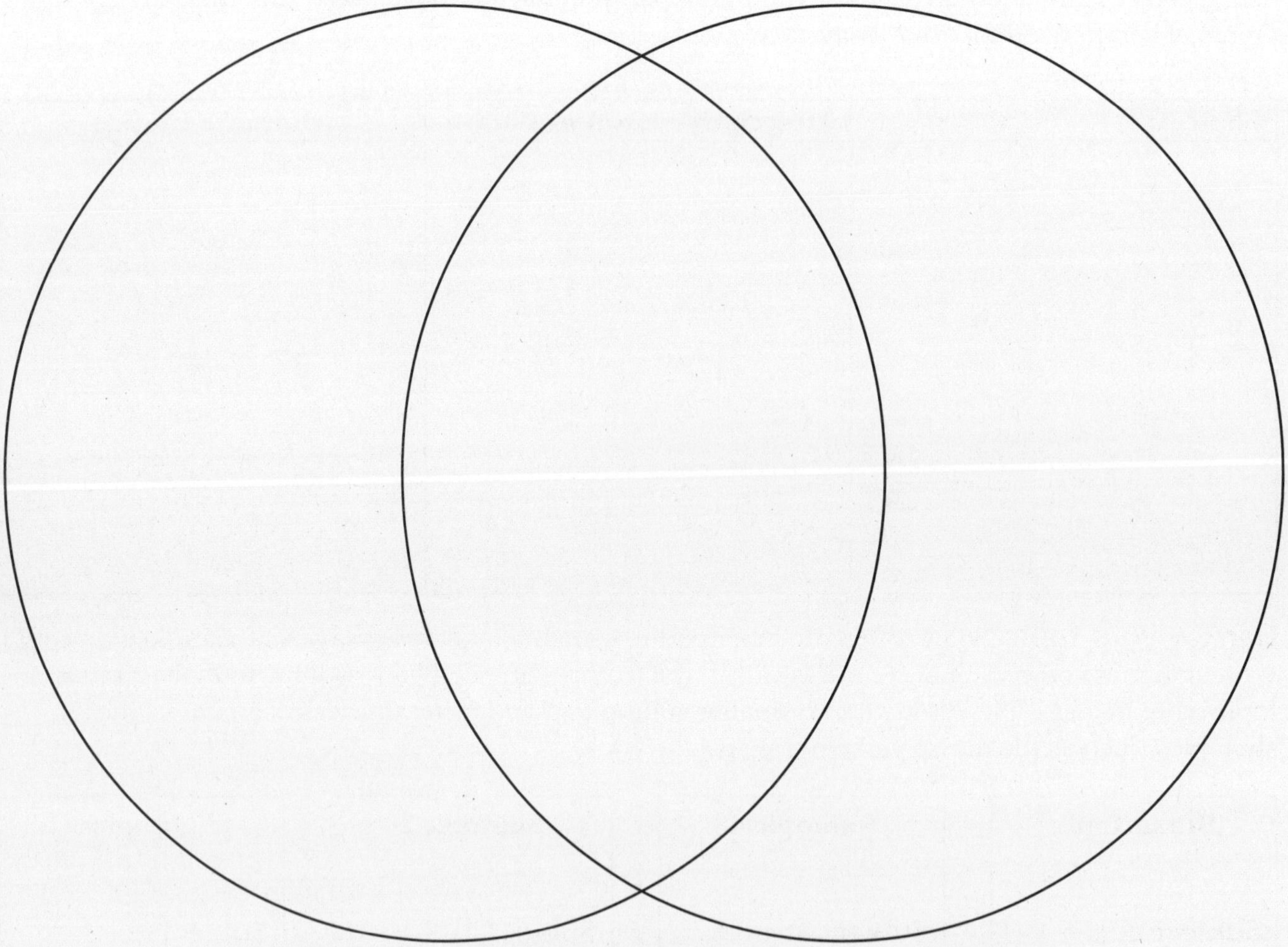

Subject 2. ....

Name ______________________ Date ____________ Assignment ______________

Drafting Strategies

Choose an organizational pattern. Most comparison-and-contrast essays are organized in one of two ways.

- **Block Method:** Present all of your details about one subject first. Then, present all of your details about the second subject. This method works well when you are writing about more than two things, or when your topic is very complex.
- **Point-by-Point Method:** Discuss one feature of both subjects, then another feature of both subjects, and so on.

Use the following organizers to help you decide whether the block method or the point-by-point method is a more appropriate pattern for your essay.

Block Method

List all details about **Subject 1:**

List all details about **Subject 2:**

Point-by-Point Method

Subject 1	Subject 2

For use with Writing 2

Name ______________________ Date ____________ Assignment ________________

Develop your comparison and contrast essay.

1. **Start with an effective introduction.**

   a) Draw your audience into your essay with an attention-grabbing lead sentence that appeals to their interests or invites their curiosity.

   b) Establish why the comparison is important or useful.

   c) Provide a quick overview of what your audience will learn in the rest of the essay.

2. **Use specific details.** Include details that are colorful, important, and specific. The more you distinguish similarities and differences between your subjects, the more interesting and effective your essay will be. For example, instead of saying that the movie version of a book changes the ending, explain in detail the differences in the endings.

3. **Use transitions.** Use transitional words and phrases that clearly show the relationships between your subjects' features. Transitions that show comparison include *similarly, also, just as,* and *like*. Transitions that show contrast include *although, but, on the other hand, whereas, however,* and *while*.

4. **Note formatting ideas.** Jot down formatting ideas you might use to highlight important points in your essay. Include a variety of elements such as headings or bold print for key terms, photographs, illustrations, charts, diagrams, and video and audio clips. Choose elements that help readers better understand your ideas.

My Comparison-Contrast	
Subject 1:	Subject 2: ....
Formatting Notes	

For use with Writing 2

Style

Establish a formal style. Establishing a formal style in a written essay communicates respect for your audience and shows that your ideas have value.

- By maintaining a formal style, writers encourage their audiences to keep an open mind. Writers express their ideas through statements of facts, logical reasoning, and appeals to shared values.
- By contrast, an informal style involves expressing personal reactions and assuming the audience knows something from experience or prior knowledge.

Examples:

Informal: The bread looked like it was supposed to, just like when you make a perfect grilled-cheese sandwich on a grill. *(The writer assumes readers know how a grilled cheese sandwich looks when cooked on a grill and share the writer's opinion of the perfect grilled-cheese sandwich.)*

Formal: Dark grill marks formed a crisscrossed pattern on the crispy, golden-brown bread. Silky smooth cheddar cheese oozed out from between the slices. For me, it was the perfect grilled-cheese sandwich.

Use precise language and domain-specific vocabulary. Supporting ideas with precise nouns, verbs, adjectives, and adverbs, as well as domain-specific vocabulary gives your writing a knowledgeable, authoritative voice.

Precise language adds impact and interest to your ideas.

General: The sneakers are very comfortable.

Precise: The thick soles and seamless lining of the 490 Rev Sneaker provide added comfort when walking or jogging.

Domain-specific terms are words and phrases that are specific to a subject area. When using subject-specific vocabulary, consider your audience. If you think that readers may not recognize or understand a specific term, then provide a definition or clear example.

Audience of Students: He plays a variation of swing, a form of jazz music that was popular in the 1930s. *(Students may not know what swing is, so the writer includes a definition)*

Audience of Music Teachers: He plays a variation of swing. *(The writer knows that music teachers are familiar with music genres.)*

Name ______________________ Date ______________ Assignment ________________

Conclusion

Provide a strong conclusion. Your comparison-and-contrast essay should end with a strong conclusion that follows from and supports ideas that you presented in body of the essay. Use the following strategy to construct your conclusion.

- Begin with a summary statement that restates your main idea in a new way: *The next time you are about to buy lunch at a fast food restaurant, why not consider making your own lunch?*
- Remind readers why the comparison is important: *You can control the freshness and nutritional value of the ingredients, and it will probably cost less.*
- End by inviting readers to think about the topic in a fresh way. Make the value of your comparison clear: *Not only will you be eating a healthier meal, you may discover that you have the creativity of a great chef.*

My Conclusion	Evaluating My Conclusion
	❑ Does it begin with a restatement of my main idea? ❑ Does it sum up the main points of my comparison and contrast? ❑ Does it end with a memorable statement that gives readers something to think about?

Name ______________________ Date ____________ Assignment ______________

Revising

Evaluate organization and balance. Your essay should follow one organizational pattern from beginning to end and give equal space to each of your subjects. To check the balance of your essay, review it point by point.

You can use different colored markers to underline or highlight details for each subject.

- If one color appears much more than the other, revise to add more details about the other subject.
- If the colors first appear in large blocks and then appear to alternate, you may have started your essay using a block organization pattern and then switched to the point-by-point pattern. Revise to follow one organizational pattern throughout the essay.

Use the chart to evaluate the organization and balance in your essay. You may also ask a partner to review your essay and then revise based on your partner's comments.

	Subject 1	**Subject 2**
Point 1:		
Point 2:		
Point 3:		

Do I need to add more information? Yes No

If yes, list new information here: ....

....

....

....

Name ____________________ Date ______________ Assignment ____________________

Revising Strategies

Put a checkmark beside each question as you revise.

	Questions to Ask as You Revise
Writing Task	❑ Have I written an essay that compares and contrasts two subjects and helps readers make a decision or see things in a fresh way? ❑ Do I use specific details to show how the two subjects are similar? ❑ Do I use specific details to show how the two subjects are different?
Purpose	❑ Does my introduction identify my two subjects and establish why the comparison is important? ❑ Do I develop the comparison with relevant facts, definitions, concrete details, quotations, examples, or other information? ❑ Does all the information support or elaborate on my main idea, or thesis? ❑ Is my essay balanced with an equal number of details for each subject? ❑ Do I use one pattern of organization throughout the essay? ❑ Does my conclusion follow logically from and support ideas presented in my essay?
Audience	❑ Do I use precise language and domain-specific terms that are appropriate for my audience? ❑ Is my comparison easy to follow and understand? ❑ Do I draw my audience in with an attention-grabbing introduction? ❑ Do I use transitions to signal similarities and differences? ❑ Is there anywhere that I can add a surprising comparison, strong image, or thought-provoking question to heighten interest? ❑ Does my conclusion give my audience something to think about? ❑ Is there anywhere that I can add formatting to make my ideas clearer?

For use with Writing 2

Revising

Revise adjectives and adverbs. Problems with adjectives and adverbs often occur when these words are placed in the wrong spot in a sentence. Another common problem is confusing adjectives and adverbs that have similar meanings.

Identifying Adjective and Adverb Errors

The common modifiers *just* and *only* often cause problems in both speaking and writing. When used as an adverb, *just* often means "no more than." When *just* has this meaning, place it right before the word it modifies.

Incorrect: Do you *just* want an average pair of sneakers?

Correct: Do you want *just* an average pair of sneakers?

The position of the adverb *only* can affect the entire meaning of a sentence.

Only she enjoyed the book. (Nobody else enjoyed the book.)

She *only* enjoyed the book. (She did nothing else with the book.)

She enjoyed *only* the book. (She enjoyed nothing else.)

Adjectives and adverbs with similar meanings are easy to confuse.

Commonly Confused Adjectives and Adverbs	
bad: (adjective) He was a *bad* skater.	**badly:** (adverb) I played *badly* at the recital.
fewer: answers "How many?" He had *fewer* questions.	**less:** answers "How much?" He drank *less* water today.

Fixing Errors in Adjective and Adverb Usage

Reread the draft of your essay. Underline every sentence that contains an error in adjective and adverb usage. Correct the errors using the following methods.

- **For *only*:** If you're using *only* as an adverb meaning "no more than," place it right before the word that it modifies.
- **For *just*:** Identify the intended meaning of the sentence. Then position *just* in the sentence so that the meaning is clear.
- **For commonly confused adjectives and adverbs:** Make sure you are using the correct word. Remember that adjectives modify nouns, and adverbs modify verbs, adjectives, and other adverbs.

Revision Checklist

❑ Have I placed *just* and *only* in sentences correctly?

❑ Have I used *bad* and *badly,* and *fewer* and *less* correctly?

❑ Have I avoided usage problems with other adjectives and adverbs?

Editing and Proofreading

Review your draft to correct errors in capitalization, spelling, and punctuation.

Focus on Capitalization: Review your draft carefully to find and correct capitalization errors. If your comparison-and-contrast essay names places, people, or official groups and organizations, be sure that you have capitalized the proper names correctly.

Incorrect capitalization	**Correct capitalization**
The little mermaid café	The Little Mermaid Café

If your essay includes the titles of works, such as books or movies, capitalize the first word, the last word, and every word in between except the articles *a, an,* and *the*; short prepositions such as *to* and *of*; and coordinating conjunctions such as *and, but,* and *or.*

Example: *The Chronicles of Narnia: Prince Caspian*

Focus on Spelling: Take time to check the spelling of each word in your draft. Look for words that you frequently misspell and make sure that they are correct. If you have typed your draft on a computer, use the spell-check feature to double-check for errors. Keep in mind that spell-checkers will not find words that are typed incorrectly but spell another word, such as *no* instead of *not.* Proofread carefully even after you run spell-check.

Check the spelling of name brands online and of domain-specific words in the dictionary. In some cases, you may have to consult a specialized dictionary.

Focus on Punctuation: Titles Proofread your writing to find and address punctuation errors. If your essay includes titles of literary works or works of art, follow these rules.

- Use quotation marks around the titles of songs, short poems, short stories, book chapters, specific episodes of television programs, and news articles.
- Underline or use italics for titles of magazines, newspapers, books, plays, films, videos, radio and television programs, CDs, paintings, symphonies and other long musical works, ships, and aircraft.

Examples:

"Trees" *(poem)* "All Summer in a Day" *(short story)* "America the Beautiful" *(song)*

Mona Lisa (painting) San Francisco Chronicle (newspaper)

Revision Checklist

- ❑ Have you reviewed your essay for words, names, and titles that should be capitalized? Have you used quotation marks and italics for titles of works?
- ❑ Have you read each sentence and checked that all of the words are spelled correctly?
- ❑ Do all your sentences have the correct end punctuation?

Name ______________________ Date ____________ Assignment ______________

Publishing and Presenting

Consider one of the following ways to present your writing:

Submit to a magazine. Submit your essay to a magazine that publishes writing by students. You can find publishing information and an address in a recent edition of the magazine. If the magazine has an online edition, find out how you can submit your essay using the Internet.

Create a photo essay. Turn your comparison into a photo essay. Gather photographs and other visuals to enhance your text. Use whatever technology you have available to create and share your photo essay with the class. For example, if you used a computer to type your essay, scan photos and other graphics and add them to your document. Then print out your photo essay or upload it to the class Web site.

Rubric for Self-Assessment

Find evidence in your writing to address each category. Then use the rating scale to grade your work. Circle the score that best applies for each category.

Evaluating Your Comparison-and-Contrast Essay	not very very
Focus: How clearly have you stated how two or more subjects are alike and different?	1 2 3 4 5 6
Organization: How effectively are points of comparison organized?	1 2 3 4 5 6
Support/Elaboration: How well do you use facts, descriptions, and examples to describe similarities and differences?	1 2 3 4 5 6
Style: How precise is your language and how well have you maintained a formal style?	1 2 3 4 5 6
Conventions: How free of errors in grammar, usage, spelling, and punctuation is your essay?	1 2 3 4 5 6

Writing 3

3. Write narratives to develop real or imagined experiences or events using effective technique, relevant descriptive details, and well-structured event sequences.

Writing Workshop: Short Story

When you write a short story, you can let your imagination soar. A **short story** is a brief, creative fictional narrative that develops around a conflict, or struggle between opposing forces. A well-constructed short story can transport readers to a whole new world, where anyone and anything is possible. The purpose of a short story is to entertain, but short stories often also teach important life lessons.

Assignment

Write a short story about an interesting, puzzling, or extraordinary situation that will capture readers' attention. Include these elements:

✓ well-developed major and minor characters

✓ an interesting conflict, or struggle

✓ a clear plot, or story line told in sequence

✓ a consistent point of view

✓ narrative techniques, including dialogue, suspense, and other literary elements and devices

✓ precise vocabulary and sensory details

✓ effective use of transitions

✓ correct use of language conventions, especially the use of comparatives

*Additional Standards

Writing

3. Write narratives to develop real or imagined experiences or events using effective technique, relevant descriptive details, and well-structured event sequences.

3.a. Engage and orient the reader by establishing a context and point of view and introducing a narrator and/or characters; organize an event sequence that unfolds naturally and logically.

3.b. Use narrative techniques, such as dialogue, pacing, and description, to develop experiences, events, and/or characters.

3.c. Use a variety of transition words, phrases, and clauses to convey sequence and signal shifts from one time frame or setting to another.

3.d. Use precise words and phrases, relevant descriptive details, and sensory language to capture the action and convey experiences and events.

3.e. Provide a conclusion that follows from and reflects the narrated experiences or events.

6. Use technology, including the Internet, to produce and publish writing and link to and cite sources as well as to interact and collaborate with others, including linking to and citing sources

Language

2. Demonstrate command of the conventions of standard English capitalization, punctuation, and spelling when writing.

Name ______________________ Date ____________ Assignment ______________

Prewriting/Planning Strategies

Choose a topic. Use a "what if" strategy to find a story idea. Fill in the blanks of a sentence frame like the one shown below. Try several different situations and choose the one that interests you most.

What if .... (describe a person)
suddenly .... (describe a problem)?

Another good way to generate story ideas is to write down snippets of interesting conversation that you overhear during the day. Jot down words and phrases from these conversations in a journal. At the end of the day, read them over to see if any of them captures your imagination. Select one and develop a story around it.

Explore the conflict. The basic elements of a short story are characters, setting, and plot. The plot consists of the main **conflict,** or struggle, and the events that show how the conflict is resolved. The conflict may be *external,* as when a girl has a disagreement with her best friend; or it may be *internal,* as when the girl finds her friend's diary and struggles with her conscience about whether or not to read it. Once you have a chosen an idea for a story, take some time to explore and develop the conflict. Keep in mind that a conflict can be a difficult challenge the character must face, a decision the character must make, or a goal the character wants to achieve. Answer the questions in the chart.

1. What does my main character want?	
2. Who or what is preventing him or her from getting it?	
3. What will the character do to overcome the person or thing that is getting in the way?	

For use with Writing 3

Name ______________________ Date ____________ Assignment ______________

Understand your main character. Get to know your main character before you write. Then you will know what he or she is likely to do and say in certain situations. Use the web to explore your character's physical appearance, personality traits, likes, dislikes, special interests, and goals. Feel free to add additional categories as you develop your character.

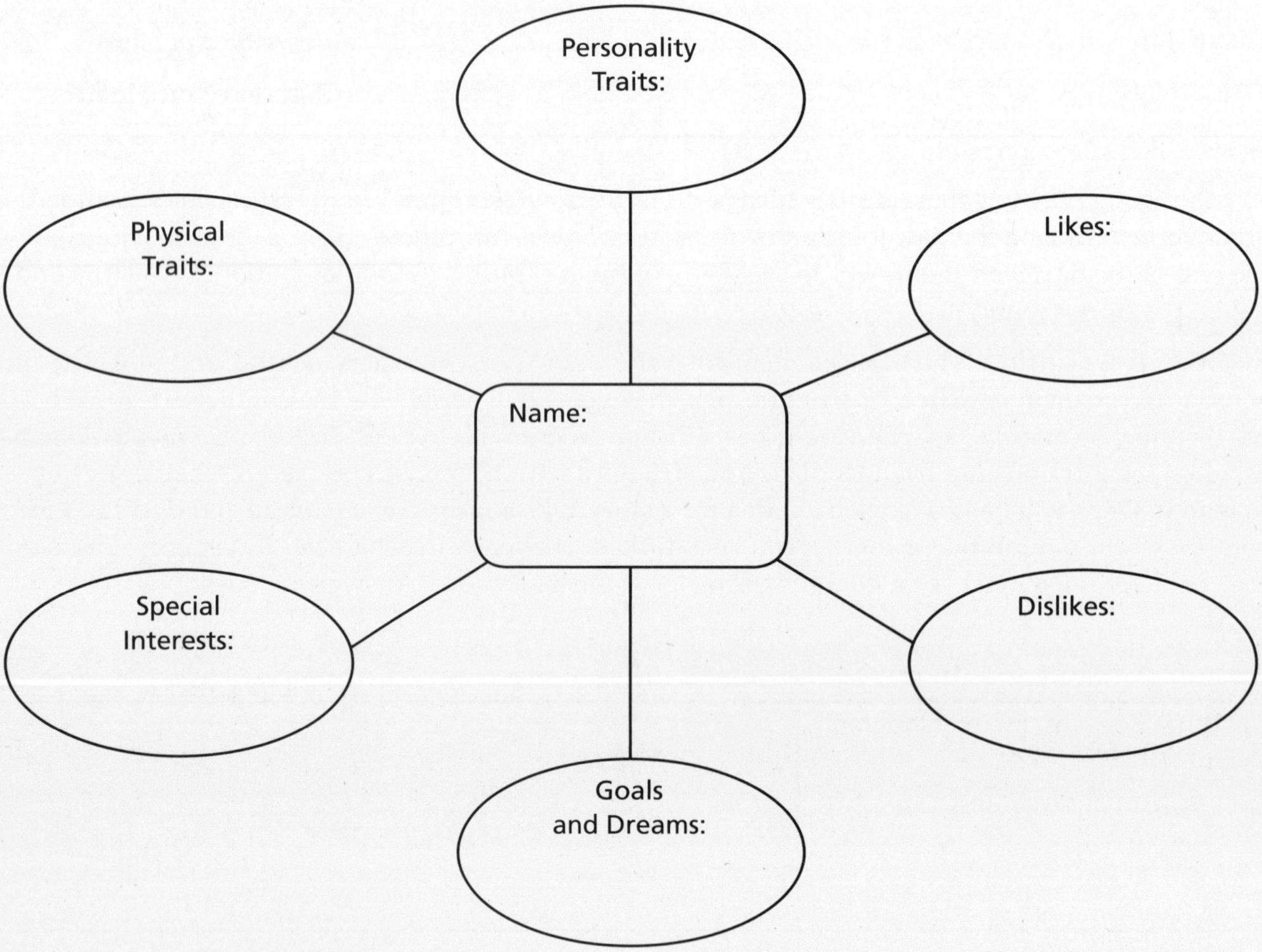

List two or three other minor, or less important characters in your story. Explain their relationship to the main character.

....

....

....

For use with Writing 3

Name ______________________ Date ______________ Assignment ______________

Drafting Strategies

Identify Setting: In some stories, the setting provides a realistic backdrop for the main character's struggle. For example, if you write about a character competing with other students to make the school's track team, some story events would likely take place at the track. In some stories, the setting actually provides the main character's conflict, for example in a story in which the main character gets stranded in a boat in a stormy sea. Use the chart to establish and describe a setting for your story.

Where and when does the story take place?	What details help describe the setting?	What does the setting mean to the conflict?

Develop a plot outline. Use the plot diagram below to organize events in your short story. Plot usually follows this pattern:

- **Exposition** introduces the characters, setting, and central conflict, or problem.
- The **rising action** includes two or three important events that show how the character tries to solve the conflict. Here the conflict intensifies and builds to the climax.
- The **climax** is the high point and most exciting part of the story. It is where the main character finally deals with the conflict.
- The **falling action** leads to the final **resolution,** where the conflict is resolved in some way and all the loose ends are tied up.

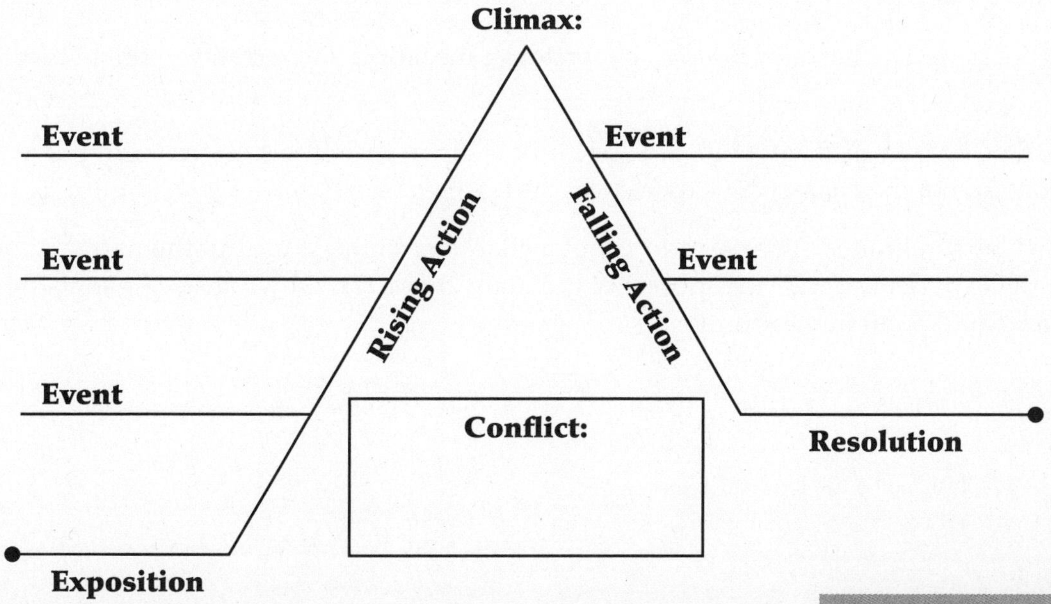

Narrative Techniques

As you draft your story, be sure to balance all the parts of the plot. Set the right pace by varying sentence length and structure so that your story does not drag in some spots or move too quickly in other spots. A good story builds naturally and logically to a single exciting moment. To accomplish this, use a variety of narrative techniques.

Use precise language and sensory details. Good writers use precise language and sensory details to show readers what is happening instead of simply telling them. Using precise language and sensory details to describe setting can also help you convey a specific mood. **Mood** is the general feeling that a story or scene conveys to the reader.

Light, peaceful mood: *Bright beams of sunlight streamed through the open window and danced playfully on Olivia's face, waking her with a warm nudge.*

Dark and threatening: *Olivia was startled awake as a heavy gust of wind slammed the shutters closed, trapping in the suffocating heat.*

Use dialogue effectively. The use of lively dialogue can help move the plot along and also help you reveal more about your characters' thoughts and attitudes. When writing dialogue, keep your characters' personalities in mind. Use words and phrasing that the character would naturally use, including slang, idioms, and contractions.

Use the narrative techniques of foreshadowing and flashback. You can use foreshadowing to build suspense and make readers want to keep reading. **Foreshadowing** gives clues about what happens later in a story. You can use flashback to provide important background information about characters and events in your story. **Flashback** interrupts the story to switch back to an earlier time.

- **Foreshadowing:** *Ben was about to ask his mother to explain when she subtly shook her head at him and smiled secretly.*
- **Flashback:** *Lightning flashed, and suddenly Kara was once again a terrified six-year-old, hiding under the bed, waiting for someone to rescue her.*

Write from a consistent point of view. Tell your story from a single, consistent point of view. Choose from these types of point of view:

- first person: The narrator is also a character in the story; the narrator refers to him- or herself as *I.*
- third person omniscient: The narrator is not a character in the story and can relate details about any of the characters' experiences and perceptions.
- third person limited: The narrator is not a character in the story, but the narrator focuses on the experiences and perceptions of the main character, showing story events from that character's point of view only.

Name _______________ Date _______________ Assignment _______________

Organize your narrative. Use the graphic organizer to organize events in your narrative. As you write, use a variety of transitional words, phrases, and clauses to convey sequence and to signal shifts from one time frame or setting to another.

- **Transitional words:** *first, next, then, meanwhile, before, during, now, yesterday, finally*
- **Transitional phrases:** *at the same time, last week, a month ago, some years back*
- **Transitional clauses:** *Before this event took place, While he was sleeping, When I was a child, After she left, As I walked into another room*

.... ***(Title)***	1. Give your story a title. It should convey the real meaning of your story and capture your readers' interest. 2. Introduce your main characters, the setting, and the conflict. 3. Describe what happens up to and including the climax of the story. Remember to • maintain a consistent point of view. • use vivid, precise language, sensory details, and dialogue. • use flashbacks to shift back to an earlier time. • use foreshadowing to give hints about future events • use transitions to show sequence and to shift to a different setting or time frame.

Name ______________________ Date ____________ Assignment ______________

Conclusion

Provide a strong, satisfactory conclusion. Write an effective resolution, or conclusion to your story that leaves your readers satisfied. Use these tips.

- End with emphasis, not abruptly or vaguely by trailing off. The last event you narrate or scene you describe should help to summarize and reflect on the narrative by clearly showing the results of what has happened. For example, if through the events in the story, the main character has changed in some significant way, then the last scene should show this change. If the character has learned a specific lesson, then the last scene should show how the character applies or plans to apply this lesson to his or her life in the future.
- Tie up loose ends. Unless you are planning to write a sequel to your story, you should not leave readers wondering what happened to an important character or whether an important problem was solved. Include answers to such questions in your resolution.
- As you tie up loose ends, be careful not to cram answers to all unresolved questions into the resolution. The most significant problems or conflicts need to be fully developed and explored through the course of the story. The resolution is the point at which you give the final outcome, not tell a whole story in a sentence or two.

My Conclusion	Evaluating My Conclusion
	☐ Does my conclusion show what happens to the main character after the conflict is resolved? ☐ Does it flow naturally and logically from story events? ☐ Does it wrap up all the loose ends in the story?

For use with Writing 3

Name ______________________ Date ____________ Assignment ______________

Revising Strategies

Evaluate your story

Use the organizer to explain how you plan to revise and edit your story to make it better. If you wish you can give a partner a copy of your draft and this graphic organizer and have your partner suggest ways to improve your story.

Focus Questions		How to Revise
Does my title capture the essence of my story and my readers' interest?	Yes .... No	
Do I introduce characters, setting, and conflict early in the story?	Yes .... No	
Do I use precise language, sensory details, and dialogue to help readers visualize setting, characters, and events?	Yes .... No	
Do I use natural-sounding dialogue that advances the plot and makes my characters believable?	Yes .... No	
Do all the events show how the main character deals with the conflict?	Yes .... No	
Do I use transitions to make the sequence of events clear and to show shifts in time and place?	Yes .... No	
Does the ending leave readers with any unanswered questions?	Yes .... No	
Do I maintain a consistent point of view throughout?	Yes .... No	
Do I use a variety of words and sentence lengths to set a good pace?	Yes .... No	

Revising

Comparison of Adjectives and Adverbs

Most adjectives and adverbs have three degrees of comparison; the *positive,* the *comparative,* and the *superlative.*

Identify degrees of adjectives and adverbs. The positive is used when no comparison is made. The comparative is used when two things are being compared. The superlative is used when three or more things are being compared.

Positive: Hannah is a *fast* runner.

Comparative: Eva is a *faster* runner than Hannah.

Superlative: Emmy is the *fastest* runner on the team.

Forming Comparative and Superlative Degrees	
Rules	**Examples**
Use *-er* or *more* to form the comparative degree.	faster, taller, narrower, sunnier, more intelligent, more expressive
Use *-est* or *most* to form the superlative degree.	fastest, tallest, sunniest, most nutritious, most sorrowful
Use *more* or *most* with modifiers of three or more syllables.	more popular, more intelligently, most popular, most intelligently

Fixing Incorrect Use of Comparative and Superlative Degrees

As you revise your draft, look for places where you made comparisons. Use one or more of the following methods to fix the incorrect use of comparative and superlative degrees of adjectives and adverbs in your draft:

1. **Identify the number of things being compared.** Review the rules for comparison and use the correct word or word ending.
2. **Identify the number of syllables in the modifier.** Review the rules for modifiers with a specific number of syllables and use the correct word or word ending.
3. **Read the words aloud.** If the words sound awkward, combine the modifier with a different word or word ending.

Editing and Proofreading

Review your draft to correct errors in capitalization, spelling, and punctuation.

Focus on Capitalization: Review your draft carefully to find and correct capitalization errors. Make sure you have capitalized the title of your story correctly. Remember that the first and last word of a title are always capitalized. Articles *(a, an, the)* and short prepositions *(in, on, of)* are not capitalized.

Incorrect capitalization:	The Day The Cow Flew through the Window
Correct capitalization:	The Day the Cow Flew Through the Window

Focus on Spelling: Check the spelling of each word in your story. Look for words that you frequently misspell and make sure that they are correct. Pay particular attention to the spelling of the past tenses of irregular verbs. Check a dictionary if you are unsure of the spelling of an irregular verb's past tense. The correct spellings of irregular verb tenses are usually listed right after the pronunciation of the word. If you have typed your draft on a computer, use the spell-check feature to double-check for errors. Proofread carefully even after you run spell-check. Spell checkers will not find words that are used incorrectly, such as *its* instead of *it's* when the incorrect word is spelled correctly.

Focus on Punctuation: Proofread your writing to find and correct punctuation errors. Specifically, make sure you have punctuated dialogue correctly. Enclose a character's exact words in quotation marks. If dialogue comes *before* the speech tag (the words announcing speech), use a comma, question mark, or exclamation point at the end of the quotation—not a period. If dialogue comes *after* the speech tag, use a comma before the quotation. Always place a period at the end of a sentence inside the quotation marks.

Examples:

"I heard the siren," Benjamin said.

Sally jumped and shouted, "So did I, but it still surprised me!"

Benjamin added, "You do seem a little jumpy today."

Revision Checklist

- ❑ Have you reviewed your story to make sure your title, names, and other proper nouns are capitalized?
- ❑ Have you read each sentence and checked that all of the words are spelled correctly, especially the past tenses of irregular verbs?
- ❑ Have you punctuated dialogue correctly?

Name ______________________ Date ______________ Assignment ______________

Publishing and Presenting

Consider one of the following ways to present your writing:

Submit your story. Submit your story to your school's literary magazine, a national publication, an online journal, or a writing contest. Many publications have online Web sites where you can find writer's guidelines for submitting your writing. Follow the guidelines exactly to increase your chances of having your work published. Ask your teacher for additional help if necessary.

Give a reading. Read your story aloud to your class or to a group of friends. Prepare posters announcing your reading. Include intriguing dialogue or descriptions from your story on your poster to build interest in your story. To enhance your reading, find and play soft background music appropriate for the content of the story. After the event, distribute signed copies of your story to members of the audience.

Rubric for Self-Assessment

Find evidence in your writing to address each category. Then use the rating scale to grade your work.

Evaluating Your Short Story	not very					very
Focus: How well-developed are your characters?	1	2	3	4	5	6
Organization: How clearly organized is the story line or sequence of events?	1	2	3	4	5	6
Support/Elaboration: How well do the dialogue and descriptive details build suspense and support the plot?	1	2	3	4	5	6
Style: How precise is your word choice?	1	2	3	4	5	6
Conventions: How correct is your grammar, especially your use of comparative adjectives and adverbs?	1	2	3	4	5	6

For use with Writing 3

Writing 4

4. Produce clear and coherent writing in which the development, organization, and style are appropriate to task, purpose, and audience.

Explanation

Readers appreciate writing that is presented clearly and coherently. To produce writing that grabs your readers' attention and holds their interest from the very first sentence until the final one, you must first consider your task, purpose, and audience.

- Your **task** is the specific reason you are writing. For example, your task may be to write a problem-and-solution essay or a business letter. Business tasks require conciseness and clarity; friendly emails, on the other hand, might ramble and jump all over from one subject to the next.
- Your **purpose** is your main goal for writing or the effect you want your writing to have. For example, your purpose may be to identify a problem at school and suggest reasonable solutions; or, it may be to get a local official to change his or her position on an important issue. Keep your purpose in mind as you write, and be sure your purpose is clear to the readers.
- Your **audience** is the people for whom you are writing. Often you will write for your teachers and classmates. You may also write for students in other grades, family members, or a wider audience, such as readers of the local newspaper or website. As a writer, keep in mind how much background your audience has on the subject, as well as how they might react to your ideas.

The choices you make as you write should reflect your specific task, purpose, and audience. For example, if you are writing a how-to-essay for younger students, you will likely organize it step-by-step, putting each step in the correct order and using simple, precise language that younger readers can grasp. However, if your task is to write a lab report for your science teacher, an email to a friend, or a letter to the editor of a magazine then the **organization,** development, and **style** of each will be very different. To produce clear and coherent writing, always consider the relationship of the organization, development, and style of your writing to your task, purpose, and audience.

Academic Vocabulary

organization the way in which details are arranged in a piece of writing

style the author's unique way of writing

Apply the Standard

Use the worksheet that follows to help you apply the standard as you write. Several copies of the worksheet have been provided for you to use with different assignments.

- Writing to a Specific Task, Purpose, and Audience

Name ______________________ Date ______________ Assignment ________________

Writing to a Specific Task, Purpose, and Audience

Use the organizer to identify the task, purpose, and audience of your writing assignment. Then note how each will affect your choice of organization, development, and style.

Assignment:	
Writing task	**Note:**
Purpose	**Note:**
Audience	**Note:**

A

Name ______________________ Date ______________ Assignment ________________

Writing to a Specific Task, Purpose, and Audience

Use the organizer to identify the task, purpose, and audience of your writing assignment. Then note how each will affect your choice of organization, development, and style.

Assignment:	
Writing task	**Note:**
Purpose	**Note:**
Audience	**Note:**

Name ______________ Date ______________ Assignment ______________

Writing to a Specific Task, Purpose, and Audience

Use the organizer to identify the task, purpose, and audience of your writing assignment. Then note how each will affect your choice of organization, development, and style.

Assignment:	
Writing task	**Note:**
Purpose	**Note:**
Audience	**Note:**

C

Name ______________________ Date ____________ Assignment ______________

Writing to a Specific Task, Purpose, and Audience

Use the organizer to identify the task, purpose, and audience of your writing assignment. Then note how each will affect your choice of organization, development, and style.

Assignment:	
Writing task	**Note:**
Purpose	**Note:**
Audience	**Note:**

Name ____________________ Date ______________ Assignment ______________

Writing to a Specific Task, Purpose, and Audience

Use the organizer to identify the task, purpose, and audience of your writing assignment. Then note how each will affect your choice of organization, development, and style.

Assignment:	
Writing task	**Note:**
Purpose	**Note:**
Audience	**Note:**

E

For use with Writing 4

Name ______________________ Date ____________ Assignment ______________

Writing to a Specific Task, Purpose, and Audience

Use the organizer to identify the task, purpose, and audience of your writing assignment. Then note how each will affect your choice of organization, development, and style.

Assignment:	
Writing task	**Note:**
Purpose	**Note:**
Audience	**Note:**

Writing 5

5. With some guidance and support from peers and adults, develop and strengthen writing as needed by planning, revising, editing, rewriting, or trying a new approach, focusing on how well purpose and audience have been addressed.

Explanation

Experienced writers know the importance of having a good writing plan in place before they begin to write. They also know that to be successful, they must keep purpose and audience in mind as they develop a writing plan. Yet, even with sufficient planning, most writers should expect their first draft to need some revisions.

After you write a first draft, your teacher and **peers** can help point out where your writing succeeds and where it still needs work. With their assistance, you can often strengthen your writing quite a bit and ensure that you successfully address purpose and audience. Here are some ways to get that guidance and support from your teacher and peers.

- Arrange for a one-on-one conference with your teacher to discuss his or her written suggestions for **revising** your first draft.
- Read aloud your draft to a partner and ask for feedback. Provide a checklist that will help your partner focus on the main goals of the assignment.
- During a peer group session, discuss ideas for strengthening your writing, focusing on how well you address purpose and audience.
- Ask a peer to review your writing for errors in **conventions** and to check for varied sentence patterns, the use of transitions, and consistency in style and tone.

On occasion, your teacher or peers may suggest that you rewrite your draft or try a whole new approach. Sometimes starting over may be your best chance at success, so be open to their suggestions, even if they require more work on your part.

Academic Vocabulary

peer a person who is the same age or has the same status as another person

revising rewriting to improve and strengthen writing

conventions correct use of punctuation, capitalization, grammar, and spelling

Apply the Standard

Use the worksheets that follow to help you apply the standard as you write. Several copies of each worksheet have been provided for you to use with different assignments.

- Evaluating Writing with Peers
- Revising and Editing

Name ______________________ Date ____________ Assignment ______________

Evaluating Writing with Peers

Work with a partner to evaluate one another's first drafts of a writing assignment. Use the organizer below to focus your evaluation. 1 is *not very* and 6 is *very*.

Focus Questions	Comments and Suggestions for Revising
How clear is my purpose? 1 2 3 4 5 6	
How well do my choice of details, vocabulary, and overall style show a consideration of my audience? 1 2 3 4 5 6	
How clear is my focus or main idea? 1 2 3 4 5 6	
How effective are my details at clarifying and elaborating each important idea? 1 2 3 4 5 6	
How clear is the organizational plan? 1 2 3 4 5 6	
How clear is the relationship between ideas in sentences and paragraphs? 1 2 3 4 5 6	
How effectively do I use transitions, and how smoothly does the writing flow? 1 2 3 4 5 6	
How well do I use precise nouns and vivid adjectives, adverbs, and verbs to create clear, strong images? 1 2 3 4 5 6	
How well do I use verbs in the active voice and vary sentence patterns and length? 1 2 3 4 5 6	

Name ____________________ Date ____________ Assignment ______________

Evaluating Writing with Peers

Work with a partner to evaluate one another's first drafts of a writing assignment. Use the organizer below to focus your evaluation. 1 is *not very* and 6 is *very*.

Focus Questions	Comments and Suggestions for Revising
How clear is my purpose? 1 2 3 4 5 6	
How well do my choice of details, vocabulary, and overall style show a consideration of my audience? 1 2 3 4 5 6	
How clear is my focus or main idea? 1 2 3 4 5 6	
How effective are my details at clarifying and elaborating each important idea? 1 2 3 4 5 6	
How clear is the organizational plan? 1 2 3 4 5 6	
How clear is the relationship between ideas in sentences and paragraphs? 1 2 3 4 5 6	
How effectively do I use transitions, and how smoothly does the writing flow? 1 2 3 4 5 6	
How well do I use precise nouns and vivid adjectives, adverbs, and verbs to create clear, strong images? 1 2 3 4 5 6	
How well do I use verbs in the active voice and vary sentence patterns and length? 1 2 3 4 5 6	

Name ______________________ Date ____________ Assignment ______________

Evaluating Writing with Peers

Work with a partner to evaluate one another's first drafts of a writing assignment. Use the organizer below to focus your evaluation. 1 is *not very* and 6 is *very*.

Focus Questions	Comments and Suggestions for Revising
How clear is my purpose? 1 2 3 4 5 6	
How well do my choice of details, vocabulary, and overall style show a consideration of my audience? 1 2 3 4 5 6	
How clear is my focus or main idea? 1 2 3 4 5 6	
How effective are my details at clarifying and elaborating each important idea? 1 2 3 4 5 6	
How clear is the organizational plan? 1 2 3 4 5 6	
How clear is the relationship between ideas in sentences and paragraphs? 1 2 3 4 5 6	
How effectively do I use transitions, and how smoothly does the writing flow? 1 2 3 4 5 6	
How well do I use precise nouns and vivid adjectives, adverbs, and verbs to create clear, strong images? 1 2 3 4 5 6	
How well do I use verbs in the active voice and vary sentence patterns and length? 1 2 3 4 5 6	

Name ______________________ Date ______________ Assignment ______________

Evaluating Writing with Peers

Work with a partner to evaluate one another's first drafts of a writing assignment. Use the organizer below to focus your evaluation. 1 is *not very* and 6 is *very*.

Focus Questions	Comments and Suggestions for Revising
How clear is my purpose? 1 2 3 4 5 6	
How well do my choice of details, vocabulary, and overall style show a consideration of my audience? 1 2 3 4 5 6	
How clear is my focus or main idea? 1 2 3 4 5 6	
How effective are my details at clarifying and elaborating each important idea? 1 2 3 4 5 6	
How clear is the organizational plan? 1 2 3 4 5 6	
How clear is the relationship between ideas in sentences and paragraphs? 1 2 3 4 5 6	
How effectively do I use transitions, and how smoothly does the writing flow? 1 2 3 4 5 6	
How well do I use precise nouns and vivid adjectives, adverbs, and verbs to create clear, strong images? 1 2 3 4 5 6	
How well do I use verbs in the active voice and vary sentence patterns and length? 1 2 3 4 5 6	

Name ______________________ Date ____________ Assignment ______________

Evaluating Writing with Peers

Work with a partner to evaluate one another's first drafts of a writing assignment. Use the organizer below to focus your evaluation. 1 is *not very* and 6 is *very*.

Focus Questions	Comments and Suggestions for Revising
How clear is my purpose? 1 2 3 4 5 6	
How well do my choice of details, vocabulary, and overall style show a consideration of my audience? 1 2 3 4 5 6	
How clear is my focus or main idea? 1 2 3 4 5 6	
How effective are my details at clarifying and elaborating each important idea? 1 2 3 4 5 6	
How clear is the organizational plan? 1 2 3 4 5 6	
How clear is the relationship between ideas in sentences and paragraphs? 1 2 3 4 5 6	
How effectively do I use transitions, and how smoothly does the writing flow? 1 2 3 4 5 6	
How well do I use precise nouns and vivid adjectives, adverbs, and verbs to create clear, strong images? 1 2 3 4 5 6	
How well do I use verbs in the active voice and vary sentence patterns and length? 1 2 3 4 5 6	

Name ______________________ Date ______________ Assignment ________________

Evaluating Writing with Peers

Work with a partner to evaluate one another's first drafts of a writing assignment. Use the organizer below to focus your evaluation. 1 is *not very* and 6 is *very*.

Focus Questions	Comments and Suggestions for Revising
How clear is my purpose? 1 2 3 4 5 6	
How well do my choice of details, vocabulary, and overall style show a consideration of my audience? 1 2 3 4 5 6	
How clear is my focus or main idea? 1 2 3 4 5 6	
How effective are my details at clarifying and elaborating each important idea? 1 2 3 4 5 6	
How clear is the organizational plan? 1 2 3 4 5 6	
How clear is the relationship between ideas in sentences and paragraphs? 1 2 3 4 5 6	
How effectively do I use transitions, and how smoothly does the writing flow? 1 2 3 4 5 6	
How well do I use precise nouns and vivid adjectives, adverbs, and verbs to create clear, strong images? 1 2 3 4 5 6	
How well do I use verbs in the active voice and vary sentence patterns and length? 1 2 3 4 5 6	

Name ________________ Date ____________ Assignment ____________

Revising and Editing

Use the organizer to explain how you plan on revising and editing your writing.

Passage from my writing (note where it appears, such as "second and third paragraphs")	**How successful is it?**	**How can I revise or edit to improve and strengthen my writing?**
Beginning:		
Middle:		
End:		

Name ______________________ Date ______________ Assignment ______________

Revising and Editing

Use the organizer to explain how you plan on revising and editing your writing.

Passage from my writing (note where it appears, such as "second and third paragraphs")	**How successful is it?**	**How can I revise or edit to improve and strengthen my writing?**
Beginning:		
Middle:		
End:		

Name ______________________ Date ____________ Assignment ______________

Revising and Editing

Use the organizer to explain how you plan on revising and editing your writing.

Passage from my writing (note where it appears, such as "second and third paragraphs")	**How successful is it?**	**How can I revise or edit to improve and strengthen my writing?**
Beginning:		
Middle:		
End:		

Name ______________________ Date ______________ Assignment ________________

Revising and Editing

Use the organizer to explain how you plan on revising and editing your writing.

Passage from my writing (note where it appears, such as "second and third paragraphs")	**How successful is it?**	**How can I revise or edit to improve and strengthen my writing?**
Beginning:		
Middle:		
End:		

Name ____________________ Date ____________ Assignment ______________

Revising and Editing

Use the organizer to explain how you plan on revising and editing your writing.

Passage from my writing (note where it appears, such as "second and third paragraphs")	**How successful is it?**	**How can I revise or edit to improve and strengthen my writing?**
Beginning:		
Middle:		
End:		

Name ______________________ Date ____________ Assignment ________________

Revising and Editing

Use the organizer to explain how you plan on revising and editing your writing.

Passage from my writing (note where it appears, such as "second and third paragraphs")	**How successful is it?**	**How can I revise or edit to improve and strengthen my writing?**
Beginning:		
Middle:		
End:		

Writing 6

6. Use technology, including the Internet, to produce and publish writing and link to and cite sources as well as to interact and collaborate with others, including linking to and citing sources.

Explanation

The Writing Process The use of computers, word processing software, the Internet, and other **technology** can simplify each step of the writing process, especially when you write a research report.

- You can use the Internet to explore a topic and determine if it is too narrow or too general.
- Once you have a suitable topic and a thesis, you can use an Internet search engine to find facts, details, and examples to support your main ideas.
- You can use computer software to take neat, organized notes, incorporating links to each online resource by copying and pasting the web addresses into your notes.
- You can copy and paste from your notes to create a rough outline, easily reordering ideas and whole sections to create a final working outline.
- You can use the links within your notes to verify and expand on facts as you write your draft and to create a Works Cited page.
- You can enhance your final report with photographs, charts, graphs, videos, and sound, when appropriate.

Collaboration The Internet is also an excellent tool for interacting and **collaborating** with other writers. For example, you can create a class website to upload drafts for peer review, post constructive comments on another student's work, and publish final reports. When working on a group project, you can use email and the class website to post links to important sources. You can also use the Internet to access professional authors' blogs or to create your own writer's blog to share your thoughts and ideas about writing and get feedback from your readers.

Academic Vocabulary

technology advanced electronic tools, such as computers, scanners, printers, word-processing and design programs, and the Internet

collaborate work with others for one purpose

Apply the Standard

Use the worksheets that follow to help you apply the standard as you write. Several copies of each worksheet have been provided for you to use with different assignments.

- Using Technology
- Collaborating with Others

Name ______________________ Date ____________ Assignment ________________

Using Technology

Use the organizer to plan how you will use technology during each stage of the writing process. Then answer the question at the bottom of the page.

Stage	What technology will you use?	What is its purpose?
Prewriting		
Drafting		
Writing		
Revising and Editing		
Publishing		

During which stage do you expect technology to be the most helpful? Explain your answer.

____

____

____

Name ______________ Date ______________ Assignment ______________

Using Technology

Use the organizer to plan how you will use technology during each stage of the writing process. Then answer the question at the bottom of the page.

Stage	What technology will you use?	What is its purpose?
Prewriting		
Drafting		
Writing		
Revising and Editing		
Publishing		

During which stage do you expect technology to be the most helpful? Explain your answer.

____

____

____

Name ______________________ Date ______________ Assignment ________________

Using Technology

Use the organizer to plan how you will use technology during each stage of the writing process. Then answer the question at the bottom of the page.

Stage	What technology will you use?	What is its purpose?
Prewriting		
Drafting		
Writing		
Revising and Editing		
Publishing		

During which stage do you expect technology to be the most helpful? Explain your answer.

___

___

___

Name ______________________ Date ______________ Assignment ________________

Using Technology

Use the organizer to plan how you will use technology during each stage of the writing process. Then answer the question at the bottom of the page.

Stage	What technology will you use?	What is its purpose?
Prewriting		
Drafting		
Writing		
Revising and Editing		
Publishing		

During which stage do you expect technology to be the most helpful? Explain your answer.

____

____

____

Name ____________________ Date ______________ Assignment ______________

Using Technology

Use the organizer to plan how you will use technology during each stage of the writing process. Then answer the question at the bottom of the page.

Stage	What technology will you use?	What is its purpose?
Prewriting		
Drafting		
Writing		
Revising and Editing		
Publishing		

During which stage do you expect technology to be the most helpful? Explain your answer.

____

____

____

Name _______________ Date _______________ Assignment _______________

Using Technology

Use the organizer to plan how you will use technology during each stage of the writing process. Then answer the question at the bottom of the page.

Stage	What technology will you use?	What is its purpose?
Prewriting		
Drafting		
Writing		
Revising and Editing		
Publishing		

During which stage do you expect technology to be the most helpful? Explain your answer.

____

____

____

Name ______________________ Date ____________ Assignment ______________

Collaborating with Others

After you complete a writing assignment, use the organizer below to evaluate how effectively you used technology to collaborate with other students.

Plan

What was your plan for using technology to interact and collaborate with others for this assignment?

Review

For each item, circle a number to rate how well you used technology to collaborate with other students. 1 is poor, and 6 is excellent.

Gathering information	1	2	3	4	5	6
Organizing details	1	2	3	4	5	6
Sharing feedback for drafts	1	2	3	4	5	6
Revising to improve	1	2	3	4	5	6
Citing sources	1	2	3	4	5	6
Editing	1	2	3	4	5	6
Publishing	1	2	3	4	5	6

Choose one item from the rating scale, and explain why you gave it the rating that you did.

Name ______________________ Date ______________ Assignment ______________

Collaborating with Others

After you complete a writing assignment, use the organizer below to evaluate how effectively you used technology to collaborate with other students.

Plan What was your plan for using technology to interact and collaborate with others for this assignment?

Review For each item, circle a number to rate how well you used technology to collaborate with other students. 1 is poor, and 6 is excellent.						
Gathering information	1	2	3	4	5	6
Organizing details	1	2	3	4	5	6
Sharing feedback for drafts	1	2	3	4	5	6
Revising to improve	1	2	3	4	5	6
Citing sources	1	2	3	4	5	6
Editing	1	2	3	4	5	6
Publishing	1	2	3	4	5	6

Choose one item from the rating scale, and explain why you gave it the rating that you did.

Name ______________________ Date ______________ Assignment ____________________

Collaborating with Others

After you complete a writing assignment, use the organizer below to evaluate how effectively you used technology to collaborate with other students.

Plan

What was your plan for using technology to interact and collaborate with others for this assignment?

Review

For each item, circle a number to rate how well you used technology to collaborate with other students. 1 is poor, and 6 is excellent.

Gathering information	1	2	3	4	5	6
Organizing details	1	2	3	4	5	6
Sharing feedback for drafts	1	2	3	4	5	6
Revising to improve	1	2	3	4	5	6
Citing sources	1	2	3	4	5	6
Editing	1	2	3	4	5	6
Publishing	1	2	3	4	5	6

Choose one item from the rating scale, and explain why you gave it the rating that you did.

Name ____________________ Date ____________ Assignment ______________

Collaborating with Others

After you complete a writing assignment, use the organizer below to evaluate how effectively you used technology to collaborate with other students.

Plan What was your plan for using technology to interact and collaborate with others for this assignment?						
Review For each item, circle a number to rate how well you used technology to collaborate with other students. 1 is poor, and 6 is excellent.						
Gathering information	1	2	3	4	5	6
Organizing details	1	2	3	4	5	6
Sharing feedback for drafts	1	2	3	4	5	6
Revising to improve	1	2	3	4	5	6
Citing sources	1	2	3	4	5	6
Editing	1	2	3	4	5	6
Publishing	1	2	3	4	5	6
Choose one item from the rating scale, and explain why you gave it the rating that you did.						

Name ______________________ Date ____________ Assignment ______________

Collaborating with Others

After you complete a writing assignment, use the organizer below to evaluate how effectively you used technology to collaborate with other students.

Plan What was your plan for using technology to interact and collaborate with others for this assignment?						
Review For each item, circle a number to rate how well you used technology to collaborate with other students. 1 is poor, and 6 is excellent.						
Gathering information	1	2	3	4	5	6
Organizing details	1	2	3	4	5	6
Sharing feedback for drafts	1	2	3	4	5	6
Revising to improve	1	2	3	4	5	6
Citing sources	1	2	3	4	5	6
Editing	1	2	3	4	5	6
Publishing	1	2	3	4	5	6
Choose one item from the rating scale, and explain why you gave it the rating that you did.						

Name ______________________ Date ______________ Assignment ________________

Collaborating with Others

After you complete a writing assignment, use the organizer below to evaluate how effectively you used technology to collaborate with other students.

Plan

What was your plan for using technology to interact and collaborate with others for this assignment?

Review

For each item, circle a number to rate how well you used technology to collaborate with other students. 1 is poor, and 6 is excellent.

Gathering information	1	2	3	4	5	6
Organizing details	1	2	3	4	5	6
Sharing feedback for drafts	1	2	3	4	5	6
Revising to improve	1	2	3	4	5	6
Citing sources	1	2	3	4	5	6
Editing	1	2	3	4	5	6
Publishing	1	2	3	4	5	6

Choose one item from the rating scale, and explain why you gave it the rating that you did.

Writing 7

7. Conduct short research projects to answer a question, drawing on several sources and generating additional related, focused questions for further research and investigation.

Explanation

A short research project usually answers one or more closely related, focused questions about a specific topic. For example, a short research project focusing on the short story writer O. Henry might include these questions:

- For what literary element or device are O. Henry's stories best known?
- What are two of O. Henry's most famous stories?

A short research project focusing on dangerous storms might include these questions:

- What is a hurricane?
- Where are hurricanes most likely to occur?

To begin your **inquiry,** or process of looking for information, consult different print and online sources, including encyclopedias, newspapers, magazines, textbooks, and reliable websites. At first, limit yourself to three or four sources, and record only facts and details that directly answer your questions. Locate **primary sources**—firsthand original accounts, such as interview transcripts and newspaper articles. In addition, find **secondary sources**—accounts that are not original, such as encyclopedia entries. Then **synthesize,** or combine creatively, ideas from the different sources.

As you conduct your research, you may generate additional related questions about your topic that require further research and investigation. Researching these questions may take more time than you have for a particular assignment. In that case, write your additional questions down so you can investigate them in the future as part of a larger research project.

Academic Vocabulary

inquiry the process of looking for information to answer specific questions about a topic

synthesize to pull together information from different sources and present it in a new way

Apply the Standard

Use the worksheets that follow to help you apply the standard as you write. Several copies of each worksheet have been provided for you to use with different assignments.

- Researching to Answer a Question
- Synthesizing Information from Different Sources

Name ______________________ Date ______________ Assignment ________________

Researching to Answer a Question

Use the organizer to gather information to answer your questions about a topic. Identify each source, such as magazine articles, books, or websites.

Topic: ....

	Research Question 1:	**Research Question 2:**
Source:		
Source:		
Source:		

Based on the facts and details gathered here, write two follow-up questions for your topic to research and investigate in the future.

1. ....
2. ....

Name ______________________ Date ____________ Assignment ______________

Researching to Answer a Question

Use the organizer to gather information to answer your questions about a topic. Identify each source, such as magazine articles, books, or websites.

Topic: ....

	Research Question 1:	**Research Question 2:**
Source:		
Source:		
Source:		

Based on the facts and details gathered here, write two follow-up questions for your topic to research and investigate in the future.

1. ....

2. ....

Name ______________________ Date ____________ Assignment ______________

Researching to Answer a Question

Use the organizer to gather information to answer your questions about a topic. Identify each source, such as magazine articles, books, or websites.

Topic: ....

	Research Question 1:	**Research Question 2:**
Source:		
Source:		
Source:		

Based on the facts and details gathered here, write two follow-up questions for your topic to research and investigate in the future.

1. ....

2. ....

Name ______________________ Date ____________ Assignment ______________

Synthesizing Information from Different Sources

Use the organizer to synthesize information from different sources. Write only the most relevant information from each source. Then put it all together to write a paragraph answering your research questions.

Research Questions:	
Information from Source 1:	
Information from Source 2:	
Information from Source 3:	

Synthesis Paragraph:

A

For use with Writing 7

Name ______________________ Date ______________ Assignment ______________

Synthesizing Information from Different Sources

Use the organizer to synthesize information from different sources. Write only the most relevant information from each source. Then put it all together to write a paragraph answering your research questions.

Research Questions:

Information from Source 1:

Information from Source 2:

Information from Source 3:

Synthesis Paragraph:

Name ______________________ Date ____________ Assignment ______________

Synthesizing Information from Different Sources

Use the organizer to synthesize information from different sources. Write only the most relevant information from each source. Then put it all together to write a paragraph answering your research questions.

Research Questions:

Information from Source 1:

Information from Source 2:

Information from Source 3:

Synthesis Paragraph:

C

For use with Writing 7

Writing 8

8. Gather relevant information from multiple print and digital sources, using search terms effectively; assess the credibility and accuracy of each source; and quote or paraphrase the data and conclusions of others while avoiding plagiarism and following a standard format for citation.

Writing Workshop: Research Report

When you write a **research report,** you choose a topic that interests you and that stimulates your curiosity. Then you gather information about that topic from reference materials, observations, interviews, or other credible sources. Finally, you combine that information into a unified whole that gives a clear and accurate picture of a specific aspect of the topic. Research reports require time and effort, but the knowledge and experience you gain will more than compensate for your efforts.

Assignment

Write a research report about a contemporary issue that interests you or affects you in some way. Include these elements:

✓ a focused topic or main idea for inquiry

✓ answers to relevant questions on the topic

✓ a clearly defined thesis statement

✓ a clear organization and smooth transitions

✓ appropriate and relevant facts and details to support the thesis

✓ information that is accurate, relevant, valid, and current

✓ visuals or media to support key ideas

✓ a bibliography and accurate, complete citations

✓ a strong introduction and conclusion

✓ correct use of language conventions, including the correct use of pronoun case

*Additional Standards

Writing

8. Gather relevant information from multiple print and digital sources, using search terms effectively; assess the credibility and accuracy of each source; and quote or paraphrase the data and conclusions of others while avoiding plagiarism and following a standard format for citation.

2. Write informative/explanatory texts to examine a topic and convey ideas, concepts, and information through the selection, organization, and analysis of relevant content.

6. Use technology, including the Internet, to produce and publish writing and link to and cite sources as well as to interact and collaborate with others, including linking to and citing sources.

9. Draw evidence from literary or informational texts to support analysis, reflection, and research.

Language

2. Demonstrate command of the conventions of standard English capitalization, punctuation, and spelling when writing.

Name ______________________ Date ______________ Assignment ________________

Prewriting/Planning Strategies

Choose a general idea. Begin the search for a good topic for your report. Look through recent magazines or newspapers, listen to the news, and review your notebooks. List current events, issues, or subjects of interest and the questions they spark. Choose your topic from among these ideas.

Use a topic web to narrow your topic. After you have a general idea for a topic, do some quick research. If you find a massive amount of information, your topic is too broad. Narrow your topic to make it more specific and more manageable for a research report. Use the topic web to narrow your topic. Each row should contain smaller and smaller aspects of your general topic. For example, "illiteracy" is too broad a topic for a research paper. Narrow the topic by asking focused questions, such as "How serious a problem is illiteracy in the United States?"

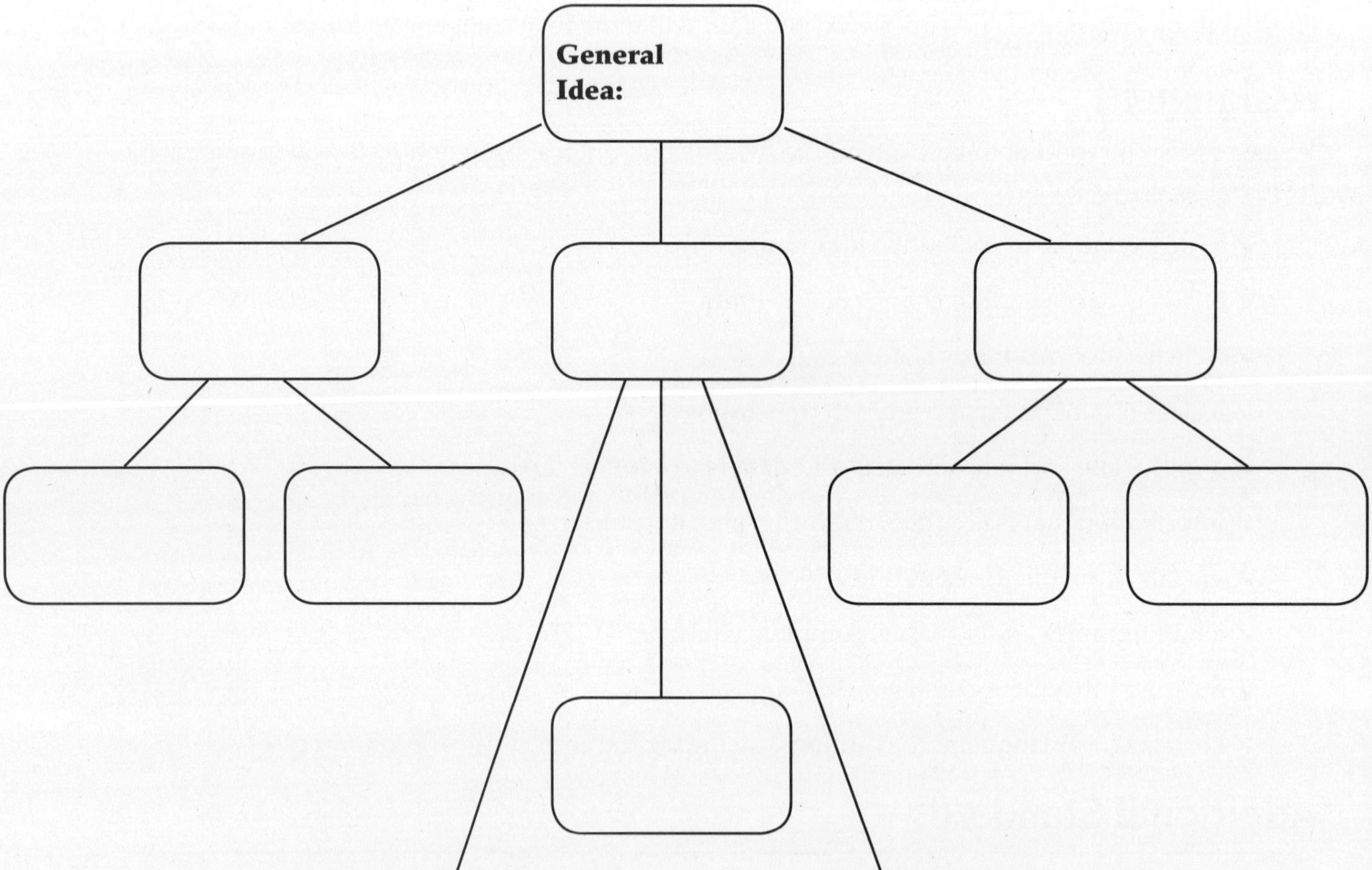

Write your narrowed topic: ....

For use with Writing 8

Name ______________________ Date ____________ Assignment ______________

Ask questions about your topic. Decide what you want your report to explain about your topic. Then ask questions that will help you help you focus your research. For example, in a report about illiteracy in a specific region of the United States, you might ask questions about its causes and its effects on the economy of the region. Next make a list of primary and secondary sources where you plan to look to find information that answers your questions.

Primary sources: firsthand or original accounts. Examples include interview transcripts and personal observations recorded in news reports journals, and diaries.

Secondary sources: accounts that are not first hand or original. Examples include encyclopedia entries, the Internet, books, television, and magazine articles.

Use the graphic organizer to write your research questions and list specific sources. List both primary and secondary sources.

Topic:				
	Question 1:	**Question 2:**	**Question 3:**	**Question 4:**
Source 1				
Source 2				
Source 3				
Source 4				

Evaluating Sources

You will use a variety of print and digital sources to gather information for your report. That information should be interesting and relevant, but first it must be accurate, which is why you should evaluate the credibility of your sources.

Print Sources: You can usually find accurate information in encyclopedia articles; textbooks; nonfiction books; autobiographies; interview transcripts; and in magazines published by respected organizations, such as the Smithsonian. Keep in mind that facts and details on the Internet and in recently published specialized magazines, such as science journals, may be more accurate than information found in some older books.

Digital Sources: You can also use digital sources for your research. These include CDs; radio and television documentaries produced by respected organizations, such as the Public Broadcasting System (PBS); videos and slide programs; and the Internet.

Use caution when doing research on the Internet. Check the professional background of a Web site's writer or sponsor before accepting that the facts on that site are accurate. Be wary of Web sites sponsored by companies or organizations that want to influence your political choices or consumer purchases. Facts on these sites may be tilted to suit the purpose of these sponsors. Internet sources sponsored by the government (ending in *.gov*) or educational institutions (ending in *.edu*) are generally more credible than those established by businesses (ending in *.com*). Check that university sites are actually sponsored by the university and are not private sites of students at the school.

You can waste a lot of time browsing digital sources if your search terms are too broad. To save time and get effective results, use highly specific terms, such as a person's full name, or slightly less general terms. For example, "birds" is too general and will generate too many useless, irrelevant hits. However, "habits or behavior of water birds" is general, but more focused. It should yield fewer and relevant hits.

News Media Sources: Many news outlets slant their reports so that they favor specific groups or policies. Before using facts from a news outlet in your report, confirm the facts with at least two other reliable sources.

To evaluate the credibility of your sources, ask yourself these questions:

- Is this a primary source or a secondary source?
- Is the information current?
- Is the author or subject of the interview an authority in the field?
- Is the information objective and complete?
- Does the source have any hidden purpose, such as wanting me to support a cause or buy a product?
- Is the information accurate? Can I confirm it in at least one other source?

Name ______________________ Date ____________ Assignment ______________

Record source information. At the end of your report, you will provide a bibliography of every source you cite in your report. This task will be less tedious if you keep accurate details about your sources as you conduct your research.

Use the **source cards** to record details about each source you use. Include the title, author, publication date and place, and page numbers on which you find information. Use the "Other" line, to list a Web address if the source is an Internet site, or other notes about the source, for example, if it is a CD or an interview transcript. Use as many source cards as you need. Be sure to record information carefully and accurately.

Title:
Author:
Publication Date and Place:
Page Numbers:
Other:

Title:
Author:
Publication Date and Place:
Page Numbers:
Other:

Name ______________________ Date ____________ Assignment ______________

Take notes. Follow these guidelines for taking notes efficiently.

- Take complete and accurate notes. This will save you from having to go back and check every source when you draft and revise.
- Keep your notes organized and focused. Write one of your research questions at the top of each card. Use different colored markers to highlight each question. Then, write only facts and details that answer that question on the note card. If your note cards get mixed up, you can see at a glance by the color which notes go together.
- Use a new note card for each new source. Go back and number your source cards. Then, write that source number on the note card. If you prefer, you can write an abbreviated form of the title of the source or the author's last name.
- Use quotation marks when you copy words exactly. Indicate the author's last name and page number on which the quotation appears in parentheses after the quotation. This will be helpful if you have go back to check the quotation when you draft and if you decide to use the exact quotation in your report.
- In most cases, you should take notes in your own words. This will protect you from accidentally **plagiarizing,** or copying someone else's ideas and words, when you write your draft.

Record facts, details, examples, and explanations about your topic on note cards like this. Use as many note cards as you need.

Research Question:
Facts and Details:
Source Notation:

For use with Writing 8

Name ______________________ Date ____________ Assignment ______________

Drafting Strategies

Create an outline to organize information. When your notes are complete, use the graphic organizer to create an outline for your draft. A detailed, well-constructed outline will keep you on track as you draft your report.

- First, (I) write a strong thesis statement that expresses the main point you want to make about your topic. Refer to your thesis frequently as you write your draft to help stay focused.
- Next, group your notes by category and turn these categories into subtopics, or main points. You can also turn your prewriting questions into subtopics. Use Roman Numerals (I, II, III, IV) to number your subtopics. Use capital letters (A, B, C) for the supporting details.
- For the conclusion, write a sentence that restates your main idea.

Thesis Statement ....

(Subtopic 1) I. ....

(Detail) A. ....

(Detail) B. ....

(Detail) C. ....

(Subtopic 2) II. ....

(Detail) A. ....

(Detail) B. ....

(Detail) C. ....

(Subtopic 3) III. ....

(Detail) A. ....

(Detail) B. ....

(Detail) C. ....

Conclusion IV. ....

For use with Writing 8

Use your outline as a guide. Use your outline to stay focused as you write your draft. Each Roman numeral and capital letter in your outline will probably require a paragraph in your report. Each paragraph should have a clear topic sentence that expresses the main idea of that paragraph. All other sentences in the paragraph should contain facts, examples, and details that illustrate or further explain the topic sentence. All topic sentences should relate to the main idea of the report, expressed in the thesis statement.

Create smooth transitions between paragraphs. As you write the body of your draft, create smooth transitions between the paragraphs. One effective way to do this is to repeat a word or phrase from the end of one paragraph in the opening sentence of the next paragraph. This also helps to create a unified, cohesive report.

Cite sources as you draft. As you continue to draft, choose the most relevant and interesting facts, details, examples, and explanations from your notes. Try to **summarize** or **paraphrase** the information by putting it into your own words. This will prevent you from committing **plagiarism**—stealing another writer's words and ideas and presenting them as your own.

Whether you are summarizing, paraphrasing, or using a direct quotation, you must credit another writer's ideas within your report and with a full bibliography. Use these tips to avoid plagiarism and to give proper credit within your report.

- For *summarized or paraphrased information,* insert parentheses for the author's last name and the page number(s) from which the information came:
  Male black bears in the wild can weigh as much as 500 pounds (Faulk 16-17).

- For a *direct quotation,* use quotation marks. After the end quotation mark, insert in parentheses the author's last name and the page number(s) from which the quotation came:
  In his book on bears, Faulk states that "before entering full hibernation, black bears fortify their bodies for the long sleep by storing a great deal of extra body fat" (Faulk 121).

Include visuals to support key ideas. Use charts or other visual aids to highlight and expand key points in the body of your report or to add interesting related information that might otherwise interrupt the flow of your report. In your writing, refer to the visuals and explain what points they prove or explain. Direct your readers to use these visuals as needed.

Crediting Sources

A **bibliography** at the end of your report provides readers with complete bibliographic information of each source you cited in your report. Readers can use the author and page number citations within your report to find the specific source in your bibliography. Readers who are interested can use the bibliography to learn more about your topic.

This chart shows the Modern Language Association (MLA) format for crediting sources.

MLA Style for Listing Sources

Book with one author	Pyles, Thomas. *The Origins and Development of the English Language.* 2nd ed. New York: Harcourt Brace Jovanovich, Inc., 1971.
Book with two or three authors	McCrum, Robert, William Cran, and Robert MacNeil. *The Story of English.* New York: Penguin Books, 1987.
Book with an editor	Truth, Sojourner: *Narrative of Sojourner Truth.* Ed. Margaret Washington. New York: Vintage Books, 1993.
Signed article in a weekly magazine	Wallace, C. (2000, February 14). A Vodacious Deal. *Time,* 155, 63.
Signed article in a monthly magazine	Gustatitis, Joseph. "The Sticky History of Chewing Gum." *American History* Oct. 1998: 30–38.
Unsigned editorial or story	"Selective Silence" Editorial. *Wall Street Journal* 11 Feb. 2000: A14.
Filmstrips, slide programs, videocassettes, DVDS	*The Diary of Anne Frank.* Dir. George Stevens. Perf. Millie Perkins, Shelly Winters, Joseph Schildkraut, Lou Jacobi, and Richard Beymer. Twentieth Century Fox, 1959.
Internet	"Fun Facts About Gum." NACGM site. National Association of Chewing Gum Manufacturers. 19 Dec. 1999 <http://www.nacgm.org/consumer/funfacts.html>
Newspaper	Thurow, Roger. "South Africans Who Fought for Sanctions Now Scrap for Investors." *Wall Street Journal* 11 Feb. 2000: A1+
Personal Interview	Smith, Jane. Personal interview. 10 Feb. 2000.
CD (with multiple publishers)	Simms, James, ed. *Romeo* and *Juliet.* By William Shakespeare. CD- ROM. Oxford: Attica Cybernetics Ltd.; London: BBC Education; London: HarperCollins Publishers, 1995.

Name ______________________ Date ____________ Assignment ______________

Create a bibliography. Use the graphic organizer to create a bibliography for your research report. Use the entries in the MLA style sheet on the previous page as a model. Arrange your sources in the order that you cited them for the first time in your report.

Bibliography

Name ______________________ Date ____________ Assignment ______________

Revising Strategies

Evaluate your draft for organization, unity, and interest. Use the organizer to evaluate the organization, unity, and interest level of your research report. If you wish, you can give a classmate a copy of your outline, your draft, and this graphic organizer. Have your classmate suggest ways to improve your report.

Focus Questions	
Does the organization of ideas in my draft follow my outline?	Yes .... No ....
If the answer to the first question is no, will changing the order of ideas improve the sense and structure of my report?	Yes .... No ....
Do I vary sentence length and patterns? Is there anywhere that I can I combine short, choppy sentences or break up longer sentences?	Yes .... No ....
Does my introduction contain a clear thesis statement that focuses the report?	Yes .... No ....
Does every paragraph help to develop the thesis?	Yes .... No ....
Do all of my paragraphs contain clear topic sentences that support my main idea?	Yes .... No ....
Do I use sufficient facts, details, or examples to illustrate and elaborate my main ideas?	Yes .... No ....
Do I introduce any details or ideas that are not related to my thesis statement?	Yes .... No ....
Do I create a smooth flow between paragraphs by repeating words and phrases from one paragraph to the next; or do I use transitions, such as *first, finally,* and *as a result?*	Yes .... No ....
Does the conclusion restate the thesis statement and summarize all the main points in the report? Does it give readers something more to think about?	Yes .... No ....
Do I use visual aids effectively to highlight and prove points in the body of my essay?	Yes .... No ....

Revising to Correct Use of Pronoun Case

As you revise your draft, check that you have used the correct forms of pronouns. Many pronouns change form according to usage. *Case* is the relationship between a pronoun's form and its use.

Personal Pronouns	
Nominative Case	**Objective Case**
I, we you he, she, it, they	me, us you him, her, it, them

Using Personal Pronouns Personal pronouns in the **nominative case** may be the subject of a verb or a predicate nominative—a noun or pronoun that renames the subject.

Subject: She plays soccer. Cassie and I play soccer, too.

Predicate Nominative: Beckham's biggest fans are Jenna and I.

Personal pronouns in the **objective case** have three uses: as a direct object, as an indirect object, and as the object of a preposition.

Direct Object: Jason invited Raf and me to the game.

Indirect Object: Paul had given him two extra tickets.

Object of a Preposition: All three of us were grateful to him.

Fixing Incorrect Use of Personal Pronouns Mistakes with pronouns usually occur when the subject or object is compound.

1. **To test a pronoun in a compound subject, use just the pronoun with the verb in the sentence.** For example, in the sentence, "Cassie and me play soccer," "me play" clearly sounds wrong. The nominative case *I* is needed.

2. **To test a pronoun in a compound object, use just the pronoun by itself after the verb or the preposition.** For example, in the sentence, "Jason invited Raf and I to the game," "Jason invited I" sounds wrong. The objective case *me* is needed.

Editing and Proofreading

Review your draft to correct errors in capitalization, spelling, and punctuation.

Focus on Capitalization: Review your draft carefully to find and correct capitalization errors. Make sure every sentence begins with a capital letter. Focus on the citations in your report and bibliography. Make sure titles of sources are capitalized correctly. If you have made specific references to experts on your topic who have titles, make sure you have capitalized their titles correctly.

Representative Ellie Dickenson **Professor Jon Stephens**

Focus on Spelling: Check the spelling of each word in your story. Pay particular attention to the spelling of authors' names. When in doubt, go back to source materials to double check for accuracy. Remember that a spell checker cannot offer corrections for proper names. In addition, a spell checker will not find words that are spelled correctly but used incorrectly, such as *too, to,* and *two.* Proofread carefully to find misused words.

Focus on Punctuation: Proofread your writing to find and correct punctuation errors. Make sure every sentence has end punctuation. Check that you have put parentheses around citations within your report. If you are using the MLA style, citations should appear in parentheses directly after the information cited. Make sure that you have used quotation marks around direct quotations and short works, and that you have underlined or italicized long written works or periodicals. Check sure that all the entries in your bibliography are punctuated correctly.

Revision Checklist

- ❑ Have you reviewed your research report for correct capitalization?
- ❑ Have you read each sentence and checked that all of the words are spelled correctly?
- ❑ Have you punctuated all your sentences and your bibliography correctly?

Name ______________________ Date ____________ Assignment ______________

Publishing and Presenting

Consider one of the following ways to present your writing:

Give an oral presentation. Use your report as the basis for an oral presentation on your topic. Have on hand graphs, charts, maps, photographs, videos, or any other visuals that will enhance your presentation and further explain important ideas in your report. If your report is about an important person from recent times, you may be able to find a recording in his or her voice that you can play as a dramatic introduction to the presentation.

Put your report on file in the library. Print out a clean copy of your report and put it in a sturdy binder. Ask the school librarian to keep your report on the shelf with other reference sources on the same topic. Then other students in your school who choose to write a research report on a topic related to your topic can use your report as a source.

Rubric for Self-Assessment

Find evidence in your writing to address each category. Then use the rating scale to grade your work.

Evaluating Your Research Report	not very					very
Focus: How clearly stated is your thesis?	1	2	3	4	5	6
Organization: How effective is your organization of information?	1	2	3	4	5	6
Support/Elaboration: How accurate and thorough are your supporting facts and details?	1	2	3	4	5	6
Style: How smooth are your transitions?	1	2	3	4	5	6
Conventions: How complete and accurate are citations in your report and in your bibliography?	1	2	3	4	5	6

Writing 9a

9a. Draw evidence from literary or informational texts to support analysis, reflection, and research.

- **Apply *grade 7 Reading standards to literature* (e.g., "Compare and contrast a fictional portrayal of a time, place, or character and a historical account of the same period as a means of understanding how authors of fiction use or alter history").**

Explanation

You may be asked to write an essay comparing and contrasting a fictional portrayal of a time, place, or character and a **historical account** of the same period. Comparing a fictional to a historical account can help you figure out whether the fiction writer used historical details accurately or altered them. When you write such an essay, discuss the similarities and differences in the ways that historical details are used in the two texts.

For your essay, select a fictional story about a character from history and a historical account of the same person. Then gather details to identify similarities and differences between how the character is portrayed in both texts. Transitional words and phrases such as *similarly, likewise, unlike, on the other hand,* and *in contrast* can help make the similarities and differences between the two works clear.

Choose one of these patterns to organize details in the body of your essay.

- **Block Method:** Present all the details about the character in the fictional story. Then, present all the details about the character in the historical account.
- **Point-by-Point Method:** Alternate discussion of the character in each work, point by point.

Keep in mind that **historical fiction** writers are not bound by the same strict rules as history writers. Fiction writers often change and embellish the facts to fit the story. As you take notes, think about how the fiction writer uses or alters history and how it affects your understanding and enjoyment of the story. Include these ideas in your conclusion.

Academic Vocabulary

historical account factual description of a specific period in history

historical fiction made-up stories that are based on actual places, characters, and events in history

Apply the Standard

Use the worksheet that follows to help you apply the standard as you write. Several copies have been provided for you to use with different assignments.

- Comparing and Contrasting

Name ______________________ Date ____________ Assignment ________________

Comparing and Contrasting

Use the Venn diagram to compare and contrast a fictional account of a person from the past with a historical account of the same person. First, note the title and author of each work, and name the character whose portrayal you will be comparing. Then write the differences you find between their portrayals in the outer circles and the similarities in the space where the circles overlap.

Title and Author of Fictional Story: ....

Title and Author of Historical Account: ....

Character I will compare in my essay: ....

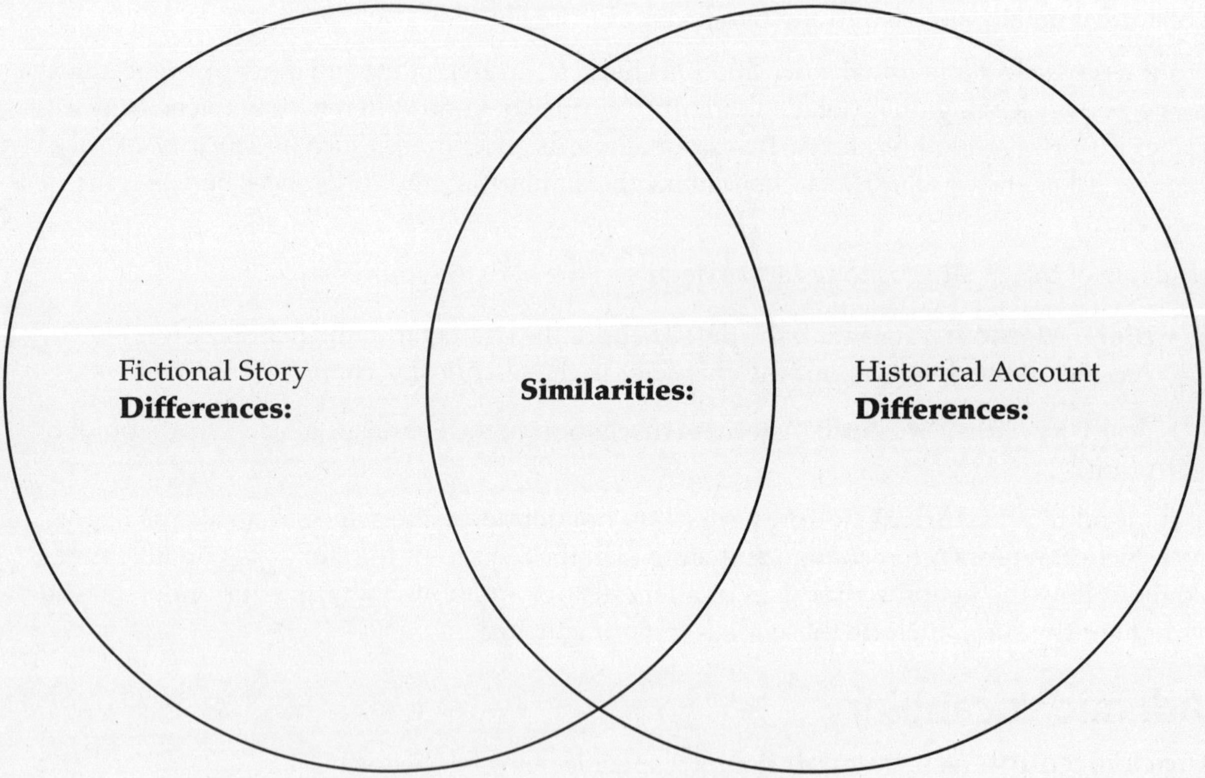

Name ______________________ Date ____________ Assignment ______________

Comparing and Contrasting

Use the Venn diagram to compare and contrast a fictional account of a person from the past with a historical account of the same person. First, note the title and author of each work, and name the character whose portrayal you will be comparing. Then write the differences you find between their portrayals in the outer circles and the similarities in the space where the circles overlap.

Title and Author of Fictional Story: ....

Title and Author of Historical Account: ....

Character I will compare in my essay: ....

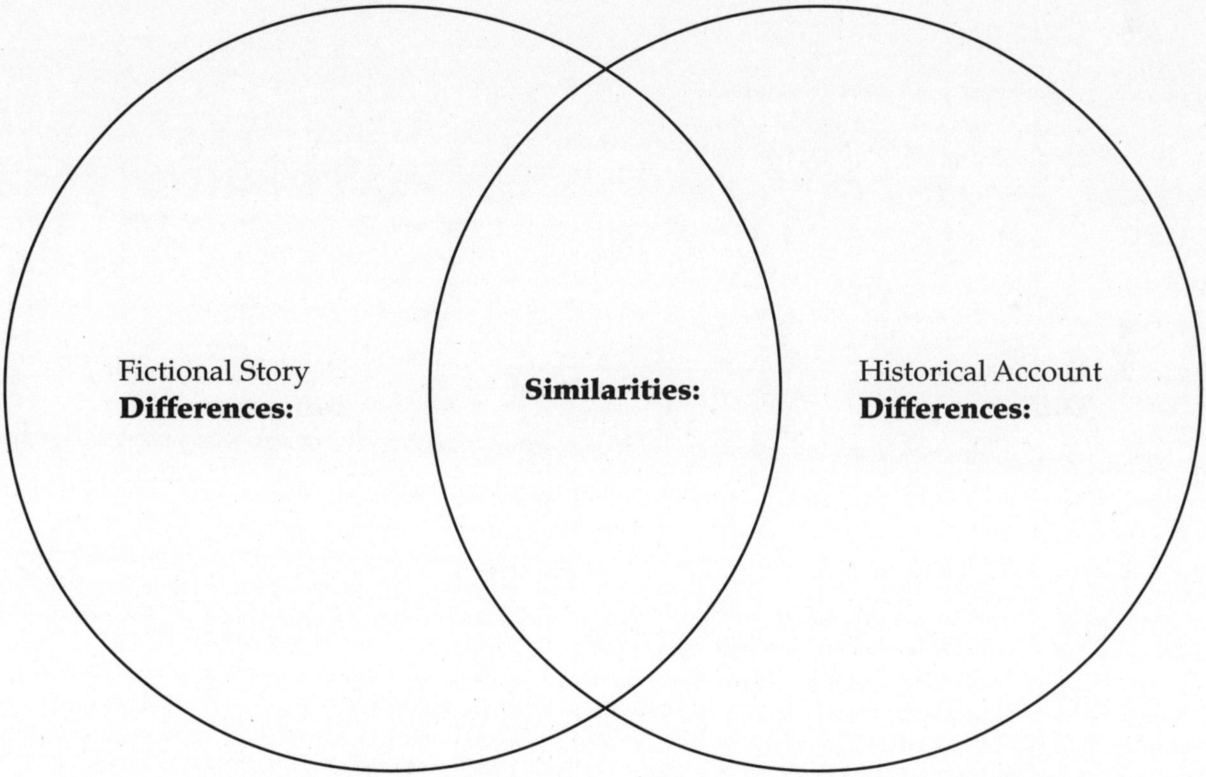

Name ______________________ Date ______________ Assignment ________________

Comparing and Contrasting

Use the Venn diagram to compare and contrast a fictional account of a person from the past with a historical account of the same person. First, note the title and author of each work, and name the character whose portrayal you will be comparing. Then write the differences you find between their portrayals in the outer circles and the similarities in the space where the circles overlap.

Title and Author of Fictional Story: ....

Title and Author of Historical Account: ....

Character I will compare in my essay: ....

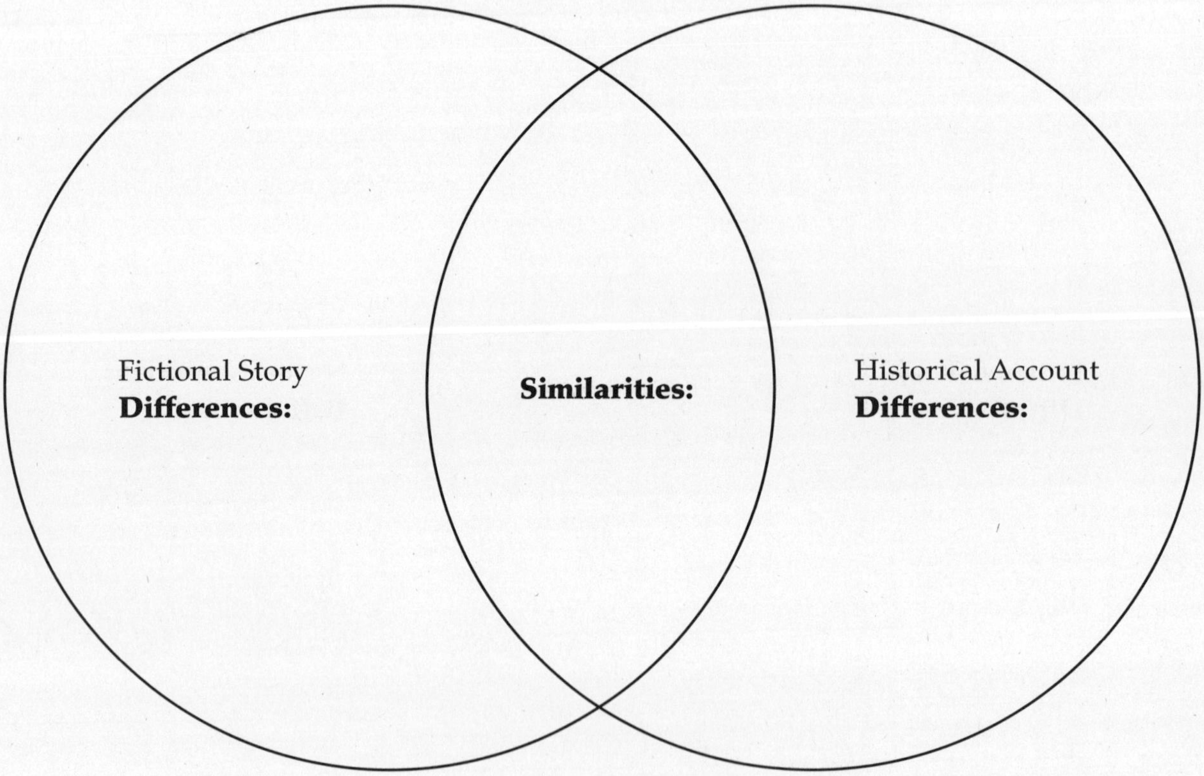

C

For use with Writing 9a

Writing 9b

9b. Draw evidence from literary or informational texts to support analysis, reflection, and research.

- **Apply *grade 7 Reading standards* to literary nonfiction (e.g., "Trace and evaluate the argument and specific claims in a text, assessing whether the reasoning is sound and the evidence is relevant and sufficient to support the claims").**

Explanation

In editorials, reviews, and speeches, writers argue their positions on specific issues. When you write an evaluation of an argument, focus on its strengths and weaknesses. Decide if the reasoning is sound and the **claim** makes sense. Based on your examination, tell whether the writer successfully argued his or her position.

Select a text with an argument. Then take notes for an essay about it. Here are some points to keep in mind:

- A sound argument contains a clearly stated position or claim.
- A valid claim is supported by relevant and sufficient **evidence,** such as facts, statistics, anecdotes, quotations from experts, and examples.
- The writer provides verifiable sources for his or her evidence.
- Reasons are logical and presented in an organized way.
- The writer gives evidence against opposing points of view.
- The evidence is based on facts, not opinions.

Before you write, look over your notes. Decide whether you have been persuaded to accept the author's claim. Then choose examples from the text to support your evaluation. Use your notes to stay focused as you write.

Begin your draft by stating the writer's position. Then, write a thesis statement that expresses your opinion of the writer's claim. In the body of your essay, show how the writer builds the argument. Explain why his or her claim is or is not valid. Use evidence from the text to support your evaluation. In your conclusion, restate your thesis and sum up your ideas.

Academic Vocabulary

claim a writer's position on an issue

evidence factual details that support a claim

Apply the Standard

Use the worksheet that follows to help you apply the standard as you write. Several copies have been provided for you to use with different assignments.

- Evaluating an Argument

Name ______________________ Date ____________ Assignment ______________

Evaluating an Argument

Use the organizer to take notes for your essay evaluating an argument. Include specific details from the text to explain your responses.

Title:	**Form (e.g. editorial, review):**	
Writer's position:		
What does the writer want readers to believe or do?		
Evaluation Questions	**Response**	**Explain**
Is an opinion clearly stated?	❑ Yes ❑ No	
Is the opinion supported by reasons and evidence?	❑ Yes ❑ No	
Do the reasons make sense? Are they logical?	❑ Yes ❑ No	
Is the evidence sufficient and relevant?	❑ Yes ❑ No	
Does the author provide sources than can be verified?	❑ Yes ❑ No	
Are transitions used to make the argument easy to follow?	❑ Yes ❑ No	
Does the writer maintain a reasonable voice throughout the argument and avoid biased or overly emotional language?	❑ Yes ❑ No	
Does the writer give evidence against an opposing point of view?	❑ Yes ❑ No	
Are readers likely to agree or disagree with the writer's position?	❑ Yes ❑ No	

Name ______________________ Date ____________ Assignment ____________

Evaluating an Argument

Use the organizer to take notes for your essay evaluating an argument. Include specific details from the text to explain your responses.

Title:	**Form (e.g. editorial, review):**	
Writer's position:		
What does the writer want readers to believe or do?		
Evaluation Questions	**Response**	**Explain**
Is an opinion clearly stated?	❑ Yes ❑ No	
Is the opinion supported by reasons and evidence?	❑ Yes ❑ No	
Do the reasons make sense? Are they logical?	❑ Yes ❑ No	
Is the evidence sufficient and relevant?	❑ Yes ❑ No	
Does the author provide sources than can be verified?	❑ Yes ❑ No	
Are transitions used to make the argument easy to follow?	❑ Yes ❑ No	
Does the writer maintain a reasonable voice throughout the argument and avoid biased or overly emotional language?	❑ Yes ❑ No	
Does the writer give evidence against an opposing point of view?	❑ Yes ❑ No	
Are readers likely to agree or disagree with the writer's position?	❑ Yes ❑ No	

Name ______________________ Date ____________ Assignment ________________

Evaluating an Argument

Use the organizer to take notes for your essay evaluating an argument. Include specific details from the text to explain your responses.

Title:	**Form (e.g. editorial, review):**	
Writer's position:		
What does the writer want readers to believe or do?		
Evaluation Questions	**Response**	**Explain**
Is an opinion clearly stated?	❑ Yes ❑ No	
Is the opinion supported by reasons and evidence?	❑ Yes ❑ No	
Do the reasons make sense? Are they logical?	❑ Yes ❑ No	
Is the evidence sufficient and relevant?	❑ Yes ❑ No	
Does the author provide sources than can be verified?	❑ Yes ❑ No	
Are transitions used to make the argument easy to follow?	❑ Yes ❑ No	
Does the writer maintain a reasonable voice throughout the argument and avoid biased or overly emotional language?	❑ Yes ❑ No	
Does the writer give evidence against an opposing point of view?	❑ Yes ❑ No	
Are readers likely to agree or disagree with the writer's position?	❑ Yes ❑ No	

Writing 10

10a. Write routinely over extended time frames (time for research, reflection, and revision) and shorter time frames (a single sitting or a day or two) for a range of discipline-specific tasks, purposes, and audiences.

Explanation

Writing assignments are a part of every student's regular routine. Some writing assignments, such as research reports or responses to literature, are long term and require several days or weeks to complete. Other assignments are short term and require only a single class period or a day or two to write. A friendly letter is an example of a short-term writing assignment.

A friendly letter has the same basic parts as a business letter: the heading, the salutation or greeting, the body, the closing, and the signature. However, a friendly letter is informal in style and personal in tone. In class, you might be asked to write a friendly letter to an author whose work you have read or a letter from the viewpoint of a character in a story. Use these strategies to plan and write a friendly letter.

- First, identify your task, purpose, and audience. Ask yourself: Who will receive my letter? What do I want this person to know? If you have been given a **writing prompt,** read the prompt carefully to make sure you understand its key ideas.
- Plan how you will use the time available. If you have 50 minutes, you might use 15 minutes to plan, 25 minutes to write, and 10 minutes to revise and edit.
- Take a few minutes to write down the main points you want to make in your letter. Then number your ideas in the order that you will discuss them.
- Draft your letter. Keep the language friendly and conversational but polite.
- Reread your letter to make sure it is complete and your ideas make sense.
- Correct any errors in punctuation, capitalization, spelling, and grammar. Avoid using slang. Check that your format is correct.

Academic Vocabulary

writing prompt a sentence or sentences that provide a specific writing idea

Apply the Standard

Use the worksheet that follows to help you apply the standard as you write.

- Writing a Friendly Letter

Name ______________________ Date ____________ Assignment ______________

Writing a Friendly Letter

Use the organizer to plan and organize your friendly letter.

Task:	Purpose:	Audience: ....
Plan your time Prewrite: .... minutes	Draft: .... minutes	Revise and Edit: .... minutes

Organize Ideas

.... ← address

....

....

.... ← date

greeting → ....,

message →

....

....

....

....

....

....

....

....

....

....

....

....

closing → ....,

signature → ....,

For use with Writing 10a

Writing 10

10. Write routinely over extended time frames (time for research, reflection, and revision) and shorter time frames (a single sitting or a day or two) for a range of discipline-specific tasks, purposes, and audiences.

Explanation

Students are often asked to write descriptions of people, places, things, and events for reading, social studies, and other classes. Some descriptive writing assignments are short, such as a one-paragraph description of a special person. Other assignments, such as a descriptive essay of a meaningful event in history, would take longer to complete.

A well-written description should present a subject so clearly that readers will be able to picture it in their minds. The use of **sensory details** and vivid **imagery** can bring a person, place, thing, or event to life. Read the sample descriptions below. The first is vague and lifeless; the second uses vivid, precise language.

Vague: *The sunset over the ocean was amazing. A bird called in the sky.*

Vivid: *The blazing orange sun sank into a steel-blue sea. A gull screeched overhead.*

When asked to describe something, first define your task, purpose, and audience. Then, make an outline of your ideas. Next, gather sensory details. The amount of time you spend on the description and the details you gather depends on whether you are writing a short paragraph or an essay. The overall impression you want to create should also affect the details. To begin, introduce your topic and explain its significance. List details in an order that will make sense to readers, and use transitions to link ideas. Then, write a conclusion that ties all your ideas together.

Academic Vocabulary

imagery vivid mental pictures created with figurative language and sensory details

sensory details language that explains how something looks, sounds, feels, tastes, or smells

Apply the Standard

Use the worksheet that follows to help you apply the standard as you write. Several copies have been provided for you to use with different assignments.

- ❑ Writing a Description

Name ______________________ Date ____________ Assignment ________________

Writing a Description

Use the organizer to plan your description.

Task:		Purpose:	Audience:	
Plan your time Prewrite: .... minutes		Draft: .... minutes	Revise and Edit: .... minutes	
Topic:				
Gather Sensory Details				
Sound	Sight	Feel/Touch	Smell	Taste

Choose a General Organizational Pattern (You may end up using more than one pattern in a long essay or report.)

❑ **Chronological order** works well for descriptions of events. Use transition words such as *first, next, then,* and *finally.*

❑ **Spatial order** works well for descriptions of places and people. Use transition words such as *near, far, above,* and *below.*

❑ **Order of importance** works well for descriptions of significant events and people. Use transition words or phrases such as *first of all, especially,* and *most importantly.*

❑ **Other** ....
Transition words: ....

Name ______________________ Date ____________ Assignment ______________

Writing a Description

Use the organizer to plan your description.

Task:		Purpose:	Audience:	
Plan your time Prewrite: .... minutes		Draft: .... minutes	Revise and Edit: .... minutes	
Topic:				
Gather Sensory Details				
Sound	Sight	Feel/Touch	Smell	Taste

Choose a General Organizational Pattern (You may end up using more than one pattern in a long essay or report.)

- ❑ *Chronological Order:* works well for descriptions of events; use transition words such as *first, next, then,* and *finally.*
- ❑ *Spatial Order:* works well for descriptions of places and people; use transition words such as *near, far, above,* and *below.*
- ❑ *Order of Importance:* works well for descriptions of significant events and people; use transition words, such as *first of all, especially,* and *most importantly.*
- ❑ Other: ....
  Transition words: ....

B

Name ______________________ Date ____________ Assignment ______________

Writing a Description

Use the organizer to plan your description.

Task:	Purpose:	Audience:		
Plan your time Prewrite: .... minutes	Draft: .... minutes	Revise and Edit: .... minutes		
Topic:				
Gather Sensory Details				
Sound	Sight	Feel/Touch	Smell	Taste

Choose a General Organizational Pattern (You may end up using more than one pattern in a long essay or report.)

- ❑ *Chronological Order:* works well for descriptions of events; use transition words such as *first, next, then,* and *finally.*
- ❑ *Spatial Order:* works well for descriptions of places and people; use transition words such as *near, far, above,* and *below.*
- ❑ *Order of Importance:* works well for descriptions of significant events and people; use transition words, such as *first of all, especially,* and *most importantly.*
- ❑ Other: ....
  Transition words: ....

Writing 10

10. Write routinely over extended time frames (time for research, reflection, and revision) and shorter time frames (a single sitting or a day or two) for a range of discipline-specific tasks, purposes, and audiences.

Explanation

A **character sketch** is a brief description of a person that highlights key traits. Because character sketches can be completed in a short time frame, they are routinely assigned as in-class writing activities or as overnight homework. A character sketch can show your insight into fictional or historical characters after reading. It is also very useful for outlining characters before writing a short story.

Like a sharply focused snapshot, a character sketch captures the essential qualities of a person. It is not a biography. Imagine that you want to describe a good friend to your parents or another adult. What details would you give about your friend's appearance and behavior to help your listener form a clear picture of your friend?

To write a character sketch, follow these steps.

- Identify the subject of your sketch. Your subject may be a person you know, a character from literature, a person from history, or a character you make up.
- Decide what you want readers to understand most about your subject.
- Take notes about your subject that will help you accomplish your task. Ask and answer questions about your subject's age and appearance, actions, beliefs, and other **personality traits.** List evidence you might use to illustrate specific traits.
- Gather your notes, and write a brief description of your subject. Remember to focus only on his or her most important or revealing traits.

Academic Vocabulary

character sketch a brief description of a person that highlights key traits

personality trait basic characteristic or quality of a person

Apply the Standard

Use the worksheet that follows to help you apply the standard as you write.

- Writing a Character Sketch

Name ______________________ Date ____________ Assignment ______________

Writing a Character Sketch

Use the organizer below to gather ideas for a character sketch.

Task:	Purpose:	Audience: ....
Plan your time Prewrite: .... minutes	Draft: .... minutes	Revise and Edit: .... minutes

Gather ideas for a character sketch	
Who is the subject of the character sketch?	
What is your subject's age and gender?	
What do you want readers to understand most about your subject?	

Answer the questions to explore your subject in detail. When appropriate, give evidence from your subject's life that you can use in your sketch to illustrate a specific quality or trait.

Questions	Responses	Evidence
What does your subject look like? What is unique about your subject's appearance?		
What are your subject's most important beliefs and values?		
How does your subject treat other people?		
What adjectives would you and others use to describe your subject?		
What outstanding traits does your subject have? (Include traits that show your subject's strengths and weaknesses.)		

For use with Writing 10c

Writing 10

10. Write routinely over extended time frames (time for research, reflection, and revision) and shorter time frames (a single sitting or a day or two) for a range of discipline-specific task, purposes, and audiences.

Explanation

A **how-to essay** explains how to do something or make something in a step-by-step **process.** Most people encounter process writing daily in instructional booklets, manuals, guides, and sets of directions. When you choose a topic for a how-to paper, select a process that interests you. Be sure you know the topic well enough to explain it clearly and completely. Consider what your audience may already know about the topic to determine how much extra information you need to include. Your paper should feature these elements:

- a narrow, focused topic that can be fully explained in the time and space available
- a list of materials needed to achieve a specific end result
- multi-step directions, organized in sequential order
- transitional words and phrases to make the order clear; for example, *first of all, next, after you have, in an hour, once you have,* and *finally*
- explanation of any unfamiliar or technical terms
- diagrams or illustrations to clarify the directions, if needed

Create a plan that allows time for prewriting, drafting, revising, editing, and producing a final, clean copy. When you revise, make sure the introduction focuses the essay on the topic. Also, check that the middle explains the steps in order and that no steps are missing. You may wish to set off the actual directions in a numbered or bulleted list.

Academic Vocabulary

how-to essay a short, focused piece of expository writing that explains a process

process a series of steps or actions that lead to a specific result

Apply the Standard

Use the worksheet that follows to help you apply the standard as you write.

- Writing a How-to Essay

Name ______________________ Date ____________ Assignment ______________

Writing a How-to Essay

Use the organizer below to gather and organize details for your how-to essay.

Task:	Purpose:	Audience: ....
Plan your time Prewrite: .... minutes	Draft: .... minutes	Revise and Edit: .... minutes
Gather Details		
List of Materials		
Organize Ideas for Your Draft		
Title: **Introduction:**		

Step 1:

Step 2:

Step 3:

Step 4:

Step 5:

Conclusion:

For use with Writing 10

Speaking and Listening Standards

Speaking and Listening 1

1. Engage effectively in a range of collaborative discussions (one-on-one, in groups, and teacher-led) with diverse partners on grade 7 topics, texts, and issues, building on others' ideas and expressing their own clearly.*

Workshop: Present a Critique of a Literary Work

While a review is a general description and evaluation of a literary work, a critique is a detailed, critical analysis of a work or some aspect of it. Oral and written critiques are used in science, mathematics, and social studies as well as in literature.

In a detailed analysis of a literary work, the speaker's purpose is to persuade listeners to believe an idea or share the speaker's position. Speakers use different strategies in crafting a critique so that it is clear and persuasive.

Assignment

Present a critique of a literary selection you have read. In your critique, include these elements:

- ✓ an evaluation of the work that expresses a single, clear point of view
- ✓ a number of points supporting that point of view, such as relevant examples, quotations, and key details
- ✓ a coherent, easy-to-follow organization
- ✓ appropriate eye contact, adequate volume, and clear pronunciation
- ✓ language that is formal and precise and that follows the rules of standard English

*Additional Standards

Speaking and Listening

1. Engage effectively in a range of collaborative discussions (one-on-one, in groups, and teacher-led) with diverse partners on *grade 7 topics, texts, and issues,* building on others' ideas and expressing their own clearly.

1.a. Come to discussions prepared, having read or researched material under study; explicitly draw on that preparation by referring to evidence on the topic, text, or issue to probe and reflect on ideas under discussion.

1.b. Follow rules for collegial discussions, track progress toward specific goals and deadlines, and define individual roles as needed.

1.c. Pose questions that elicit elaboration and respond to others' questions and comments with relevant observations and ideas that bring the discussion back on topic as needed.

1.d. Acknowledge new information expressed by others and, when warranted, modify their own views.

4. Present claims and findings, emphasizing salient points in a focused, coherent manner with pertinent descriptions, facts, details, and examples; use appropriate eye contact, adequate volume, and clear pronunciation.

5. Include multimedia components and visual displays in presentations to clarify claims and findings and emphasize salient points.

6. Adapt speech to a variety of contexts and tasks, demonstrating command of formal English when indicated or appropriate.

Language

3.a. Choose language that expresses ideas precisely and concisely, recognizing and eliminating wordiness and redundancy

Organize Your Oral Presentation

An oral presentation needs to be well organized so that your listeners can follow along with you and understand your position. Take time before you begin writing your presentation to think through your talk.

Start with a claim. As you plan and draft your presentation, focus on the claim or idea you want to make. Try to state your position in one clear sentence.

Support your claim. Be sure that each additional point you make supports your critical analysis and evaluation of the work. You can support your claim with examples, quotations, and details from the work.

Use clear, precise language. Avoid wordiness or other details that do not support your claim. Use language that is precise and specific to the literary work you are discussing. Note these examples:

> **Vague, imprecise language:** *The writer keeps you kind of on edge.*
> **Precise language:** *The writer creates suspense.*

Finish rewriting this vague statement to make it more precise and subject specific:

> **Vague:** *The writer pushes the story forward.*
> **Precise:** The writer advances the ___________.

Conclude your critique. At the conclusion of your presentation, restate your position or claim and reinforce the major reasons supporting it. Try to end your presentation on a memorable note. Highlight again your position and why your listeners should believe it too. Make sure you leave time to answer your classmates' questions.

Name ______________________ Date ____________ Assignment ______________

Organize Your Critique

Organize your critique so that the audience can easily follow it. Use the graphic organizer below to be sure you have sufficient support for your position:

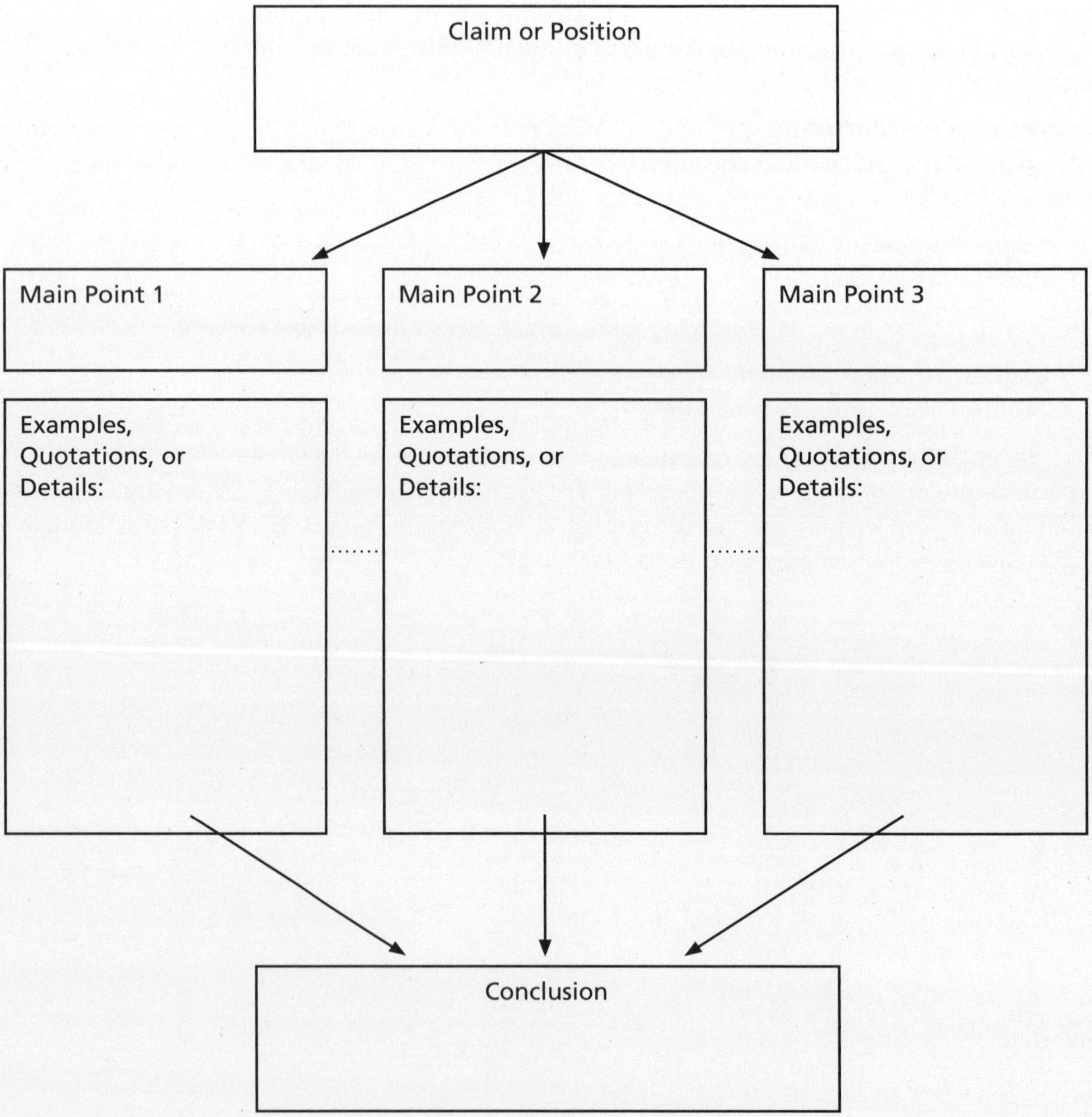

Name ______________________ Date ____________ Assignment ______________

Visuals and Multimedia

You can enhance almost any presentation with the right visual displays, such as charts and diagrams, as well as with multimedia.

Use visual displays and multimedia components. Visual displays, such as charts and diagrams, can add clarity to a presentation by conveying complex information quickly and easily. Multimedia components, such as online graphics or audio clips, can also highlight parts of a presentation. However, be sure to use such items with moderation and only to emphasize a major point. Integrate these items into your presentation by introducing each one. Take time to explain how the visual or multimedia supports your point. Use a chart like the one below to integrate multimedia elements:

Type of Visual Display or Multimedia Component	Main Point It Supports	Where to Include It and How to Introduce It

Name ______________________ Date ____________ Assignment ______________

Presentation Techniques

The way you deliver your critique is often as important as how well you have organized and written it.

Use presentation techniques. Throughout your critique, use these presentation tips to help you with the delivery:

- **Eye contact:** Make eye contact with members of the audience so listeners will feel you are speaking to them rather than at them.
- **Volume:** Adjust your volume so everyone in the audience can hear you without straining. You can also increase or decrease your volume for dramatic effect, but do not overuse this device.
- **Pronunciation:** Speak clearly so listeners can understand every word you say. If you know you have trouble pronouncing a word, practice saying it beforehand.
- **Natural gestures:** Gestures you would naturally use in conversation can help you maintain a friendly but appropriately formal tone.
- **Language conventions:** Your manner should be relaxed, but your language should follow the rules of standard, written English. Errors in grammar will distract listeners from your message.

As you listen to your fellow students' presentations, use the rubric below to assess their presentation techniques.

Speaking Techniques	Listening Rubric
Eye contact	❑ Did the speaker make eye contact? ❑ Did listeners feel the speaker was speaking to them?
Speaking volume	❑ Did the speaker talk loud enough for everyone to hear? ❑ Did the speaker change volume during different points in the talk?
Pronunciation	❑ Did the speaker speak each word and sentence clearly and accurately?
Gestures and Posture	❑ Did the speaker stand up straight and exhibit good posture? ❑ Did the speaker use hand gestures to emphasize key parts of the talk?
Language	❑ Did the speaker use standard English? ❑ Did the speaker use language precisely and avoid vague words and phrases and filler words such as "um"?

Name ______________________ Date ____________ Assignment ______________

Discuss and Evaluate

After you finish presenting your critique, participate with classmates in a discussion of its content and delivery.

Discuss and evaluate the critique. If possible, reach a consensus on the strengths of the critique and on aspects of it that can be improved. If it is not possible to agree, summarize points of agreement and disagreement. Refer to the guidelines below in order to make your discussion as productive as possible.

Guidelines for Discussion

Prepare for the discussion by reviewing the guidelines below for holding a productive discussion.

- Help the group set goals for the discussion and assign roles, such as leader and notetaker, as necessary.
- Ask questions and answer others' questions in a way that helps the group keep focused and meet its goals.
- Be receptive to new ideas suggested by others and, when appropriate, change your own thinking to take new ideas into account.
- Make sure everyone has a chance to participate and express his or her views.

Guidelines for Group Discussion

Discussion Rubric	Notes
❑ Did everyone participate in the discussion? ❑ Was each member of the group able to express his or her opinion?	
❑ Was there a leader guiding the discussion? ❑ Did someone take notes to share with everyone at the end of the discussion?	
❑ Did participants ask questions and answer questions posed by others? ❑ Did participants stay focused on the topic?	
❑ Were participants open to comments from others? ❑ Were people in the group open to any new ideas suggested by other participants?	

Name ______________________ Date ____________ Assignment ______________

Self-Assessment

When the class discussion and evaluation is completed, take a few moments to reflect on your critique. How do you think it went? Consider how your classmates reacted to the critique—did the group discussion help you to realize anything about your critique?

Use a rubric for self-assessment. Based on your own and your classmates' opinions of your critique, fill out the following rubric. Try to assess your critique and delivery as if you were an audience member instead of the person who gave the critique. Use the rating scale to grade your work. Circle the score that best applies for each category.

Criteria	Rating Scale Not very very
Focus: Did my critique provide a critical analysis and evaluation of a literary work from the textbook?	1 2 3 4 5
Organization: Was my critique organized so that listeners could easily follow it?	1 2 3 4 5
Support/Elaboration: Did I support main points with examples, quotations, and details from the text, using visual displays and multimedia components where appropriate?	1 2 3 4 5
Delivery: Did I create a relaxed but formal tone, making eye contact with listeners, maintaining an adequate volume, and speaking clearly?	1 2 3 4 5
Conventions: Was my presentation free from errors in grammar, spelling, and punctuation?	1 2 3 4 5

Speaking and Listening 2

2. Analyze the main ideas and supporting details presented in diverse media and formats (e.g., visually, quantitatively, orally) and explain how the ideas clarify a topic, text, or issue under study.

Explanation

When you are studying a particular topic, text, or issue, the ideas and details in a variety of sources may help clarify your understanding. Different sources provide different perspectives and help you sharpen your focus on what you are studying. You can learn more about many topics, texts, and issues by looking in books, magazines, newspapers, or other print sources. You can also check a variety of non-print sources, such as video documentaries, internet articles, and radio programs. Both print and non-print media contain information presented in a variety of **formats,** including:

- visual elements, such as photographs and illustrations
- quantitative details, such as statistics and graphs
- oral elements, such as speeches and interviews

Successful listeners and speakers are able to **analyze** the main ideas and supporting details presented in all kinds of media and formats. Analyzing the ideas and details in such diverse ways should give you a better understanding of your topic, text, or issue. It should also help you better explain how the ideas in the source clarified your understanding.

Examples

- **Visual** elements can present details not available in text sources. For example, if you are studying pollution, a diagram may show you how pollution from a smokestack enters the air. Visual elements, such as images and videos, can also express emotionally powerful ideas. For example, a photograph of a badly polluted river, lake, or stream can communicate the idea that pollution causes terrible damage to our world.
- **Quantitative** details, which offer information expressed in numbers and charts, will also provide strong support for ideas. Charts and graphs are two formats that make complex data easy to understand. For example, a graph that shows an increase in pollution rates worldwide over the last 50 years provides strong support for the idea that pollution is a growing problem. To analyze quantitative details, ask yourself: What does this chart or graph show? Does the data in the chart or graph provide strong support for the main idea?
- **Oral** elements are ideas and details that are spoken, or even sung. For example, you might listen to a radio broadcast about pollution in the United States. The broadcast may include narration and an interview with an expert on pollution. Listen carefully and take notes. The ideas and details presented in audio sources can be challenging to identify and analyze.

Academic Vocabulary

format the way in which something is presented and published
analyze to examine the relationship among the ideas and details in a source

Apply the Standard

Use the worksheet that follows to help you apply the standard. Several copies of the worksheet have been provided for you to use with different assignments.

- Analyzing Information from Different Media

Name ______________________ Date ____________ Assignment ______________

Analyzing Information from Different Media

When you are studying a particular topic, text, or issue, use this worksheet to keep track of each source you consult. Provide information about the source below. Then, use the organizer to analyze the main idea and supporting details. Finally, answer the question at the bottom of the page.

Topic, Text, or Issue:
Source:
Type of Media:
Format(s) Used:

Main Idea:

Supporting Detail:	**Supporting Detail:**	**Supporting Detail:**

Explain how the main idea and supporting details clarify your understanding of the topic, text, or issue that you are studying. ....

....

....

....

A

For use with Speaking and Listening 2

Name ______________________ Date ____________ Assignment ______________

Analyzing Information from Different Media

When you are studying a particular topic, text, or issue, use this worksheet to keep track of each source you consult. Provide information about the source below. Then, use the organizer to analyze the main idea and supporting details. Finally, answer the question at the bottom of the page.

Topic, Text, or Issue:
Source:
Type of Media:
Format(s) Used:

Main Idea:

Supporting Detail:	**Supporting Detail:**	**Supporting Detail:**

Explain how the main idea and supporting details clarify your understanding of the topic, text, or issue that you are studying. ....

....

....

....

B

Name ______________________ Date ____________ Assignment ______________

Analyzing Information from Different Media

When you are studying a particular topic, text, or issue, use this worksheet to keep track of each source you consult. Provide information about the source below. Then, use the organizer to analyze the main idea and supporting details. Finally, answer the question at the bottom of the page.

Topic, Text, or Issue:
Source:
Type of Media:
Format(s) Used:

Main Idea:

Supporting Detail:	**Supporting Detail:**	**Supporting Detail:**

Explain how the main idea and supporting details clarify your understanding of the topic, text, or issue that you are studying. ....

....

....

....

Speaking and Listening 3

3. Delineate a speaker's argument and specific claims, evaluating the soundness of the reasoning and the relevance and sufficiency of the evidence.

Explanation

Successful listeners are able to delineate, or clearly outline, the argument and specific claims a speaker is making. By identifying the specific claims, you can then **evaluate** whether the evidence the speaker offers in support of the claims is relevant and sufficient.

Examples

- Most good speakers will make a main specific **claim** and provide reasons and evidence to support it. There may be smaller claims made as well to support the main claim. When listening to a speaker, listen for the main claim being made. It may be presented as a cause-and-effect statement, such as "Because we are not recycling enough, our city landfills are overflowing."
- Once you've identified a speaker's main claim, evaluate the soundness of the **reasoning,** or the arguments and proof used to support the claim. Listen for how the message is organized. It should be relatively clear and easy to follow the logic of the speaker's argument as it unfolds.
- When a speaker presents support for a claim, evaluate the **relevance** of the evidence. Strong evidence used in an argument includes specific numbers and facts from important studies, quotes from experts in the field, and research done by highly regarded institutions or organizations. The main claim should always have at least a few strong points of evidence to back it up.

Academic Vocabulary

evaluate to judge or determine the quality or value of something

reasoning the arguments, proof, and analysis used to support an assertion or claim

relevance whether or not something applies to or is connected to something else

Apply the Standard

Use the worksheets that follow to help you apply the standard. Several copies of the worksheet have been provided for you.

- Understanding a Speaker's Argument
- Evaluating Evidence and Reasoning

Name ______________________ Date ____________ Selection ________________

Understanding a Speaker's Argument

Use the organizer to help delineate a speaker's argument and identify specific claims. Then answer the question.

MAIN CLAIM: ....

....

....

Specific Supporting Claim	**Specific Supporting Claim**	**Specific Supporting Claim**	**Specific Supporting Claim**
....	....	....	....
....	....	....	....
....	....	....	....
....	....	....	....
Ask: Does this claim logically support the main claim and connect to the claims that came before it?	Ask: Does this claim logically support the main claim and connect to the claims that came before it?	Ask: Does this claim logically support the main claim and connect to the claims that came before it?	Ask: Does this claim logically support the main claim and connect to the claims that came before it?

Is the speaker's argument logically organized? ....

....

....

Name ______________________ Date ______________ Selection ____________________

Understanding a Speaker's Argument

Use the organizer to help delineate a speaker's argument and identify specific claims. Then answer the question.

MAIN CLAIM: ....

....

....

Specific Supporting Claim	**Specific Supporting Claim**	**Specific Supporting Claim**	**Specific Supporting Claim**
....	....	....	....
....	....	....	....
....	....	....	....
....	....	....	....
Ask: Does this claim logically support the main claim and connect to the claims that came before it?	Ask: Does this claim logically support the main claim and connect to the claims that came before it?	Ask: Does this claim logically support the main claim and connect to the claims that came before it?	Ask: Does this claim logically support the main claim and connect to the claims that came before it?

Is the speaker's argument logically organized? ....

....

....

Name ______________________ Date ______________ Selection ______________________

Understanding a Speaker's Argument

Use the organizer to help delineate a speaker's argument and identify specific claims. Then answer the question.

MAIN CLAIM: ....

....

....

Specific Supporting Claim	Specific Supporting Claim	Specific Supporting Claim	Specific Supporting Claim
....	....	....	....
....	....	....	....
....	....	....	....
....	....	....	....
Ask: Does this claim logically support the main claim and connect to the claims that came before it?	Ask: Does this claim logically support the main claim and connect to the claims that came before it?	Ask: Does this claim logically support the main claim and connect to the claims that came before it?	Ask: Does this claim logically support the main claim and connect to the claims that came before it?

Is the speaker's argument logically organized? ....

....

....

C

Name _______________ Date _______________ Selection _______________

Evaluating Evidence and Reasoning

Use the organizer to evaluate the soundness of the reasoning and the relevance and sufficiency of the evidence in a speaker's argument. Then answer the question.

Specific Claim	**Evidence Cited**	**Is It Relevant? (Y or N)** Explain your answer	**Sufficient Support? (Y or N)** Explain your answer
1.			
2.			
3.			
4.			

Based on your evaluation, how would you assess the strength or weakness of the speaker's argument? ....

....

....

Name ______________________ Date ______________ Selection ____________________

Evaluating Evidence and Reasoning

Use the organizer to evaluate the soundness of the reasoning and the relevance and sufficiency of the evidence in a speaker's argument. Then answer the question.

Specific Claim	**Evidence Cited**	**Is It Relevant? (Y or N)** Explain your answer	**Sufficient Support? (Y or N)** Explain your answer
1.			
2.			
3.			
4.			

Based on your evaluation, how would you assess the strength or weakness of the speaker's argument? ....

....

....

Name ______________________ Date ____________ Selection ________________

Evaluating Evidence and Reasoning

Use the organizer to evaluate the soundness of the reasoning and the relevance and sufficiency of the evidence in a speaker's argument. Then answer the question.

Specific Claim	Evidence Cited	Is It Relevant? (Y or N) Explain your answer	Sufficient Support? (Y or N) Explain your answer
1.			
2.			
3.			
4.			

Based on your evaluation, how would you assess the strength or weakness of the speaker's argument? ....

....

....

Speaking and Listening 4

4. Present claims and findings, emphasizing salient points in a focused, coherent manner with pertinent descriptions, facts, details, and examples; use appropriate eye contact, adequate volume, and clear pronunciation.

Explanation

When you speak to an audience, your goal is to present your claim and findings about a topic. Ensure that your audience is able to follow your presentation by emphasizing your most **salient**, or important and relevant, points. To emphasize key points in a focused and **coherent** manner, include descriptions, facts, details, and examples that are **pertinent** to your claim. Keep your audience engaged by maintaining eye contact, speaking with adequate volume, and using clear pronunciation.

Examples

- Make sure that your presentation is focused and coherent by creating an outline. Start your outline with your main claim. Then write down the points you want to make and the descriptions, facts, and details you will use to support your points. Organize your findings so that they will make sense to your audience. For example, if your claim is that the school library should have more books available online, give facts about how many books are available online now *before* you suggest changes.
- Emphasize each key point by including pertinent facts, descriptions, details, and examples. The more specific your information is, the stronger your presentation will be. Make sure all the information in your presentation directly applies to your claim. For example, data about how often students access online library resources is pertinent, while a description of the library website may not be. Always use clear, precise, and descriptive language to deliver your facts. Vague, unclear language will confuse your audience.
- Engaging the audience is essential when delivering a presentation. Maintaining eye contact with listeners is one way to keep them interested. Try picking out the people who appear most interested and maintain eye contact with them. Also, speak loudly enough so that everyone can hear you, and pronounce your words clearly. Try to keep an even pace as you speak—you do not want to speak too quickly or slowly—but vary the tone and volume of your voice for dramatic effect.

Academic Vocabulary

coherent clear and focused; connected in a way that makes logical sense
pertinent related to the subject or idea being discussed or examined
salient important; relevant

Apply the Standard

Use the worksheets that follow to help you apply the standard. Several copies of each worksheet have been provided for you to use with different assignments.

- Organizing Information
- Presenting Information Effectively

Name ______________________ Date ____________ Assignment ______________

Organizing Information as a Speaker

Use the organizer below to arrange your key points, descriptions, facts, details, and examples in a logical order. Then answer the questions at the bottom of the page.

CLAIM:	
Salient Points	**Descriptions, Facts, Details, and Examples**
1.	
2.	
3.	
4.	

To what extent are your salient points emphasized in a coherent and focused manner? ....

....

How clear is the connection between your claim and your main points ? ....

....

Name ______________________ Date ____________ Assignment ________________

Organizing Information as a Speaker

Use the organizer below to arrange your key points, descriptions, facts, details, and examples in a logical order. Then answer the questions at the bottom of the page.

CLAIM:	
Salient Points	**Descriptions, Facts, Details, and Examples**
1.	
2.	
3.	
4.	

To what extent are your salient points emphasized in a coherent and focused manner? ....

....

How clear is the connection between your claim and your main points ? ....

....

Name ______________________ Date ______________ Assignment ________________

Organizing Information as a Speaker

Use the organizer below to arrange your key points, descriptions, facts, details, and examples in a logical order. Then answer the questions at the bottom of the page.

CLAIM:	
Salient Points	**Descriptions, Facts, Details, and Examples**
1.	
2.	
3.	
4.	

To what extent are your salient points emphasized in a coherent and focused manner? ....

....

How clear is the connection between your claim and your main points ? ....

....

Name ______________________ Date ______________ Assignment ______________

Presenting a Speech Effectively

Use the organizer below to prepare your presentation and assess your delivery.

	Presentation Checklist
Preparation	❑ Is my speech focused and logically organized? ❑ Have I emphasized my most important points? ❑ Have I included pertinent descriptions, facts, details, and examples? ❑ Did I create an outline? ❑ Is my language clear and precise?
Eye Contact	❑ Did I maintain eye contact with people in the audience? ❑ Did I look around at different people in the audience? ❑ Was I able to keep my audience engaged by maintaining eye contact?
Volume	❑ Was my speaking volume loud enough for everyone in the audience to hear me? ❑ Did I vary my tone for dramatic effect at important points in my speech? ❑ Did I maintain a steady pace in my delivery?
Pronunciation	❑ Was my delivery of the words natural? ❑ Did I pronounce each word clearly and correctly?

Name ______________________ Date ______________ Assignment ________________

Presenting a Speech Effectively

Use the organizer below to prepare your presentation and assess your delivery.

	Presentation Checklist
Preparation	❑ Is my speech focused and logically organized? ❑ Have I emphasized my most important points? ❑ Have I included pertinent descriptions, facts, details, and examples? ❑ Did I create an outline? ❑ Is my language clear and precise?
Eye Contact	❑ Did I maintain eye contact with people in the audience? ❑ Did I look around at different people in the audience? ❑ Was I able to keep my audience engaged by maintaining eye contact?
Volume	❑ Was my speaking volume loud enough for everyone in the audience to hear me? ❑ Did I vary my tone for dramatic effect at important points in my speech? ❑ Did I maintain a steady pace in my delivery?
Pronunciation	❑ Was my delivery of the words natural? ❑ Did I pronounce each word clearly and correctly?

Name ______________________ Date ____________ Assignment ______________

Presenting a Speech Effectively

Use the organizer below to prepare your presentation and assess your delivery.

	Presentation Checklist
Preparation	❑ Is my speech focused and logically organized? ❑ Have I emphasized my most important points? ❑ Have I included pertinent descriptions, facts, details, and examples? ❑ Did I create an outline? ❑ Is my language clear and precise?
Eye Contact	❑ Did I maintain eye contact with people in the audience? ❑ Did I look around at different people in the audience? ❑ Was I able to keep my audience engaged by maintaining eye contact?
Volume	❑ Was my speaking volume loud enough for everyone in the audience to hear me? ❑ Did I vary my tone for dramatic effect at important points in my speech? ❑ Did I maintain a steady pace in my delivery?
Pronunciation	❑ Was my delivery of the words natural? ❑ Did I pronounce each word clearly and correctly?

Speaking and Listening 5

5. Include multimedia components and visual displays in presentations to clarify claims and findings and emphasize salient points.

Explanation

Using **multimedia,** such as photos, video, music, and sound, can turn an average presentation into an outstanding one. Adding graphs, diagrams, and other visual displays to a speech can help clarify your **claims,** or opinions, and findings and emphasize your most salient points.

Examples

- When you plan a presentation, consider how multimedia components and visual displays can improve it. After you have determined your key claims and most important points, think about which points would benefit most from using multimedia. Where might the audience get a better understanding by seeing photos or video or listening to sound recordings? Which key point would be made stronger with some kind of multimedia component? For example, if you want to make a point about how cell phones can help teenagers in an emergency, you could play a recording or show a news clip about a teenager who used her cell phone to call for help when someone was in danger.
- Make sure the media you incorporate into your presentation helps clarify or emphasize the specific points you are trying to make. Visuals or sounds that do not have a purpose can distract or even confuse your audience. Before introducing multimedia into a presentation, ask yourself these questions:
    - How does the media actually help clarify or emphasize a point I am making?
    - How well is this media component related to the subject matter?
    - How easy is it to understand the media I want to use?
    - How should I introduce each media component to help the audience see its link to my point?
- Practice your presentation several times to make sure your use of the various media components is smooth and seamless.

Academic Vocabulary

claim opinion or argument

multimedia different forms of electronic communication, such as sound, images, and video

Apply the Standard

Use the worksheet that follows to help you apply the standard.

- Using Multimedia and Visuals

Name ______________________ Date ____________ Assignment ______________

Using Multimedia and Visuals

Use the organizer to identify multimedia components you will include in your presentation. Describe how each component will help clarify or emphasize an important point. Then decide how you will introduce each component.

Media Type *(video, graphic, etc.)*	**How It Will Clarify or Emphasize a Key Point**	**Introductory Information**

Speaking and Listening 6

6. Adapt speech to a variety of contexts and tasks, demonstrating command of formal English when indicated or appropriate.

Explanation

When you have to speak to different audiences and for different reasons, you need to **adapt** your speech. Consider your **task** and the **context** in which you are speaking. Are you delivering a formal presentation or an informal talk? Who is your audience, and what do they know about your topic? Are you trying to persuade your audience? Are you trying to entertain them?

Adapt your language to your task and context. Using **formal English** shows respect for your subject and audience. It will also ensure that your audience understands you. Avoid using casual language or slang.

Examples

- Your task, audience, and subject should determine how you adapt your speech. For example, in a campaign speech your language should be clear and formal. With a group of classmates, your speech may be less formal.
- Effective public speakers use precise, engaging language and formal English. Keep in mind the points below when you are preparing to deliver a speech or presentation:

  Sentence Variety: Make sure to vary the length and tempo of your sentences. If you use the same sentence patterns too often, your speech will seem dull. Use short, simple sentences to emphasize key points.

  Pronouns: Unclear pronoun references can easily confuse your audience. Avoid using too many pronouns and use specific nouns and names to prevent confusion. When you do use pronouns, be sure your audience will recognize their referents.

Academic Vocabulary

adapt to change something in order to fit a different purpose or situation

context the general situation in which a given thing happens

formal English language that strictly follows rules of grammar

task assignment; piece of work that someone is given to do

Apply the Standard

Use the worksheets that follow to help you apply the standard. Several copies of each worksheet have been provided for you to use with different assignments.

- Adapting a Speech to an Audience
- Using Appropriate Language

Name ______________________ Date ____________ Assignment ______________

Adapting a Speech to an Audience

Use the organizer below to adapt your speech to different audiences. Then answer the question at the bottom of the page.

Speaking Task: ....

....

Audience *(Describe the audience for which your speech is intended.)*	
Adaptation / Change	**Reason for Change**
1.	
2.	
3.	
4.	

Which changes do you think will have the greatest effect on your audience?

....

....

Name ______________________ Date ____________ Assignment ______________

Adapting a Speech to an Audience

Use the organizer below to adapt your speech to different audiences. Then answer the question at the bottom of the page.

Speaking Task: ....

....

Audience *(Describe the audience for which your speech is intended.)*	
Adaptation / Change	**Reason for Change**
1.	
2.	
3.	
4.	

Which changes do you think will have the greatest effect on your audience?

....

....

Name ______________________ Date ____________ Assignment ______________

Adapting a Speech to an Audience

Use the organizer below to adapt your speech to different audiences. Then answer the question at the bottom of the page.

Speaking Task: ....

....

Audience *(Describe the audience for which your speech is intended.)*	
Adaptation / Change	**Reason for Change**
1.	
2.	
3.	
4.	

Which changes do you think will have the greatest effect on your audience?

....

....

Name ______________________ Date ____________ Assignment ______________

Using Appropriate Language

Before you give a speech, use the checklist to evaluate your use of language. Then answer the question at the bottom of the page.

Audience: ....

Speaking Task: ....

	Speech Checklist
Language	❑ Is my language appropriate for the context and speaking task? ❑ Am I using formal English consistently? ❑ Are my language and word choices precise and engaging enough to keep the listeners interested?
Sentences	❑ Am I using the same sentence patterns too often? ❑ Can I vary sentence lengths to change my pace and tempo? ❑ Do I use short sentences for dramatic effect, or to emphasize a key point?
Pronouns	❑ Am I overusing pronouns? ❑ Can I substitute proper names and specific nouns to avoid pronoun confusion? ❑ Is who or what my pronouns refer to absolutely clear?

Which of the areas above need the most work? Explain how you will fix the problem(s).

....

....

....

....

....

....

Name ____________________ Date ____________ Assignment ______________

Using Appropriate Language

Before you give a speech, use the checklist to evaluate your use of language. Then answer the question at the bottom of the page.

Audience: ....

Speaking Task: ....

	Speech Checklist
Language	❑ Is my language appropriate for the context and speaking task? ❑ Am I using formal English consistently? ❑ Are my language and word choices precise and engaging enough to keep the listeners interested?
Sentences	❑ Am I using the same sentence patterns too often? ❑ Can I vary sentence lengths to change my pace and tempo? ❑ Do I use short sentences for dramatic effect, or to emphasize a key point?
Pronouns	❑ Am I overusing pronouns? ❑ Can I substitute proper names and specific nouns to avoid pronoun confusion? ❑ Is who or what my pronouns refer to absolutely clear?

Which of the areas above need the most work? Explain how you will fix the problem(s).

....

....

....

....

....

....

Name ______________________ Date ______________ Assignment ______________

Using Appropriate Language

Before you give a speech, use the checklist to evaluate your use of language. Then answer the question at the bottom of the page.

Audience: ....

Speaking Task: ....

	Speech Checklist
Language	❑ Is my language appropriate for the context and speaking task? ❑ Am I using formal English consistently? ❑ Are my language and word choices precise and engaging enough to keep the listeners interested?
Sentences	❑ Am I using the same sentence patterns too often? ❑ Can I vary sentence lengths to change my pace and tempo? ❑ Do I use short sentences for dramatic effect, or to emphasize a key point?
Pronouns	❑ Am I overusing pronouns? ❑ Can I substitute proper names and specific nouns to avoid pronoun confusion? ❑ Is who or what my pronouns refer to absolutely clear?

Which of the areas above need the most work? Explain how you will fix the problem(s).

....

....

....

....

....

....

Language Standards

Language 1a

1a. Demonstrate command of the conventions of standard English grammar and usage when writing or speaking.
- **Explain the function of phrases and clauses in general and their function in specific sentences.**

Explanation

A **phrase** is a group of words that does not contain both a subject and a verb. Two types of phrases are **prepositional phrases** and **infinitive phrases**.

A **prepositional phrase** is a group of words that includes a **preposition** (*at, in, under, for*) and either a noun or a pronoun that is the **object of the preposition**. There are **two types** of prepositional phrases: an **adjective phrase** and an **adverb phrase**.

- **An adjective phrase modifies a noun or pronoun,** giving more information about the noun or pronoun. It answers such questions as *Which one?*, *What kind?*, or *How many?*.
- **An adverb phrase modifies a verb, an adjective, or an adverb.** It answers such questions as *Where?*, *When?*, *How?*, *Why?*, or *To what extent?*.

An **infinitive phrase** contains an **infinitive** (*to speak, to see*) and its **modifiers or complements.** In a sentence, an infinitive phrase can act as a noun, an adjective, or an adverb.

A **clause** is a group of words that ***does*** contain a subject and a verb. There are two types of clauses: **main** (or **"independent"**) **clauses** and **subordinate** (or **"dependent"**) **clauses**.

- **A main (or "independent") clause expresses a complete thought.** Therefore, it can stand alone as a complete sentence.
- **A subordinate (or "dependent") clause does *not* express a complete thought.** Therefore, it cannot stand alone as a complete sentence. A subordinate clause begins with a **subordinate conjunction** (*if, when, because, who, which*), and modifies a noun or a verb.

Examples

1. **Prepositional phrases: Adjective phrase:** *The man* ***in that apartment*** *is my uncle.* (*Which* man?)
   Adverb phrase: *He lives* ***in that apartment***. (*Where* does he live?)
2. **Infinitive phrases**: *My goal is* ***to be an astronaut.*** (functions as a noun)
   This is the gift ***to buy for Stella.*** (functions as an adjective, modifying the noun *gift*)
   Everyone went ***to see the show.*** (functions as an adverb, modifying the verb *went*)
3. **Main and subordinate clauses:** *We drove to Seattle.* (**main clause**; expresses a complete thought)
   When we drove to Seattle (**subordinate clause;** does not express a complete thought)
   When we drove to Seattle, we visited Gloria. **(subordinate clause, main clause)**

Name ______________________ Date ____________ Assignment ______________

Apply the Standard

A. Underline the prepositional phrase in each sentence. Circle the word that it modifies. Then write whether the phrase is an *adjective* or *adverb* phrase.

1. Yesterday, we walked to a farmer's market. ....

2. The woman at the first booth was selling apples. ....

3. I bought some apples from the first bin. ....

4. The woman put the apples in a sturdy bag. ....

5. On the way home, I ate two apples. ....

B. Underline the infinitive phrase in each sentence. Then write whether the phrase functions as a *noun, adjective,* or *adverb.*

1. Stephen decided to buy ingredients for a dessert. ....

2. His goal was to make an apple pie. ....

3. I knew my grandmother was the woman to call for a recipe. ....

4. We got a paper and pencil to write it down. ....

5. To make this pie will be difficult, Stephen! ....

C. In each sentence, underline the subordinate clause once and the main clause twice.

1. Here's the recipe that Grandma uses for pies.

2. Whenever she makes her apple pie, everyone scrambles for a piece.

3. If I can make a pie as delicious as that, will you try it?

4. My dad, who learned about baking from Grandma, will be pleased to try our pie.

5. Let's gather all the ingredients before we start to measure and mix.

For use with Language 1a

Language 1b

1b. Demonstrate command of the conventions of standard English grammar and usage when writing or speaking.

- **Choose among simple, compound, complex, and compound-complex sentences to signal differing relationships among ideas.**

Explanation

Sentences are made with clauses. A main clause has a subject and a verb and expresses a complete thought. A subordinate clause also has a subject and a verb, but it does *not* express a complete thought.

There are **four types** of sentences.

- A **simple sentence** is one main clause that expresses a single complete thought.
- A **compound sentence** has two or more main clauses linked by a comma and a word such as *and, or,* or *but.* Each of the clauses expresses a complete thought.
- A **complex sentence** has one main clause and one or more subordinate clauses.
- A **compound-complex sentence** has two or more main clauses and one or more subordinate clauses.

Examples

- **Simple:** *Emma went to soccer practice.* (a single complete thought)
- **Compound:** *Emma went to soccer practice, and Joy watched from the sidelines.* (two related complete thoughts joined by a comma and *and*)
- **Complex:** *Emma went to soccer practice after the school day ended.* (one main clause expressing a complete thought and one subordinate clause)
- **Compound-complex:** *Emma went to soccer practice, and Joy watched from the sidelines because she wanted to cheer for Emma.* (two related main clauses and one subordinate clause)

Name ______________________ Date ______________ Assignment ______________

Apply the Standard

A. Identify each sentence as *simple, compound, complex,* or *compound-complex.* Write your answer on the line provided.

....**1.** Joy and Emma go to the same middle school.

....**2.** Because Joy is younger than Emma, she is in a sixth-grade classroom.

....**3.** Joy may be younger, but she shares many of Emma's interests and skills.

....**4.** Joy is a dancer who has been in many recitals, and she is also a musician.

....**5.** Emma was really pleased when she learned about Joy's musical interests.

B. Look again at the sentences in Practice A. Answer each of the following questions, writing the number (1–5) of the correct sentence on the line provided.

....**1.** Which sentence signals a link between opposing ideas?

....**2.** Which sentence explains *why* something else happened?

....**3.** Which sentence explains *when* something else happened?

....**4.** Which sentence contains a subordinate clause that provides details about a person?

....**5.** Which sentence expresses a single complete thought?

C. Write an original sentence to match each description.

1. a compound sentence expressing opposing ideas ....

....

2. a simple sentence expressing a complete thought ....

....

3. a complex sentence giving details about a person ....

....

4. a compound-complex sentence telling *why* something happened ....

....

5. a compound sentence expressing related (not opposing) ideas ....

....

For use with Language 1b

Language 1c

1c. Demonstrate command of the conventions of standard English grammar and usage when writing or speaking.

- **Place phrases and clauses within a sentence, recognizing and correcting misplaced and dangling modifiers.**

Explanation

As you know, **prepositional phrases** and **subordinate clauses** are used to provide details about the main idea in a sentence. They modify, or provide information about, other words in the sentence.

- Use a prepositional **adjective phrase** to modify a noun or pronoun.
  A girl ***in my class*** *won the state championship* ***for tennis.*** (Which girl? What championship?)
- Use a prepositional **adverb phrase** to modify a verb, an adjective, or an adverb.
  After lunch*, we went* ***to the tennis match.*** (When did we go? Where did we go?)
- Use a **subordinate clause** to modify a noun—a person, place or thing.
  Do you know the boy ***who won the last tennis match?*** (Which boy?)
- Use a **subordinate clause** to also modify a verb.
  After we left the tennis match*, we stopped for lunch at a diner.* (When did we stop for lunch?)

When constructing sentences, always be careful with the placement of phrases and clauses that you use as modifiers. Two errors to avoid are **misplaced modifiers** and **dangling modifiers,** both of which can create confusion.

Examples

A **misplaced modifier** appears in the wrong place in a sentence.

Misplaced: *Bob gave a beautiful bird to his sister* ***that sang well.***
(The bird, not the sister, sang well!)

Corrected: *Bob gave a beautiful bird* ***that sang well*** *to his sister.*

A **dangling modifier** doesn't modify anything in the sentence.

Dangling: ***Baking homemade bread,*** *the kitchen smelled wonderful.*
(The kitchen didn't bake the bread.)

Corrected: ***While I was baking homemade bread,*** *the kitchen smelled wonderful.*

Name ______________________ Date ______________ Assignment ______________

Apply the Standard

A. Each sentence contains a misplaced or dangling modifier. Rewrite each sentence to correct the error.

1. We sat on folding chairs and ate pretzels that were made of iron.

....

2. After eating all the pretzels, the bag was empty.

....

3. Walking home, a huge dog charged toward us.

....

4. To distract the dog, threw a stick into a nearby bush.

....

5. We fooled that dog with a trick that was barking and leaping.

....

6. At home in my workshop, I showed Jen a picture that I drew in the basement.

....

7. Still upset about that barking dog, a snack might help her.

....

8. Filled with ham and cheese, I made a sandwich for Jen.

....

9. Noisy music suddenly blared while we were eating in a loud and disruptive way.

....

10. My brother was playing some tunes he had recorded for his faraway pen pal in the next room.

....

B. Place a check mark in the correct space to show where the boldfaced modifier belongs.

with floppy ears	1. He gave his mother .... a dog ....
that is fragile	2. This vase .... can hold only one flower ....
at 4:30	3. The school offers a late bus .... for athletes playing games ....

For use with Language 1c

Language 2a

2a. Demonstrate command of the conventions of standard English capitalization, punctuation, and spelling when writing.

- **Use a comma to separate coordinate adjectives (e.g., *It was a fascinating, enjoyable movie* but not *He wore an old[,] green shirt*).**

Explanation

A **comma** is a punctuation mark that signals a brief pause within a sentence. Here are rules to follow when two or more adjectives appear before a noun.

- Always use a comma to **separate adjectives of equal rank**.
- Do ***not*** use a comma to separate such adjectives if they must always be used in a specific order.
- Do ***not*** use a comma to separate such adjectives when one of them is considered to be part of the noun.

Study the examples below.

Examples

- **Adjectives of equal rank:**

  *Mandy is a **playful, happy** dog.*

  In this sentence, the two adjectives *playful* and *happy* have equal rank. They can be switched in order, and the sentence will still make sense. Use a comma to separate such adjectives.

  *Mandy is a **happy, playful** dog.*

- **Adjectives that must occur in a specific order:**

  *She wore a **bright green** hat.*

  In this sentence, the two adjectives *bright* and *green* do ***not*** have equal rank. If their order is switched, the sentence will not make sense. Do ***not*** use a comma to separate such adjectives.

  Incorrect: *She wore a **green bright** hat.*

  Incorrect: *She wore a **bright, green** hat.*

- **Adjectives considered part of the noun:**

  *The symbol of the United States is the **brave bald** eagle.*

  In this sentence, the two adjectives *brave* and *bald* do ***not*** have equal rank. *Bald* is considered part of the noun *bald eagle,* the name of the bird. Do ***not*** use a comma to separate such adjectives.

  Incorrect: *The symbol of the United States is the **bald brave** eagle.*

  Incorrect: *The symbol of the United States is the **brave, bald** eagle.*

Name ______________ Date ______________ Assignment ______________

Apply the Standard

A. Rewrite each of these sentences to correct any errors in the use of commas. If the sentence is correct as is, write *Correct* on the line.

1. Jen made a kettle of delicious, hot chocolate.

....

2. We ate our picnic under a blue cloudless sky.

....

3. After mowing the lawn, I wanted an icy, cold drink.

....

4. The collector had a stack of valuable golden coins.

....

5. Is there cold, sour cream on that baked potato?

....

6. We had a busy, frantic morning yesterday.

....

7. Come see our redecorated, living room.

....

8. Howard bought a bag of orange sweet potatoes.

....

B. Rewrite each phrase below, adding another adjective before the noun. Use a comma to separate the adjectives if one is necessary.

1. an old shoe ....

2. a British flag ....

3. a beautiful day ....

4. an ambitious student ....

5. New Mexico ....

For use with Language 2a

Language 2b

2b. Demonstrate command of the conventions of standard English capitalization, punctuation, and spelling when writing.
- **Spell correctly.**

Explanation

Writing can become confusing to a reader if it contains spelling errors. Here are some guidelines to prevent—or correct—spelling errors.

Examples

Homophones are words that sound alike but have different spellings and meanings. They are the cause of many spelling errors. Even spell check on the computer cannot always catch this type of error because the word is not being spelled incorrectly. You are using the *wrong* word! Here are some commonly confused homophones. Learn their definitions and their differences!

your—possessive pronoun *Your book is due at the library.*	**you're**—a contraction, meaning "you are" *You're my best friend.*
lead—"a heavy metal" *Those old water pipes are made of lead.*	**led**—past tense of the verb *to lead* *Manny led us on a hike.*
than—conjunction *An elephant is larger than a horse.*	**then**—"at the time" or "next" *Beat the eggs. Then add the flour.*
whose—possessive pronoun *Whose hat is this?*	**who's**—contraction meaning "who is" or "who has" *Who's knocking at the door?*

Words with suffixes can be tricky, too. Here are some guidelines for spelling them correctly.

- Keep the silent *e* when adding a suffix that begins with a consonant (*safe* + *ly* = *safely*).
- Drop the silent *e* when adding a suffix that begins with a vowel (*safe* + *est* = *safest*).
- If a word ends in a consonant and *y*, change the *y* to *i* before adding a suffix (*fly* + *er* = *flier*).
- If the last syllable of a multi-syllable word is accented and ends in a consonant, double the final consonant before adding a suffix that starts with a vowel (*prefer* + *ing* = *preferring*).

Tricky syllables, such as those that are barely heard, can also cause spelling errors. Here are some examples: *reference, average, governor, nuclear, privilege*

Irregular plurals are not formed by simply adding *–s*. Here are some rules to keep in mind.

- Change a final *f* to *v* and add *–es* (*hoof/hooves, leaf/leaves*).
- Add *–es* to words ending in *–sh, –ss,* or *–ch* (*wish/wishes, dress/dresses, lunch/lunches*).

Name ______________________ Date ______________ Assignment ______________

Apply the Standard

A. Each sentence contains one or more misspelled or misused words. Circle each error, and write the correct spelling on the line. If the sentence is *correct* as is, write *Correct* on the line.

1. During the winter, the temprature in Florida rarely dips below freezeing.

....

2. My grandmother, who's home is in Florida, says that on an avrage day, it is about 65 degrees.

....

3. In that warm weather, Florida grows a lot of fruits and vegtables, like strawberrys, peachs, and lettuce.

....

4. In fact, last year Florida lead all the states in the production of oranges.

....

5. Yesterday, Mom announced, "In March, we'll be makeing our usual trip to visit you're grandmother."

....

6. I think it is more fun to visit in March then any other time of year because of baseball's spring training games.

....

B. Use each of these words or pair of words in a sentence.

1. *funny* plus the *suffix –er* ....

....

2. *forget* plus the suffix *–ing* ....

....

3. *whose, who's* ....

....

4. *your, you're* ....

....

For use with Language 2b

Language 3a

3a. Use knowledge of language and its conventions when writing, speaking, reading, or listening.

- **Choose language that expresses ideas precisely and concisely, recognizing and eliminating wordiness and redundancy.**

Explanation

Two important goals for effective writing are expressing your ideas well and grabbing your readers' attention. You can reach those goals by choosing **precise** words, eliminating **wordiness,** and preventing **redundancy.**

Examples

Precise words have clear and definite meanings. When writing and editing your work, always check for such vague words as *nice, big,* and *good.* Replace them with precise words. A thesaurus can help you find the word you need to express your exact meaning.

Vague: *I hope we have a* ***good*** *day for our* ***event.*** *(What kind of day is a good day? What event?)*
Improved: *I hope we have a* ***sunny, warm*** *day for our* ***class picnic.***

Vague: *We saw a* ***big animal outside.*** *(How big? What kind of animal?)*
Improved: *We saw an* ***enormous black bear in the woods.***

Redundancy is unnecessary repetition. Avoid this error while writing, or correct it while revising and editing. Say it once and say it well!

Redundant: *The horse suddenly started galloping at a* ***frightening*** *pace, and I was really* ***scared.*** *(The reader already knows you are scared because the pace is described as frightening.)*
Improved: *I was really* ***scared*** *when the horse suddenly started galloping.*

Redundant: *This is the* ***best story that I have ever read.*** *It was* ***really great*** *and very exciting. (The reader understands that the story is really great if you consider it the best story.)*
Improved: *This* ***exciting story is the best one*** *that I have ever read.*

Wordiness involves the use of cluttered sentence structures or unnecessary details.

Wordy sentence: *When we got home,* ***I was able to change*** *out of my rain-soaked* ***shirt and pants.*** *(It doesn't matter how many clothes were changed, but that they were rain-soaked.)*
Improved: When we got home, ***I changed*** *out of my rain-soaked* ***clothes.***

Unnecessary details: *I'd like you to meet my dear friend Helen* ***who was born in Chicago.*** *Like you, she is in the school band. (The fact that Helen was born in Chicago isn't important.)*
Improved: *I'd like you to meet my dear friend Helen. Like you, she is in the school band.*

Name ______________________ Date ______________ Assignment ______________

Apply the Standard

A. Rewrite each sentence, replacing the underlined vague words with precise words.

1. We were stuck in traffic because a huge <u>thing</u> fell out of a <u>truck</u> and blocked the <u>road</u>.

....

2. Finally, <u>someone</u> arrived to <u>help solve the problem in a good way</u>.

....

3. However, <u>this</u> caused us to miss your <u>event</u>.

....

4. I hope that <u>the people</u> had a <u>good</u> time and that you <u>are having good feelings</u> about <u>it</u>.

....

5. <u>Send word</u> when you think you might be going to have <u>it</u> again.

....

B. Rewrite each sentence, eliminating redundancy and wordiness.

1. My uncle is a teacher who teaches science. He's in the science department at Ridgeway High.

....

2. During the summer months of July and August, Uncle Hal works at a seaside camp by the ocean.

....

3. He leads a large group of about 20 to 25 kids on boating trips out into the harbor in boats.

....

4. The kids are thrilled and really excited to see huge, enormous whales, which are mammals.

....

5. Every once in a while, they spot dolphins leaping and jumping out of the water. That's a rare event.

....

6. Uncle Hal, who is my mother's older brother, also teaches the kids about tide pools.

....

For use with Language 3a

Language 4a

4a. Determine or clarify the meaning of unknown and multiple-meaning words and phrases based on *grade 7 reading and content*, choosing flexibly from a range of strategies.

- **Use context (e.g., the overall meaning of a sentence or paragraph; a word's position or function in a sentence) as a clue to the meaning of a word or phrase.**

Explanation

When you come to an unfamiliar word in your reading, read the surrounding words and phrases for help. These **context clues** can help you determine the word's meaning. The unknown word's position or role in the sentence can also help provide context clues, as can the main idea of the passage or sentence. Read over the sentence, paying special attention to where the unknown word is and what type of words are around it, to help figure out what the word means.

Examples

Clues in Nearby Words and Phrases Examples of this type of context clue include:

Restatement or definition: *Sheep and cows are **herbivores,** or plant eaters.*
(The clue suggests that *herbivores* means "plant eaters.")

Opposite or contrast: *We worried about a **catastrophe** while scaling the wall, but all went smoothly.*
(The clues suggest that *catastrophe* means "disaster.")

Example: *Common **crustaceans** include clams, mussels, and oysters.*
(The clues suggest that *crustaceans* means "animals living in shells.")

Clues in the Word's Function in the Sentence Look at the position and function of the word in the sentence. If, for example, the unfamiliar word comes before a noun, it is probably an adjective. Does it follow an article or an adjective? If so, it is likely a noun. Does it express action? If so, it may be a verb. Use that information, plus any clues in surrounding words and phrases, to figure out the unknown word's meaning.

*When Luis scored a touchdown, the **exuberant** cheerleaders led the fans in a loud chorus of cheers.*
(*Exuberant* comes before a noun. Therefore, it is an adjective. That information, as well as prior knowledge about football games and cheerleaders, shows that *exuberant* means "peppy" or "in high spirits.")

Clues in the Overall Meaning of the Sentence or Passage Look for the overall meaning of the sentence or the main idea of the paragraph. Often these two elements will provide context clues.

*After a **hectic** day at the hospital, Dr. Branson was relieved to sit and relax in her peaceful apartment.*
(The overall meaning of the sentence suggests that *hectic* means "extremely busy or challenging.")

Name ______________________ Date ____________ Assignment ______________

Apply the Standard

A. Use context clues in nearby words and in the overall meaning of the sentence to determine the meaning of the underlined word in each sentence. Write its definition on the line provided.

1. This blue sweater will complement your outfit perfectly. ....

2. Students in the seventh grade were formerly in the sixth grade. ....

3. If you want to be a great pianist, you must practice diligently. ....

4. Only unkind people would spread such malicious rumors. ....

5. Because we eat both plant matter and meat, we are omnivores. ....

6. Chopping wood and shoveling snow are laborious tasks. ....

7. Eating lots of sugary foods can be detrimental to your health. ....

8. Jen and I tried to think serious thoughts in order to suppress our laughter. ....

9. To pay for the magazine subscription, enclose your remittance in this envelope. ....

10. We had to be home by four o'clock, so we couldn't tarry any longer. ....

B. Think about the underlined word's function and position in each sentence. Use that information, plus any other context clues, to define the underlined word. Write its meaning on the line.

1. I hoped that he would remain calm during the debate, but he was temperamental. ....

2. She used at least ten yards of fabric to sew the voluminous skirt. ....

3. Please pull that loose rope as hard as you can to make it taut. ....

4. Plants use seeds to propagate. ....

5. Divvy up the remaining cookies so that each child gets an equal share. ....

For use with Language 4a

Language 4b

4b. Determine or clarify the meaning of unknown and multiple-meaning words and phrases based on *grade 7 reading and content*, choosing flexibly from a range of strategies.

- **Use common, grade-appropriate Greek or Latin affixes and roots as clues to the meaning of a word (e.g., *belligerent, bellicose, rebel*).**

Explanation

When you come to an unfamiliar word in your reading, try breaking the word down into its parts. Look for **affixes** and **roots.** If you know the meanings of those word parts, you will have a good clue about the meaning of the unfamiliar word.

An **affix** is a word part that is attached to a base word in order to change the meaning of the base word. There are two kinds of affixes—**prefixes**, which are attached *before* the base word, and **suffixes**, which are attached *after* the base word. A **root** is the core of a word. Often, the root is an old word that has come into the English language from an ancient language, such as Latin or Greek.

Examples

This chart shows the meanings of some common Greek and Latin roots and affixes.

Word Part	Type	Origin	Meaning	Example
-scrib-, script-	root	Latin	"write"	*script* (the written form of a drama)
-brev-	root	Latin	"short"	*abbreviate* (to use a brief form of a word)
-dem-	root	Greek	"people"	*demography* (the science of collecting data regarding populations of people)
-path-	root	Greek	"feeling"	*sympathy* (sad feelings for someone's misfortune)
semi-	prefix	Latin	"half"	*semicircle* (half a circle)
post-	prefix	Latin	"after"	*postoperative* (occurring after an operation)
peri-	prefix	Greek	"around"	*periphery* (the boundary line around a figure or a piece of land)
-ence	suffix	Latin	"quality or state"	*excellence* (the state of excelling; superiority)
-y	suffix	Latin	"quality or condition"	*chilly* (characterized by chill; cold)
-ist	suffix	Greek	"doer," "believer"	*artist* (someone who creates art)

Name ______________ Date ______________ Assignment ______________

Apply the Standard

A. Write the definition of the underlined word. Use the meaning of its highlighted root or affix, as well as any context clues that you discover.

1. The city officials will open an inquiry to find out why the records are missing. ....

2. I wish that those **apath**etic people would show some spirit. ....

3. During the confer**ence**, several representatives discussed their views. ....

4. People eagerly bought tickets for an appearance by the famous violin**ist**. ....

5. The government in that country was a **demo**cracy. ....

B. Use the meanings of the highlighted affixes to answer the questions. Write your answers in complete sentences.

1. Where in a letter to a friend would a **postscript** appear? Explain.

....

2. Would a long-winded speaker be complimented for his **brev**ity? Explain why or why not.

....

3. Where would the **peri**meter of a field be located?

....

4. Would you want to take a test when you were **semi**conscious? Explain why or why not.

....

5. What type of literature would a sat**irist** be most likely to write?

....

C. Use the affixes and roots in these words or phrases to figure out their meanings. Write your answers on the lines.

1. *emergence* ....

2. a *postwar* period ....

3. *dependence* ....

4. a *semiaquatic* animal ....

For use with Language 4b

Language 4c

4c. Determine or clarify the meaning of unknown and multiple-meaning words and phrases based on *grade 7 reading and content,* choosing flexibly from a range of strategies.

- **Consult general and specialized reference materials (e.g., dictionaries, glossaries, thesauruses), both print and digital, to find the pronunciation of a word or determine or clarify its precise meaning or its part of speech.**

Explanation

To find the definition, pronunciation, and part of speech of any word in the English language, consult a **dictionary.** A dictionary will also provide a word's **etymology,** or origin. Many words in the English language come from Latin and Greek.

A **thesaurus** provides **synonyms**, or words with similar meanings, for many words in the English language. When writing, use a thesaurus to find precise words that will help you express the exact meaning that you want to get across to your audience.

You can usually find dictionaries and thesauruses in your school, at the library, or online.

Examples

Notice what this **dictionary entry** reveals about the word *conscience.*

con•science (kon'-sh*uh* ns) **n.** [L *conscientia*, consciousness, moral sense] **1** knowledge or sense of what is right and wrong, with an urge to do right **2** a moral judgment that steers away from unethical principles and fosters feelings of shame if unethical behavior results [a guilty *conscience*]

- A space or black dot inserted in the entry word indicates where the **syllables** break.
- Symbols in parentheses show the **pronunciation.** Note the stress mark that indicates which syllable is stressed.
- The abbreviation **n.** tells the part of speech. *Conscience* is a noun. Other abbreviations used include **v.** (verb), **adj.** (adjective), and **adv.** (adverb).
- The word's **etymology**, or origin, then appears in brackets. *Conscience* comes from the Latin word *conscientia.*
- The definition of the word follows. If there is more than one definition for the word, each is numbered. Sometimes a bracketed example appears to show the usage of the word.

Now notice what this **thesaurus entry** for the word *conscience* offers.

conscience ***n.*** inner voice, morals, principles, scruples, small voice, values

Antonym: immorality

- The part of speech follows the entry word.
- Synonyms are listed, followed by antonyms (if the word has both synonyms and antonyms).

Name ______________________ Date ____________ Assignment ______________

Apply the Standard

Use the information in these dictionary and thesaurus entries to answer the questions.

Dictionary entry:

em•ploy (em-ploi') ***v.*** [L *implicare,* to enfold or engage] **1** to make use of; to use **2** to hire or engage the services of, in return for pay **3** to keep busy or occupied [to employ oneself in crafts]

Thesaurus entry:

employ (verb)
1. make use of; apply, use, utilize
2. enlist, hire, sign up, take on
Antonyms: fire, lay off, let go
3. engage, fill time with, keep busy, occupy one's time with
Antonyms: ignore, shun

1. Which syllable in *employ* is the stressed syllable? ....

2. What part of speech is *employ*? ....

3. What language provided its etymology, and what did the original word mean? ....

4. Why is the third dictionary definition followed by material in brackets? ....

5. Which dictionary definition (1, 2, or 3) relates to the use of *employ* in the following sentence?

The copy center will *employ* five workers. ....

6. Why does the first thesaurus entry for *employ* contain no antonyms? ....

7. Rewrite this sentence, using a **synonym** for *employ. Mr. Jensen will **employ** a tutor for his son.*

....

8. Write a sentence using a **synonym** for the **first** thesaurus entry for *employ.*

....

9. Write a sentence using an **antonym** for the **third** thesaurus entry for *employ.*

....

10. Write a sentence using a **synonym and an antonym** for the **second** thesaurus entry for *employ.*

....

For use with Language 4c

Language 4d

4d. Determine or clarify the meaning of unknown and multiple-meaning words and phrases based on grade 7 *reading and content,* choosing flexibly from a range of strategies.

- **Verify the preliminary determination of the meaning of a word or phrase (e.g., by checking the inferred meaning in context or in a dictionary).**

Explanation

When you come to an unfamiliar word or phrase in your reading, look for **context clues** to figure out its meaning. Some clues might appear in **nearby words or phrases.** Others might be found in the **general meaning of the sentence.** If the meaning of the unknown word or phrase is still difficult to understand, **reread** the sentence or passage to look again for clues. Then **read ahead.** You may find clues in the sentences that follow the unknown word or phrase. To confirm of the meaning of a word, it is sometimes necessary to look up the word in a dictionary.

Examples

Clues in Nearby Words and Phrases Examples include:

Restatement or definition: *The chili contained* ***garbanzos,*** *or chickpeas, that we bought yesterday.*

(The clue suggests that *garbanzos* means "chickpeas.")

Opposite or contrast: *We expected a small room at the hotel, but we received a* ***commodious*** *one.*

(The clues suggest that *commodious* means "large" or "roomy.")

Clues or explanation: ***Torrid*** *climates exist in deserts and in regions lying along the equator.*

(The clues suggest that *torrid* means "very hot.")

Clues in the Function of the Word in the Sentence Look at the word's position and function in the sentence. Does it modify a noun? If so, it is an adjective. If it modifies a verb, it is an adverb. Use that information, plus any other context clues you find, to determine the unknown word's meaning.

When Manny broke his leg during the football game, he felt ***grievous*** *pain.* (*Grievous* modifies a noun; therefore, it is an adjective. That information, as well as prior knowledge about serious injuries and pain, tells you that *grievous* means "severe" or "terrible.")

Clues in the Overall Meaning of the Sentence or Passage Look for the overall meaning of the sentence or the main idea of the paragraph. Often, these two elements will provide context clues. If the meaning is still unclear, reread the passage to clarify, and then read ahead to seek further clues. You may also consult a dictionary.

We expended so much energy working in the hot sun that we became very thirsty and ***ravenous.***

(The overall meaning of the sentence suggests that *ravenous* means "extremely hungry.")

Name ______________________ Date ______________ Assignment ______________

Apply the Standard

A. Use context clues to find the meaning of the underlined word or phrase. Write its definition on the line.

1. My dog is very hirsute. If I don't brush him daily, he sheds hair all over the rugs. ....

2. Explain to me how nocturnal animals see well enough to hunt in the darkness. ....

3. Looking for my lost ring seemed like a fruitless task, so I was thrilled to find it so quickly. ....

4. Every year, we donate sustenance from our garden to the residents of a shelter. ....

5. To get the right color of paint, Mom took a small swatch of curtain fabric to the paint store. ....

6. Justice is usually served. However, some people commit crimes with impunity. ....

7. We missed that movie when it first came out, so we were pleased to learn of its revival. ....

8. I've heard echoes before, but the reverberation of that blaring horn was really loud today. ....

9. Suddenly, the car skewed sharply to the left. ....

10. To save time, the president did not allow additional speakers to protract the discussion. ....

B. Read each passage. Use context clues and the overall meaning of the passage to determine the meaning of each underlined word or phrase. Write its definition on the line.

1. We wrote five reasons for lowering the membership dues. At the top of the list, the paramount reason was that the poor economy meant that extra spending money was in short supply.

....

2. Some poets were comfortable writing in public places. Emily Dickinson, however, wrote in solitude. She often wrote in the attic of her home. ....

3. We can never trust that the politician is telling the truth. Time and again, news reporters have uncovered exaggerations or outright mendacities in his campaign speeches.

....

4. Two weeks had passed since her knee surgery. The doctor examined the incision on her leg and was pleased to see that it was healing nicely. ....

5. When my mother brought home the lost kitten, our dog seemed very pleased. In fact, she curled up around the little kitten to warm it. She became its surrogate mother. ....

For use with Language 4d

Language 5a

5a. Demonstrate understanding of figurative language, word relationships, and nuances in word meanings.

- **Interpret figures of speech (e.g., literary, biblical, and mythological allusions) in context.**

Explanation

Figurative language is writing or speech that is not meant to be taken literally. Based on comparisons of unlike items, it goes beyond the dictionary meaning of words. The many types of figurative language are known as **figures of speech.** Common figures of speech include **similes, metaphors, personification,** and **idioms.** Writers use these figures of speech when they want to describe things in vivid and imaginative ways. Figurative language may seem puzzling at first. However, you can use **context clues,** hints in the surrounding passage, to figure out what a figure of speech means.

Examples

- A **simile** compares two unlike things using the words *like* or *as.*
  The telephone lines buzzed like bees. Many people called, hoping to win the prize.
- A **metaphor** compares two unlike things by describing one thing as if it were another.
  When I am really tired, a long nap is the best medicine. I feel refreshed afterward.
- **Personification** gives human qualities to something that is not human.
  Raindrops danced on the roof.
- A **symbol** is anything—an object, person, animal, place, or image—that represents something else.
  The dove symbolizes peace. A skull symbolizes death, or danger.
- An **allusion** is a reference to a well-known person, event, place, literary work, or work of art.
  It rained so hard that we thought about calling Noah and asking him to build us an ark.
  (The allusion is to the biblical character Noah, who built an ark in order to survive a flood from a rainstorm lasting for forty days and forty nights.)
- An **idiom** is an expression that is not meant to be taken literally. They are common to everyday conversation.
  People who live in glass houses shouldn't throw stones.
  (Most people don't live in homes made of glass. The expression implies that if you are vulnerable to criticism then you should avoid criticizing others.)

Name ______________________ Date ______________ Assignment ________________

Apply the Standard

A. Each sentence contains an underlined word or phrase. On the line preceding the sentence, identify the type of figurative language it represents. Write *simile, metaphor, personification, symbol, allusion, or idiom.*

.... **1.** Stevie Wonder sang, "You are the sunshine of my life."

.... **2.** British soldiers were eager to fight to defend the crown.

.... **3.** We were happy to be home after our long and exciting odyssey out West.

.... **4.** In many parts of the country, the robin welcomes the arrival of spring.

.... **5.** A red heart often stands for love or romance.

.... **6.** Don't rock the boat by bringing up an alternative plan. Just accept Hal's point of view.

.... **7.** With that thick quilt on my bed, I felt as warm as toast.

.... **8.** Why don't you extend the olive branch and apologize to Mike for your harsh words?

.... **9.** The people were crowded together like bees in a hive.

.... **10.** I plodded along slowly, a modern-day version of Aesop's slow and steady tortoise.

B. Complete this chart. Tell what type of figurative language the item is. Then tell what it means.

Figurative Language	Type	What It Means
1. like birds soaring on the wind		
2. two people who are peas in a pod		
3. Defend the flag!		
4. Slow down.		
5. an "Honest Abe" kind of person		
6. Hope is an island in a sea of despair.		
7. You're on your own.		
8. as smooth as silk		
9. Flowers insist that I appreciate everyday beauty.		
10. giving someone the green light		

For use with Language 5a

Language 5b

5b. Demonstrate understanding of figurative language, word relationships, and nuances in word meanings.

- **Use the relationship between particular words (e.g., synonym/antonym, analogy) to better understand each of the words.**

Explanation

Understanding the relationships between words helps writers to grasp the precise meanings of words and the relationship between ideas. One kind of word relationship is **synonyms,** or words with similar meanings, and another kind is **antonyms,** or words with opposite meanings.

An **analogy** compares two things that are similar in a certain way but unlike in other ways. Many tests include analogy problems. An analogy item on a test contains two pairs of words. The relationship between the first pair of words is the same as the relationship between the second pair of words. Thinking about these relationships will help you better understand the meanings of words.

Examples

Working with analogies will help you analyze many different relationships between words. Each analogy features a specific type of relationship. Here are examples.

- **Synonyms, or Similar Meanings:** ***happy*** is to ***contented*** as ***small*** is to ***tiny***
- **Antonyms, or Opposite Meanings:** ***up*** is to ***down*** as ***day*** is to ***night***
- **Cause/Effect:** ***rain*** is to ***puddles*** as ***fire*** is to ***heat***
- **Part/Whole:** ***finger*** is to ***hand*** as ***room*** is to ***house***
- **Item/Category:** ***sparrow*** is to ***bird*** as ***potato*** is to ***vegetable***
- **Item/Use:** ***pen*** is to ***write*** as ***knife*** is to ***cut***
- **Characteristic/Object:** ***hot*** is to ***sun*** as ***slow*** is to ***turtle***
- **Color/Object:** ***blue*** is to ***sky*** as ***green*** is to ***grass***
- **Material/Object:** ***corn*** is to ***taco*** as ***steel*** is to ***bridge***

Noticing word relationships can help you learn new words. For example, if someone says, "He was very sweet and kind, not at all belligerent," you can figure out the meaning of *belligerent,* even if it is unfamiliar. The relationship between the words in the sentence reveals that *belligerent* means the opposite of "very sweet and kind." It means "hostile and aggressive."

Name ______________________ Date ______________ Assignment ________________

Apply the Standard

A. Study these analogies. On the line preceding each analogy, tell what type of relationship it represents. For example, write synonyms, antonyms, cause/effect, part/whole, item/category, or item/use.

Type of Analogy

.... **1.** ***stubborn*** is to ***mule*** as ***sly*** is to ***fox***

.... **2.** ***tired*** is to ***sleep*** as ***hungry*** is to ***eat***

.... **3.** ***chapter*** is to ***book*** as ***toe*** is to ***foot***

.... **4.** ***argue*** is to ***agree*** as ***early*** is to ***late***

.... **5.** ***red*** is to ***ruby*** as ***silver*** is to ***dime***

.... **6.** ***glass*** is to ***window*** as ***egg*** is to ***omelet***

.... **7.** ***puzzled*** is to ***confused*** as ***strong*** is to ***mighty***

.... **8.** ***shirt*** is to ***wear*** as ***pan*** is to ***cook***

.... **9.** ***daisy*** is to ***flower*** as ***hammer*** is to ***tool***

.... **10.** ***brick*** is to ***wall*** as ***tree*** is to ***forest***

B. Study the relationship between the first pair of words. Then write a word to complete the second pair. Make sure that the second pair of words has the same relationship as the first pair of words. Use the examples above for guidance. Write what type of analogy it is on the line preceding each analogy.

Type of Analogy

.... **1.** ***sand*** is to ***beach*** as ***grass*** is to ....

.... **2.** ***red*** is to ***tomato*** as ***yellow*** is to ....

.... **3.** ***beagle*** is to ***dog*** as ***strawberry*** is to ....

.... **4.** ***sad*** is to ***happy*** as ***young*** is to ....

.... **5.** ***cloth*** is to ***dress*** as ***wood*** is to ....

.... **6.** ***spoon*** is to ***stir*** as ***broom*** is to ....

.... **7.** ***fast*** is to ***racehorse*** as ***brave*** is to ....

.... **8.** ***listen*** is to ***hearing*** as ***exercise*** is to ....

.... **9.** ***goal*** is to ***purpose*** as ***smile*** is to ....

.... **10.** ***Monday*** is to ***day*** as ***Mars*** is to ....

For use with Language 5b

Language 5c

5c. Demonstrate understanding of figurative language, word relationships, and nuances in word meanings.

- **Distinguish among the connotations (associations) of words with similar denotations (definitions) (e.g., *refined, respectful, polite, diplomatic, condescending*).**

Explanation

A word's **denotation** is its exact dictionary meaning, or definition. A word's **connotation** is the feeling that it suggests and the associations it calls up. Connotations can be negative, positive, or neutral. While they are generally agreed upon in a society, they can also be somewhat subjective. They can also vary from place to place and time to time.

Examples

This chart shows four words that share the **same denotation** but have **different connotations**.

Word	Denotation	Connotation	Example Sentence
1. bold	willing to face situations that may be dangerous or challenging	**1.** willing to face a challenge (neutral)	**1.** *I felt bold enough to hike up the mountain.*
2. courageous		**2.** naturally fearless in the face of danger (positive)	**2.** *The courageous soldier marched into battle.*
3. valiant		**3.** very brave; heroic (positive)	**3.** *The valiant knight saved the village from its enemies.*
4. reckless		**4.** too willing to face danger; irresponsibly bold (negative)	**4.** *It was reckless to drive the car during a raging hurricane.*
5. foolhardy		**5.** daring or bold in a rash and foolish way (negative)	**5.** *Challenging the strongest member of the football team to an arm wrestling match was absolutely foolhardy.*

To fully understand a word's meaning, you must know the dictionary definition, as well as the ideas or emotions associated with the word. Writers often depend on their readers' understanding of connotations to get across their meaning.

Name ____________________ Date ____________ Assignment ____________

Apply the Standard

A. Use context clues and what you know about the meanings of words to tell whether the underlined word has a *neutral, positive,* or *negative* connotation. Circle your answer.

Type of Connotation

neutral positive negative **1.** The gymnasts had <u>slender</u> bodies.

neutral positive negative **2.** The abandoned puppies had <u>scrawny</u> bodies.

neutral positive negative **3.** The children were <u>rowdy</u>.

neutral positive negative **4.** The cold air felt <u>sharp</u> against my cheeks.

neutral positive negative **5.** The cold air felt <u>refreshing</u> against my cheek.

neutral positive negative **6.** The old man <u>strolled</u> home from the park.

neutral positive negative **7.** The old man <u>sauntered</u> home from the park.

neutral positive negative **8.** The old man <u>hobbled</u> home from the park.

neutral positive negative **9.** Give the person in front of you a <u>tap</u>.

neutral positive negative **10.** Give the person in front of you a <u>shove</u>.

B. Each row in this chart contains a group of words. They have the same denotation but different connotations. Tell whether each word's connotation is *neutral, positive,* or *negative.* Circle your answer. Then use each word in a sentence that makes its connotation clear.

Word	Denotation	Connotation	Example Sentence
1. amaze	to surprise	**1.** neutral, positive, negative	**1.**
2. bewilder		**2.** neutral, positive, negative	**2.**
3. rattle		**3.** neutral, positive, negative	**3.**
4. miss	to pass over	**4.** neutral, positive, negative	**4.**
5. scorn		**5.** neutral, positive, negative	**5.**

For use with Language 5c

Language 6

6. Acquire and use accurately grade-appropriate general academic and domain-specific words and phrases; gather vocabulary knowledge when considering a word or phrase important to comprehension or expression.

Explanation

In your schoolwork, you will come across two main types of words. Understanding them will help you achieve success:

- **Academic words** are those you use in a variety of subjects at school to solve problems, understand what you read, and express your ideas clearly and precisely. You can think of these as toolkit words, as useful in schoolwork as a hammer and saw are in carpentry. Examples include *define, characteristic, perspective,* and *focus.*
- **Domain-specific words** are words specific to a course of study. In a literature course, examples include *allusion, theme, point of view,* and *sonnet.* In a science course, examples include *photosynthesis, protoplasm,* and *nucleus.* In a social studies course, examples include *longitude, latitude,* and *topography.*

Learning the meanings of academic and domain-specific words and using them frequently will help you to complete tasks effectively and express yourself clearly.

Examples

In classroom assignments and on many tests, you must understand academic words and phrases to complete a task or answer a question. Here are examples:

Describe your *personal response* to. . .	Explain how it made you feel.
Analyze *the author's use of . . .*	Break it into parts to find connections.
Examine *the facts regarding. . .*	Study the details known to be true.

The domain-specific vocabulary that you learn in an English course helps you discuss literature more precisely. For example, you do not just "see the stuff that happens to a person in a short story." Instead, you "analyze the effect of plot events on a character." In this way, you recognize that a plot is a linked chain of events, not just a series of unrelated happenings. You also recognize that stories are not about real-life people but about characters developed by an author.

Name ______________________ Date ____________ Assignment ______________

Apply the Standard

A. Match each domain-specific word or phrase with its definition. Write the letter of the definition on the line provided.

.... **1.** antagonist

.... **2.** connotation

.... **3.** motives

.... **4.** meter

.... **5.** onomatopoeia

.... **6.** stanza

.... **7.** theme

.... **8.** exposition

.... **9.** resolution

.... **10.** protagonist

a. words that imitate sounds

b. the rhythmical pattern in a poem

c. the outcome of the conflict in a plot

d. a group of lines in a poem, similar to a paragraph in prose

e. the main character in a piece of literature

f. the reasons that drive a character to act, think, or speak

g. a character or force in conflict with the main character

h. the central message in a literary work

i. a set of ideas associated with a particular word

j. the part of the plot that introduces the setting and characters

B. Complete each statement with the correct definition of the italicized academic word or phrase. Write the letter of the correct answer on the line.

1. ***Diversity*** is ....

a. person's fate or future

b. school for higher learning

c. variety, as of groups or cultures

d. solitary place

2. To ***perceive*** means to ....

a. see or adopt a point of view

b. make or create

c. seek the truth or form an understanding

d. prove a concept to be accurate

3. Things that are ***unique*** are ....

a. easy to understand

b. difficult to understand

c. unlike any other thing

d. alike in some way

4. To make an ***assumption*** means to ....

a. investigate the facts

b. express a contrary opinion

c. believe or accept that something is true

d. evaluate or make a judgment

For use with Language 6

Performance Tasks

Name ______________________ Date ____________ Assignment ______________

Performance Task 1a

Literature 1 Cite several pieces of textual evidence to support analysis of what the text says explicitly as well as inferences drawn from the text.*

Task: Support Analysis of a Story or Poem

Write a response to literature in which you cite evidence from a story or poem to support your analysis of it. Explain both what the text says explicitly and what you infer from it.

Tips for Success

Present a response to a story or poem you have read. In your response, include these elements:

- ✓ an objective summary of the story or poem
- ✓ a sentence that sums up your response to the story or poem
- ✓ a detailed analysis of what the story or poem means to you and why
- ✓ several pieces of evidence from the text that support the ideas you present
- ✓ several pieces of evidence from the text that explicitly support your inferences and conclusions
- ✓ language that is formal, precise, and follows the rules of standard English

Rubric for Self-Assessment

Criteria for Success	not very					very
How objective and clear is your summary of the text?	1	2	3	4	5	6
How well have you communicated your response to the text?	1	2	3	4	5	6
How effective and detailed is your analysis of the text?	1	2	3	4	5	6
How well do you support your analysis with explicit evidence from the text?	1	2	3	4	5	6
How clearly do you explain the inferences and conclusions you drew from the text?	1	2	3	4	5	6
How well do you support those inferences and conclusions with evidence from the text?	1	2	3	4	5	6
How successful is your use of standard English?	1	2	3	4	5	6
How well have you succeeded in using a formal style and appropriate tone for your audience?	1	2	3	4	5	6

* Other standards covered include Writing 4, 9; Speaking 4; Language 3.

Name ______________________ Date ______________ Assignment ______________

Performance Task 1b

Speaking and Listening 5 Include multimedia components and visual displays in presentations to clarify claims and findings and emphasize salient points.

Task: Use Multimedia Components in a Presentation

Use multimedia components in a presentation of a story or poem. Use the media to help your audience understand the text and to draw focus to its most important points or ideas. In the final five minutes of your presentation, explain the text's main theme and use media to help get your ideas across to your audience.

Tips for Success

Make a multimedia presentation of a story or poem. As part of your presentation, include these elements:

- ✓ images (either sketches or photos) that illustrate the text
- ✓ video or audio of you reading the text or portion of the text aloud
- ✓ music that evokes the same emotions as the text
- ✓ sound effects that enhance the mood of the story or poem
- ✓ images, sound effects, or music that clarify your ideas about the text's theme

Rubric for Self-Assessment

Criteria for Discussion	not very					very
How convincingly did the images illustrate the text?	1	2	3	4	5	6
How well did you convey the feeling of the text when you read it aloud?	1	2	3	4	5	6
How effectively did the music enhance the text?	1	2	3	4	5	6
To what extent did the sound effects contribute to your presentation?	1	2	3	4	5	6
How effective was your use of media in describing the story's or poem's theme?	1	2	3	4	5	6

Name ______________________ Date ____________ Assignment ______________

Performance Task 2a

Literature 2 Determine a theme or central idea of a text and analyze its development over the course of the text; provide an objective summary of the text.*

Task: Determine the Theme of a Story or Poem

First, write an objective summary of a story or poem. Then using key details from your summary, write a response to literature in which you determine the theme and trace its development over the course of the text.

Tips for Success

Write a response to a story or poem you have read. In your response, include these elements:

✓ an objective summary of the text's key details

✓ a statement of the theme of the text

✓ a judgment of whether the theme is universal or specific to one time and place

✓ an explanation of how the key details convey the theme

✓ an analysis of the theme's development over the course of the text

✓ language that is formal, precise, and follows the rules of standard English

Rubric for Self Assessment

Criteria for Success	not very					very
How objective and clear is your summary of the text?	1	2	3	4	5	6
How fully have you discussed the theme of the story or poem?	1	2	3	4	5	6
How clearly have you explained whether the theme is universal or specific?	1	2	3	4	5	6
How thorough is your analysis of the key details that convey the theme?	1	2	3	4	5	6
How well supported is your analysis of the theme's development over the course of the story or poem?	1	2	3	4	5	6
How successful is your use of standard English?	1	2	3	4	5	6
How well have you succeeded in using a formal style and appropriate tone for your audience?	1	2	3	4	5	6

* Other standards covered include Writing 2e, 4; Language 3.

Name ____________________ Date ______________ Assignment ______________

Performance Task 2b

Speaking and Listening 1 Engage effectively in a range of collaborative discussions with diverse partners on *grade 7 topics, texts, and issues,* building on others' ideas and expressing their own clearly.

Task: Discuss Responses to a Literary Text

Participate in a one-on-one discussion in which you and a classmate discuss the theme of a story or poem and analyze the theme's development over the course of the text.

Tips for Success

Participate in a discussion about a story or poem you have read. Follow these tips for success:

✓ prepare by reading the story or poem and thinking about its theme

✓ work with your partner to agree on discussion guidelines

✓ clearly state your thoughts about the theme

✓ note evidence from the text that supports your analysis

✓ pose questions that encourage your partner to share his or her ideas

✓ listen carefully to your partner's opinions

✓ respond to your partner's questions and comments with relevant observations and ideas

Rubric for Self Assessment

Criteria for Discussion	not very					very
How well had you thought through your analysis of theme before the discussion?	1	2	3	4	5	6
How effective were the guidelines for the discussion?	1	2	3	4	5	6
How clearly and effectively did you state the theme of the text during discussion?	1	2	3	4	5	6
To what extent did you support your analysis with text evidence?	1	2	3	4	5	6
How carefully did you listen to your partner?	1	2	3	4	5	6
How well did you respond after hearing your partner's comments?	1	2	3	4	5	6
How effective were your discussion questions in helping you and your partner explore the development of theme?	1	2	3	4	5	6

Name ______________________ Date ____________ Assignment ______________

Performance Task 3a

Literature 3 Analyze how particular elements of a story or drama interact (e.g., how setting shapes the characters or plot).*

Task: Analyze How Elements of a Story or Drama Interact

Write a response to literature in which you analyze both how the dialogue and incidents in a story or drama reveal character and how the characters' personalities determine what they say and do.

Tips for Success

Present a response to a story or drama you have read. In your response, include these elements:

- ✓ descriptions of several plot points or incidents
- ✓ quotations from the dialogue of several characters
- ✓ vivid descriptions of the characters you will be discussing
- ✓ an analysis of what the dialogue and incidents tell the audience about the characters
- ✓ an analysis of how the characters' personalities determine what they say and do
- ✓ language that is formal, precise, and follows the rules of standard English

Rubric for Self-Assessment

Criteria for Success	not very					very
How well have you described the plot points or incidents?	1	2	3	4	5	6
To what extent does the dialogue you chose reveal character?	1	2	3	4	5	6
How fully have you described the characters?	1	2	3	4	5	6
How clear is your analysis of the way dialogue and incidents reveal information about character?	1	2	3	4	5	6
How clear is your analysis of the way characters' personalities determine what they say and do?	1	2	3	4	5	6
How successfully do you use standard English?	1	2	3	4	5	6
How well do you succeed in using a formal style and appropriate tone for your audience?	1	2	3	4	5	6

* Other standards covered include Writing 4 and Language 1.

For use with Literature 3

Name ______________________ Date ____________ Assignment ______________

Performance Task 3b

Speaking and Listening 4 Present claims and findings, emphasizing salient points in a focused, coherent manner with pertinent descriptions, facts, details, and examples; use appropriate eye contact, adequate volume, and clear pronunciation.

Task: Present Claims About a Story or Drama Effectively

Give a presentation in which you explain how dialogue, plot, and character interact in a story or drama you have read.

Tips for Success

Give a presentation on the way dialogue, plot, and character interact in a story or drama. As part of your presentation, include these elements:

- ✓ an objective summary of the plot and characters
- ✓ a focused, coherent analysis of the way dialogue, plot, and character interact
- ✓ examples of dialogue, plot, and character traits that illustrate your points and support your claims
- ✓ pertinent descriptions, facts, and details to support your analysis
- ✓ appropriate eye contact
- ✓ adequate volume and clear pronunciation

Rubric for Self-Assessment

Criteria for Discussion	not very					very
How well did you succeed in keeping your summary objective and clear?	1	2	3	4	5	6
How coherent and focused was your analysis of the interaction of elements in the story or drama?	1	2	3	4	5	6
How convincing were your examples of dialogue, plot, and character?	1	2	3	4	5	6
How useful were your descriptions, facts, and details in helping your audience understand your analysis?	1	2	3	4	5	6
How effectively did you make eye contact with your audience?	1	2	3	4	5	6
How well did you succeed in speaking clearly and loudly enough for your listeners to hear and understand you?	1	2	3	4	5	6

For use with Speaking and Listening 4

Name ______________________ Date ______________ Assignment ______________________

Performance Task 4a

Literature 4 Determine the meaning of words and phrases as they are used in a text, including figurative and connotative meanings; analyze the impact of rhymes and other repetitions of sounds (e.g., alliteration) on a specific verse or stanza of a poem or section of a story or drama.*

Task: Analyze the Figurative Meanings of Words and the Impact of Repeated Sounds

Write an essay in which you look beyond the dictionary definitions of the words you read to 1) analyze the figurative and connotative meanings of words and phrases and 2) explain the effect of repeated sounds on the meaning and tone of a story or drama.

Tips for Success

Write a response to a story or play you have read, and include these elements:

- ✓ a definition of the figurative meaning of a word or phrase from the text
- ✓ an explanation of the connotation of at least one word or phrase from the text
- ✓ an analysis, using evidence from the text, of the effect these words or phrases have on the text's meaning and tone
- ✓ an analysis of the effect of sound devices on meaning and tone
- ✓ language that is formal, precise, and follows the rules of standard English

Rubric for Self-Assessment

Criteria for Success	not very					very
How clearly have you defined the figurative meaning of the word or phrase you chose?	1	2	3	4	5	6
How clearly have you explained the connotation of the word or phrase you chose?	1	2	3	4	5	6
How well do you explain the effect of the author's word choice on the story's or play's meaning and tone?	1	2	3	4	5	6
How well do you explain the effect of repeated sounds?	1	2	3	4	5	6
How well have you supported your analysis with evidence from the text?	1	2	3	4	5	6
How successful is your use of standard English?	1	2	3	4	5	6
How well have you succeeded in using a formal style and appropriate tone for your audience?	1	2	3	4	5	6

* Other standards covered include Writing 4, 9a; Language 1, 5.

Name ______________________ Date ____________ Assignment ______________

Performance Task 4b

Speaking and Listening 1 Engage effectively in a range of collaborative discussions with diverse partners on *grade 7 topics, texts, and issues,* building on others' ideas and expressing their own clearly.

Task: Discuss Responses to a Story or Drama

Participate in a group discussion in which you and several classmates do a choral reading of a section from a story or drama and then discuss the effect of figurative language, connotations, and repeated sounds on the meaning and tone of the passage.

Tips for Success

Participate in a discussion about a story or play, and include these elements:

- ✓ prepare by reading the text and identifying a passage that contains figurative language, connotative language, and repeated sounds
- ✓ read the passage aloud on your own first as practice
- ✓ agree with all group members on guidelines and individual roles
- ✓ do a choral reading of the passage as a group
- ✓ share your opinions about the passage and the effect of figurative language, connotations, and repeated sounds on meaning and tone
- ✓ pose questions that encourage group members to elaborate on their opinions
- ✓ respond to others' questions and comments with relevant observations

Rubric for Self-Assessment

Criteria for Discussion	not very					very
How successful were you at identifying a passage with figurative and connotative language and repeated sounds?	1	2	3	4	5	6
How well did you read aloud the passage on your own?	1	2	3	4	5	6
How effective were the group's guidelines for the discussion?	1	2	3	4	5	6
How well did the group perform the choral reading?	1	2	3	4	5	6
How well did you present your analysis on the effect of figurative language, connotations, and repeated sounds?	1	2	3	4	5	6
How effective were your questions in helping the group explore the story or drama and its issues?	1	2	3	4	5	6
How relevant were your responses to others' questions and comments?	1	2	3	4	5	6
How fully and equally did each group member participate?	1	2	3	4	5	6

Name ______________________ Date ______________ Assignment ________________

Performance Task 5a

Literature 5 Analyze how a drama's or poem's form or structure (e.g., soliloquy, sonnet) contributes to its meaning.*

Task: Analyze How a Poem's Structure Adds to Its Meaning

Write an essay in which you analyze how the structure of a poem contributes to its meaning.

Tips for Success

Present a response to a poem you have read. In your response, include these elements:

- ✓ a description of the poem's form (e.g., ode, elegy, haiku, sonnet)
- ✓ a description of the poem's structure (e.g., number of stanzas, rhyme scheme, rhythm)
- ✓ an analysis of exactly how the poem's structure adds to that meaning
- ✓ evidence from the poem that supports your analysis
- ✓ language that is formal, precise, and follows the rules of standard English

Rubric for Self-Assessment

Criteria for Success	not very					very
How suitable is your choice of poem for this analysis?	1	2	3	4	5	6
How accurately have you described the poem's form?	1	2	3	4	5	6
How accurately have you described the poem's structure?	1	2	3	4	5	6
How well does your analysis explain the contribution of the poem's structure to the meaning?	1	2	3	4	5	6
How effectively have you supported your analysis with evidence from the poem?	1	2	3	4	5	6
How successful is your use of standard English?	1	2	3	4	5	6
How well have you succeeded in using a formal style and appropriate tone for your audience?	1	2	3	4	5	6

* Other standards covered include Writing 14; Speaking 4; Language 1, 3.

Name ______________________ Date ______________ Assignment ______________

Performance Task 5b

Speaking and Listening 6 Adapt speech to a variety of contexts and tasks, demonstrating command of formal English when indicated or appropriate.

Task: Adapt Speech When Performing and Analyzing a Poem

Give a presentation in which you read a poem aloud, show a printed version of it to the class, and explain how the poem's structure affects its meaning.

Tips for Success

Adapt the way you speak when performing and analyzing a poem. To prepare for your performance, follow these tips for success:

- ✓ prepare a reading copy of the poem in which you mark places to pause and words you want to emphasize
- ✓ prepare either an enlarged version of the poem for display or make enough copies to distribute for everyone to see the structure you are discussing
- ✓ read aloud the poet's exact words, no matter how informal or unusual the words are, and rehearse several times to avoid stumbling over words
- ✓ switch to a formal tone when you analyze how the poem's structure contributes to its meaning
- ✓ maintain the formal tone when you present evidence from the poem that supports your analysis
- ✓ invite questions and switch to a less formal tone when you answer them

Rubric for Self-Assessment

Criteria for Discussion	not very					very
How effectively did you mark up your reading copy of the poem?	1	2	3	4	5	6
How effectively did you perform the poem?	1	2	3	4	5	6
How well did you adapt your speech and tone for your analysis of the poem's structure?	1	2	3	4	5	6
How well did text evidence support your analysis?	1	2	3	4	5	6
How well did you adapt your speech and tone when answering audience questions?	1	2	3	4	5	6
How useful and accurate were your answers to questions?	1	2	3	4	5	6

Name ______________________ Date ____________ Assignment ______________

Performance Task 6a

Literature 6 Analyze how an author develops and contrasts the points of view of different characters or narrators in a text.*

Task: Analyze an Author's Development of Point of View

Write an essay in which you explain how the author of a literary text develops the points of view of different characters or narrators. Contrast the points of view and cite evidence from the text to support your analysis.

Tips for Success

Present an analysis of points of view in a literary text. In your response, include these elements:

✓ a thesis statement in which you reveal the main point of your analysis

✓ an identification of the different characters and points of view

✓ an analysis contrasting the characters' differing attitudes, perceptions, and reactions to people and events

✓ evidence from the text that supports your analysis

✓ language that is formal, precise, and follows the rules of standard English

Rubric for Self-Assessment

Criteria for Success	not very					very
How clear is your thesis statement?	1	2	3	4	5	6
How detailed is your analysis contrasting the characters' attitudes, perceptions, and reactions to people and events?	1	2	3	4	5	6
How well do you support your analysis with evidence from the text?	1	2	3	4	5	6
How successful is your use of standard English?	1	2	3	4	5	6
How well have you succeeded in using a formal style and appropriate tone for your audience?	1	2	3	4	5	6

* Other standards covered include: Writing 9a, 10; Speaking 6; Language 6.

Name ______________________ Date ____________ Assignment ______________

Performance Task 6b

Speaking and Listening 1 Engage effectively in a range of collaborative discussions with diverse partners on grade 7 topics, texts, and issues, building on others' ideas and expressing your own clearly.

Task: Discuss Points of View in a Literary Text

Participate in a group discussion in which you discuss how an author develops and contrasts the points of view of different characters in a literary work. Listen thoughtfully to others' ideas and build upon them in your discussion.

Tips for Success

Participate in a discussion about a response to a literary text. Follow these tips for success:

- ✓ prepare by reading or re-reading the text and taking notes on the different characters' attitudes, perceptions, and reactions to people or events
- ✓ consult with group members on specific goals and deadlines, and monitor your progress
- ✓ clearly present your analysis contrasting speakers' points of view when it is your turn to speak
- ✓ provide evidence from the text to support your analysis
- ✓ ask questions that inspire further discussion from participants and propel the discussion forward in order to explore the work fully
- ✓ respond to others' questions and comments with relevant observations and ideas

Rubric for Self-Assessment

Criteria for Discussion	not very					very
How thoroughly had you taken notes and prepared for the discussion?	1	2	3	4	5	6
How effectively did the group establish and monitor goals and deadlines for the discussion?	1	2	3	4	5	6
How clear and compelling was the text evidence that supported your analysis?	1	2	3	4	5	6
How effective were the questions you asked in moving the discussion forward?	1	2	3	4	5	6
How effectively did you build on the ideas of others during the discussion?	1	2	3	4	5	6

Name ______________________ Date ______________ Assignment ______________

Performance Task 7a

Literature 7 Compare and contrast a written story, drama, or poem to its audio, filmed, staged, or multimedia version, analyzing the effects of techniques unique to each medium.*

Task: Compare and Contrast a Short Story and Its Filmed Version

Write an essay in which you compare and contrast a written short story to a movie version of it. Take notes as you view, and analyze the effects of production techniques.

Tips for Success

In your essay, include these elements:

- ✓ a description of the similarities and differences between the plot of the story and the plot of the film
- ✓ a description of the similarities and differences between the way you pictured characters in your mind and the way they are portrayed in the film
- ✓ an analysis of production techniques in the film version and what effects those techniques create
- ✓ an evaluation of whether the production techniques improve upon or detract from the narrative
- ✓ evidence from both versions that supports your opinions
- ✓ language that is formal, precise, and follows the rules of standard English

Rubric for Self-Assessment

Criteria for Success	not very					very
How clearly have you described the similarities and differences between the plot of the story and the film?	1	2	3	4	5	6
How clearly have you described the similarities and differences between characters you envisioned and those portrayed on film?	1	2	3	4	5	6
How convincingly have you analyzed whether the production techniques in the film enhanced or detracted from the narrative?	1	2	3	4	5	6
How well does the evidence support your analysis?	1	2	3	4	5	6
How well have you succeeded in using a formal style and appropriate tone for your audience?	1	2	3	4	5	6

* Other standards covered include: Writing 9a, 10; Speaking 6; Language 6.

Name ______________________ Date ______________ Assignment ______________

Performance Task 7b

Speaking and Listening 6 Adapt speech to a variety of contexts and tasks, demonstrating command of formal English when indicated or appropriate.

Task: Adapt Speech When Comparing a Story and a Film

Give a presentation in which you read aloud a scene from a short story and show a film clip of the same scene. Then, share your analysis of the differences between the two versions of the scene. At the end of your presentation, invite questions from your audience and ask them to share their opinions.

Tips for Success

Adapt the way you speak when reading a story aloud, presenting an informative analysis, and leading a discussion. Follow these tips for success:

- ✓ prepare a reading copy of the scene in which you mark words you want to emphasize, places to pause, and any characters' accents or unusual pronunciations
- ✓ read aloud the author's words exactly, and invest your reading with inflections that suit the narrative and bring the story to life
- ✓ adopt a formal tone when discussing your analysis of the two versions of the scene
- ✓ use a more informal tone when leading the group discussion and responding to questions and comments

Rubric for Self-Assessment

Criteria for Discussion	not very					very
How detailed was your reading copy of the scene?	1	2	3	4	5	6
In general, how effectively did you read the scene aloud?	1	2	3	4	5	6
How successfully did you adopt a formal tone when presenting your analysis?	1	2	3	4	5	6
How successfully did you switch to a less formal tone to lead the discussion and respond to questions and comments?	1	2	3	4	5	6

Name ______________________ Date ______________ Assignment ______________

Performance Task 8a

Literature 9 Compare and contrast a fictional portrayal of a time, place, or character and a historical account of the same period as a means of understanding how authors of fiction use or alter history.*

Task: Compare and Contrast Historical Fiction and Historical Nonfiction

Write an essay in which you compare and contrast a piece of historical fiction and a nonfiction text about that same period in history, examining how fiction writers use or alter historical facts.

Tips for Success

In your essay, include these elements:

- ✓ an identification of the historical information and background that appear in both the fiction and the nonfiction piece
- ✓ an explanation of how politics and culture and any other historical details mentioned in the nonfiction text are echoed in the fictional text
- ✓ an analysis of how the author of the story utilizes historical information
- ✓ an exploration of how the author of the story strays from historical fact, and why
- ✓ evidence from both texts that supports your analysis
- ✓ language that is formal, precise, and follows the rules of standard English

Rubric for Self-Assessment

Criteria for Success	not very					very
How clearly have you identified the historical information that appears in both works?	1	2	3	4	5	6
How clearly have you explained how historical details influence the characters in the fictional text?	1	2	3	4	5	6
How detailed is your analysis of how the author of the fictional piece conveys actual historical information?	1	2	3	4	5	6
How effectively have you shown ways in which the author of the fictional narrative alters historical fact?	1	2	3	4	5	6
How well have you succeeded in using a formal style and appropriate tone for your audience?	1	2	3	4	5	6

* Other standards covered include: Writing 4, 9a; Speaking 6; Language 1, 2, 3.

For use with Literature 9

Name ______________________ Date ______________ Assignment ______________

Performance Task 8b

Speaking and Listening 5 Include multimedia components and visual displays in presentations to clarify claims and findings and emphasize salient points.

Task: Bring to Life a Period of History

Use multimedia components in a presentation in which you bring to life a historical period that has been explored in fictional narratives and in historical texts. Use media to illustrate and emphasize the main points you make.

Tips for Success

Integrate multimedia into a presentation about a historical time and place. Follow these tips for success:

- ✓ write a script to follow as you present details about your chosen historical period
- ✓ gather photos or video footage of the historical time period
- ✓ find reproductions of arts and crafts from the historical setting
- ✓ read aloud a passage from a fictional text that takes place in that time period
- ✓ find recordings of music from the time period

Rubric for Self-Assessment

Criteria for Discussion	not very					very
How clearly did you present details about the time period?	1	2	3	4	5	6
How effectively did you integrate media into your presentation?	1	2	3	4	5	6
How effective was your reading of the fictional text that takes place in that time period?	1	2	3	4	5	6
How well did the music you chose reflect the time period?	1	2	3	4	5	6

For use with Speaking and Listening 5

Name ______________________ Date ______________ Assignment ________________

Performance Task 9a

Literature 10 By the end of the year, read and comprehend literature, including stories, dramas, and poems, in the grades 6–8 text complexity band proficiently, with scaffolding as needed at the high end of the range.*

Task: Read and Comprehend Literature

Read a text of your choice and write an essay in which you analyze how the author reveals the theme or central idea of the text.

Tips for Success

Read a drama of your choice and present a response to it. In your response, include these elements:

✓ a thesis statement in which you identify the text's main theme or central idea

✓ a brief, objective summary of the text

✓ an analysis of how the theme or central idea is developed over the course of the text

✓ evidence from the text that supports your analysis

✓ language that is formal, precise, and follows the rules of standard English

Rubric for Self-Assessment

Criteria for Success	not very					very
How clear is your thesis statement?	1	2	3	4	5	6
How thorough is your analysis of the theme or central idea of the text?	1	2	3	4	5	6
How well have you explained ways in which the theme or central idea is developed?	1	2	3	4	5	6
How well do you support your analysis with evidence from the text?	1	2	3	4	5	6
How well do you succeed in using a formal style and appropriate tone for your audience?	1	2	3	4	5	6

* Other standards covered include: Writing 4, 9a; Speaking 6; Language 1, 2, 3.

Name _______________ Date _______________ Assignment _______________

Performance Task 9b

Speaking and Listening 4 Present claims and findings, emphasizing salient points in a focused, coherent manner with pertinent descriptions, facts, details, and examples; use appropriate eye contact, adequate volume, and clear pronunciation.

Task: Present Claims About a Drama

Give an oral presentation in which you describe the theme or central idea of a text. Following your presentation, invite questions and comments from your audience.

Tips for Success

Give an oral presentation explaining the theme or central idea of a text. Follow these tips for success:

- ✓ give a clear statement of the theme or central idea
- ✓ provide a focused analysis of how the author develops the theme or central idea over the course of the text
- ✓ emphasize facts, details, and examples from the text that support your analysis
- ✓ make appropriate eye contact with your audience
- ✓ speak with adequate volume and clear pronunciation
- ✓ provide an opportunity for your audience to ask questions and make comments
- ✓ give thoughtful, relevant replies to comments

Rubric for Self-Assessment

Criteria for Discussion	not very					very
How clearly did you state the theme or central idea of the text?	1	2	3	4	5	6
How logically did you trace the development of the theme or central idea?	1	2	3	4	5	6
How convincing were the facts, details, and examples you used to support your analysis?	1	2	3	4	5	6
How effective was your use of eye contact and vocal techniques in engaging the interest of your audience?	1	2	3	4	5	6
How relevant were your replies to audience questions and comments?	1	2	3	4	5	6

Name ______________________ Date ____________ Assignment ______________

Performance Task 10a

Informational Text 1 Cite several pieces of textual evidence to support analysis of what the text says explicitly as well as inferences drawn from the text.*

Task: Support an Analysis of a News Article

Write an essay in which you cite textual evidence to support your analysis of an informational text. Explain both what the text says explicitly and any inferences and generalizations you have drawn from it.

Tips for Success

Present a response to an informational text you have read. In your response, include these elements:

✓ a statement of the text's main idea

✓ an analysis of what the text states explicitly

✓ an exploration of inferences you made while reading

✓ evidence from the text of the explicitly stated details

✓ evidence from the text that supports your inferences and generalizations

✓ language that is formal, precise, and follows the rules of standard English

Rubric for Self-Assessment

Criteria for Success	not very					very
How clear is your statement of the text's main idea?	1	2	3	4	5	6
How detailed is your analysis of the text?	1	2	3	4	5	6
How well have you supported your analysis with explicit evidence from the text?	1	2	3	4	5	6
How clearly have you explained the inferences and generalizations you drew from reading the text?	1	2	3	4	5	6
How well have you supported your inferences and generalizations with evidence from the text?	1	2	3	4	5	6
How well have you succeeded in using a formal style and appropriate tone for your audience?	1	2	3	4	5	6

*Other standards covered include: Writing 4, 9a; Language 1, 2, 3.

Name ______________________ Date ______________ Assignment ______________

Performance Task 10b

Speaking and Listening 1 Engage effectively in a range of collaborative discussions with diverse partners on grade 7 topics, texts, and issues, building on others' ideas and expressing your own clearly.

Task: Discuss an Informational Text

Participate in a discussion with a partner in which you analyze the content of an informational text and respond to and build on your partner's ideas.

Tips for Success

Participate in a discussion about the content of an informational text. Follow these tips for success:

- ✓ prepare by reading the text and taking notes on the ideas it expresses, both explicit and unstated
- ✓ with your partner, develop discussion guidelines and assign individual roles in the discussion
- ✓ share your analysis of the text, and cite information that supports your analysis
- ✓ ask questions that encourage your partner to elaborate on his or her analysis of the article
- ✓ listen closely to your partner's questions and comments, and build on them in your response

Rubric for Self-Assessment

Criteria for Discussion	not very					very
How thorough was your preparation for the discussion of the text?	1	2	3	4	5	6
How effectively did you present your analysis of the text?	1	2	3	4	5	6
How convincing was the evidence that supported your ideas?	1	2	3	4	5	6
How effective were your questions in helping you and your partner explore the text and its key ideas?	1	2	3	4	5	6
To what extent were you able to build on your partner's comments in your response?	1	2	3	4	5	6

Name ______________________ Date ____________ Assignment ______________

Performance Task 11a

Informational Text 2 Determine two or more central ideas in a text and analyze their development over the course of the text; provide an objective summary of the text.*

Task: Determine the Central Idea of an Essay

Write an essay in which you first summarize objectively an essay. Then identify two central ideas in the essay that are connected. Show how they are connected and analyze how they work together to help readers understand the main idea of the essay. List at least two key details to support each central idea.

Tips for Success

Present a response to an essay you have read. In your response, include these elements:

- ✓ an objective summary of the essay
- ✓ a statement of two central ideas in the essay that are connected
- ✓ an analysis of how those central ideas work together to reveal the main idea of the essay
- ✓ an identification of at least two key details that support each central idea you have identified
- ✓ language that is formal, precise, and follows the rules of standard English

Rubric for Self-Assessment

Criteria for Success	not very					very
How well have you summarized the essay?	1	2	3	4	5	6
How accurately have you identified two central ideas that are connected?	1	2	3	4	5	6
How effectively have you analyzed how those central ideas work together to reveal the main idea?	1	2	3	4	5	6
How accurately have you identified the essay's main idea?	1	2	3	4	5	6
How accurately have you identified key details?	1	2	3	4	5	6
How clearly have you explained the key details' connection to their central ideas?	1	2	3	4	5	6
How successful is your use of standard English?	1	2	3	4	5	6
How well have you succeeded in using a formal style and appropriate tone for your audience?	1	2	3	4	5	6

* Other standards covered include Writing 9b; Language 1, 2, 3.

Name ______________________ Date ____________ Assignment ______________

Performance Task 11b

Speaking and Listening 4 Present claims and findings, emphasizing salient points in a focused, coherent manner with pertinent descriptions, facts, details, and examples; use appropriate eye contact, adequate volume, and clear pronunciation.

Task: Present Claims About an Essay

Give a presentation in which you describe two central ideas in an essay you have read, explaining how they connect to show the main idea of the essay. In your presentation, emphasize points in a coherent manner, and provide facts, details, and examples. Be sure to use appropriate eye contact, adequate volume, and clear pronunciation.

Tips for Success

As part of your presentation, include these elements:

- ✓ a large chart (readable from a distance) showing how the two central ideas, their supporting details, and the main idea of the essay are connected
- ✓ logically sequenced explanations of the connection between the central ideas and how that connection helps readers understand the main idea of the essay
- ✓ explanations of how details support the central ideas
- ✓ descriptions, facts, and details that support your ideas
- ✓ adequate volume, varied tone of voice, and accurate pronunciation
- ✓ polite, informative responses to questions from your listeners

Rubric for Self-Assessment

Criteria for Discussion	not very					very
How informative and readable was your chart?	1	2	3	4	5	6
How clearly and logically did you explain the connection between the central ideas?	1	2	3	4	5	6
How clearly and logically did you explain the way in which key details support the central ideas you are analyzing?	1	2	3	4	5	6
How well did you provide facts and details to support your ideas?	1	2	3	4	5	6
How well did you succeed in speaking clearly and loudly enough for your listeners to understand you?	1	2	3	4	5	6
How accurate was your pronunciation of words?	1	2	3	4	5	6
How polite and useful were your responses to questions?	1	2	3	4	5	6

Name ______________________ Date ______________ Assignment ________________

Performance Task 12a

Informational Text 3 Analyze the interactions between individuals, events, and ideas in a text (e.g., how ideas influence individuals or events, or how individuals influence ideas or events).*

Task: Analyze the Interactions Among People, Events, and Ideas

Write an analysis of the interactions among individuals, events, and ideas in an informational text. Explain how the subject of a biography, autobiography, or memoir was influenced by the ideas and events of the time and place. Explain also the effects he or she had on the events and ideas of society.

Tips for Success

In your analysis of the interactions among individuals, events, and ideas, include these elements:

- ✓ a brief description of the person (birth and death dates, places of residence, accomplishments, beliefs)
- ✓ an analysis of society's influence on the person, in terms of both the events and the ideas that influenced him or her
- ✓ an analysis of the person's effect on society, including the ideas the person spread and the events he or she affected
- ✓ an evaluation of how well the author showed how the person, events, and ideas interact
- ✓ language that is formal, precise, and follows the rules of standard English

Rubric for Self-Assessment

Criteria for Success	not very					very
How clearly have you described the subject of the biography, autobiography, or memoir?	1	2	3	4	5	6
How well have you analyzed society's influence on the person?	1	2	3	4	5	6
How thoroughly have you analyzed the person's effect on society?	1	2	3	4	5	6
How thoughtfully have you evaluated the author's success at showing the interactions among the person, events, and ideas?	1	2	3	4	5	6
How successful is your use of standard English?	1	2	3	4	5	6
How well have you succeeded in using a formal style and appropriate tone for your audience?	1	2	3	4	5	6

* Other standards covered include: Writing 4, 9b; Speaking 4; Language 3.

Name ______________________ Date ____________ Assignment ______________

Performance Task 12b

Speaking and Listening 5 Include multimedia components and visual displays in presentations to clarify claims and findings and emphasize salient points.

Task: Use Multimedia Components in a Presentation

Use multimedia components in a presentation about a biography, autobiography, or memoir you have read. In your presentation, analyze both how the subject affects events and ideas and also how events and ideas affect him or her.

Tips for Success

Make a multimedia presentation about the subject of a biography, autobiography, or memoir. As part of your presentation, include these elements:

- ✓ photos (or art) or video clips of the person
- ✓ photos (or art) or video clips of events that influenced or were influenced by the person
- ✓ several memorable quotes from the person, blown up to large type on posterboard or banners
- ✓ a live presentation in which you analyze how the subject interacted with events and ideas and evaluate how well the author showed that interaction
- ✓ a chart showing graphically how the subject influenced and was influenced by events and ideas
- ✓ music that evokes the same emotions as the photos or clips
- ✓ language that is formal, precise, and follows the rules of standard English

Rubric for Self-Assessment

Criteria for Discussion	not very					very
How well did the images represent the subject?	1	2	3	4	5	6
How effectively did the audio and video clips bring the person to life?	1	2	3	4	5	6
How much did the quotes add to your audience's understanding of the person?	1	2	3	4	5	6
How informative was your analysis of how the person interacted with events and ideas?	1	2	3	4	5	6
How effectively did the graphic show the interactions of the person, events, and ideas?	1	2	3	4	5	6
How well did the music reflect the emotions of the subject?	1	2	3	4	5	6

Name ______________________ Date ____________ Assignment ________________

Performance Task 13a

Informational Text 4 Determine the meanings of words and phrases as they are used in a text, including figurative, connotative, and technical meanings; analyze the impact of a specific word choice on meaning and tone.*

Task: Analyze Connotations and Technical Terms

Write an essay in which you explain the connotative and technical meanings of certain words and phrases and analyze their impact on the meaning and tone of a science article.

Tips for Success

Present an essay in which you analyze the meanings and impacts of word choices in a science article you have read. In your essay, include these elements:

- ✓ definitions of the connotative meanings of at least two words or phrases, adding a judgment on whether the connotations are positive, negative, or neutral
- ✓ definitions of the technical or specialized meanings of at least two terms in the article
- ✓ an analysis, using evidence from the text, of the impact of these word choices on the article's meaning and tone
- ✓ language that is formal, precise, and follows the rules of standard English

Rubric for Self-Assessment

Criteria for Success	not very					very
How well do the connotative words or phrases you chose lend themselves to analysis?	1	2	3	4	5	6
How clearly have you defined the connotations of the terms?	1	2	3	4	5	6
How clearly have you defined the technical meanings of the terms?	1	2	3	4	5	6
How well have you explained the impact of the words you chose to analyze on the article's meaning and tone?	1	2	3	4	5	6
How well do you support your analysis with evidence from the article?	1	2	3	4	5	6
How well do you succeed in using a formal style, appropriate tone for your audience, and standard English?	1	2	3	4	5	6

* Other standards covered include: Writing 2e, 4, 9b; Language 3, 5a, 5c.

Name ______________________ Date ______________ Assignment ______________

Performance Task 13b

Speaking and Listening 1 Engage effectively in a range of collaborative group discussions (one-on-one, in groups, and teacher-led) with diverse partners on *grade 7 topics, texts, and issues,* building on others' ideas and expressing their own clearly.

Task: Discuss How Connotations and Technical Terms Affect Meaning and Tone

Participate in a teacher-led discussion in which you and several classmates define selected connotative and technical terms in a science article and explain how those word choices affect the article's meaning and tone.

Tips for Success

Use this checklist to prepare for the discussion:

✓ read the article and identify connotations and technical terms

✓ develop guidelines with members of the group for goals and individual roles

✓ share your opinions regarding the definitions of terms and how those word choices affect the article's meaning and tone

✓ pose questions that encourage group members to elaborate on their opinions

✓ respond to others' questions and comments

Rubric for Self-Assessment

Criteria for Discussion	not very					very
How successful were you at identifying connotations and technical terms in the article?	1	2	3	4	5	6
How thoroughly had you thought through your responses to the text before the discussion?	1	2	3	4	5	6
How effective were the group's guidelines for the discussion?	1	2	3	4	5	6
How clearly and accurately did you define connotations and technical terms in the article?	1	2	3	4	5	6
How effectively did you present your analysis of the impact of connotations and technical word choices on the article's meaning and tone?	1	2	3	4	5	6
How effective were your questions in helping the group explore the article and its meaning?	1	2	3	4	5	6

For use with Speaking and Listening 1

Name ______________________ Date ____________ Assignment ______________

Performance Task 14a

Informational Text 5 Analyze the structure an author uses to organize a text, including how the major sections contribute to the whole and to the development of the ideas.*

Task: Analyze How a Section Fits into an Article

Write an essay in which you analyze how a particular section fits into the overall structure of an article that explains how to do something. Explain how the section contributes to the development of the ideas in the text.

Tips for Success

Write an essay analyzing how a section fits into the overall article you have read. In your essay, include these elements:

- ✓ an outline of the article showing all the section heads and subheads
- ✓ an analysis of how each section contributes to the development of the ideas in the article
- ✓ an analysis of how all of the sections work together to contribute to the article as a whole
- ✓ an evaluation of whether the article as a whole flows logically and is effective
- ✓ evidence from the text that supports your analysis
- ✓ language that is formal, precise, and follows the rules of standard English

Rubric for Self-Assessment

Criteria for Success	not very					very
How accurately and thoroughly have you outlined the article?	1	2	3	4	5	6
How clearly have you analyzed the way in which each section contributes to the development of ideas?	1	2	3	4	5	6
How well does your analysis explain how all of the sections work together?	1	2	3	4	5	6
How convincingly have you evaluated whether the article flows logically and is effective?	1	2	3	4	5	6
How well do you support your analysis with explicit evidence from the article?	1	2	3	4	5	6
How successful is your use of standard English?	1	2	3	4	5	6
How well have you succeeded in using a formal style and appropriate tone for your audience?	1	2	3	4	5	6

* Other standards covered include: Writing 4, 9b; Speaking 6; Language 3.

Name ______________________ Date ____________ Assignment ______________

Performance Task 14b

Speaking and Listening 4 Present claims and findings, emphasizing salient points in a focused, coherent manner with pertinent descriptions, facts, details, and examples; use appropriate eye contact, adequate volume, and clear pronunciation.

Task: Present the Findings from an Article

Give a presentation in which you explain the outline and findings from an article. In the presentation, analyze how all the sections work together, and evaluate whether the organization is effective. Be sure to give salient facts in a focused, coherent manner, with pertinent descriptions, facts, details, and examples. Use appropriate delivery, including eye contact, adequate volume, and clear pronunciation.

Tips for Success

As part of your presentation, include these elements:

- ✓ a large chart (readable from a distance) showing the outline of the article's heads and subheads
- ✓ a logically sequenced analysis of how all the sections work together to contribute to the development of the article's ideas
- ✓ an evaluation of whether the article flows logically and is effective
- ✓ descriptions, facts, and details from the article that support your ideas
- ✓ adequate volume, varied tones of voice, and clear pronunciation
- ✓ appropriate eye contact and varied body language

Rubric for Self-Assessment

Criteria for Discussion	not very					very
How accurate, readable, and useful was your chart?	1	2	3	4	5	6
How logical was your analysis of how all the sections of the article work together?	1	2	3	4	5	6
How coherent was your evaluation of the article's flow and effectiveness?	1	2	3	4	5	6
How successfully did you support your analysis and evaluation with evidence from the essay?	1	2	3	4	5	6
How well did you succeed in speaking clearly and loudly enough for your listeners to follow you?	1	2	3	4	5	6
How effectively did you use eye contact and body language and maintain adequate volume?	1	2	3	4	5	6

Name ______________________ Date ____________ Assignment ________________

Performance Task 15a

Informational Text 6 Determine an author's point of view or purpose in a text and analyze how the author distinguishes his or her position from those of others.*

Task: Determine an Author's Point of View

Write an essay in which you identify the point of view of the author of a persuasive essay and analyze how the author shows the differences between his or her viewpoint and that of other people. Then evaluate how effectively the author presents and answers counterarguments. Cite evidence in the essay to support your analysis.

Tips for Success

Write a persuasive essay explaining the author's point of view and how it is distinguished from those of others. In your essay, include these elements:

- ✓ a brief definition of what forms an author's point of view
- ✓ an identification of the author's point of view in the persuasive essay
- ✓ an analysis of how the author shows the differences between his or her viewpoint and that of at least one other person
- ✓ an evaluation of how effectively the author answers counterarguments from people with opposing viewpoints
- ✓ evidence from the text that supports your opinions
- ✓ language that is formal, precise, and follows the rules of standard English

Rubric for Self-Assessment

Criteria for Success	not very					very
How well have you defined what forms an author's viewpoint?	1	2	3	4	5	6
How accurately have you identified the author's viewpoint?	1	2	3	4	5	6
How clear is your analysis of how the author shows the differences between his or her viewpoint and other people's?	1	2	3	4	5	6
How usefully do you evaluate how effectively the author answers counterarguments from people with opposing viewpoints?	1	2	3	4	5	6
How well do you support your analysis with text evidence?	1	2	3	4	5	6
How well do you succeed in using a formal style, appropriate tone for your audience, and standard English?	1	2	3	4	5	6

* Other standards covered include: Writing 4, 9b; Speaking 4; Language 1, 2.

Name ______________________ Date ______________ Assignment ________________

Performance Task 15b

Speaking and Listening 5 Include multimedia components and visual displays in presentations to clarify claims and findings and emphasize salient points.

Task: Use Multimedia in Analyzing Author's Viewpoint

Use multimedia in a presentation about a persuasive essay you have read in which you analyze how the author shows the differences between his or her viewpoint and those of other people. Then evaluate how effectively the author answers counterarguments.

Tips for Success

Develop a multimedia presentation about a persuasive essay. As part of your presentation, include these elements:

- ✓ charts (readable at a distance) that highlight parts of the essay in different colors (for example, blue for the thesis statement, green for evidence, red for counterarguments)
- ✓ video or audio of you reading the essay aloud, varying your volume to persuade
- ✓ video or audio of you analyzing how the author distinguishes viewpoints and whether he or she answers counterarguments effectively
- ✓ sketches or photos that illustrate the subject of the essay and the author's viewpoint
- ✓ soundtrack that peaks at emotional, persuasive passages
- ✓ question-and-answer session

Rubric for Self-Assessment

Criteria for Discussion	not very					very
How readable were the charts, and how well did they help reveal the parts of the essay?	1	2	3	4	5	6
How persuasive was the video of you reading the essay?	1	2	3	4	5	6
How informative was the video of you analyzing the viewpoints and answers to counterarguments?	1	2	3	4	5	6
How effective was your evidence from the essay to support your analysis?	1	2	3	4	5	6
How well did the images illustrate the essay's subject and the author's viewpoint?	1	2	3	4	5	6
How much did the soundtrack enhance the essay's persuasiveness?	1	2	3	4	5	6

Name ______________________ Date ____________ Assignment ______________

Performance Task 16a

Informational Text 7 Compare and contrast a text to an audio, video, or multimedia version of the text, analyzing each medium's portrayal of the subject (e.g., how the delivery of a speech affects the impact of the words).*

Task: Compare and Contrast Versions of a Speech

Write an essay in which you compare and contrast the text and video versions of a speech.

Tips for Success

Write an essay in which you compare and contrast the text and video versions of a speech you have heard and read. In your essay, include these elements:

✓ an analysis of the qualities that interesting or moving words or phrases give to the written text

✓ a description of the speaker's style and your reaction to it

✓ an analysis of how the speaker's treatment of the words you discussed (for example, pauses, increased volume, hand gestures) affected your impression of the content

✓ an analysis of your reactions to the speech as you read it and as you heard it

✓ language that is formal, precise, and follows the rules of standard English

Rubric for Self-Assessment

Criteria for Success	not very					very
How successfully have you analyzed the effect of words or phrases you found interesting or moving from the written text?	1	2	3	4	5	6
How well do you describe the speaker's style and your reaction to it?	1	2	3	4	5	6
How effectively have you analyzed the speaker's treatment of the words that most affected your impression of the content?	1	2	3	4	5	6
How thoroughly have you analyzed your reactions to the written and spoken speech?	1	2	3	4	5	6
How well have you used a formal style, appropriate tone for your audience, and standard English?	1	2	3	4	5	6

* Other standards covered include Writing 4, 9b; Speaking 1, 4, 5; Language 1, 3.

Name ______________ Date ______________ Assignment ______________

Performance Task 16b

Speaking and Listening 2 Analyze the main ideas and supporting details presented in diverse media or formats (e.g., visually, quantitatively, orally) and explain how the ideas clarify a topic, text, or issue under study.

Task: Deliver and Analyze Persuasive Speeches

Take turns with several classmates to deliver persuasive speeches, using visual aids, on topics of your choice. Take notes on each speech and discuss them in a small group.

Tips for Success

As part of your presentation and participation in the discussion, include these elements:

- ✓ make sure your speech has a clear main idea and details that support it
- ✓ accompany your speech with photos, video, charts, or other visuals
- ✓ take notes on your group members' speeches
- ✓ discuss the main idea of each persuasive speech with the other speakers
- ✓ discuss how well each speech's visual aids support its main idea
- ✓ analyze how visuals helped speakers relate their points
- ✓ share your opinions regarding how key details support the message
- ✓ respond to others' questions and comments with relevant points

Rubric for Self-Assessment

Criteria for Discussion	not very					very
How clear were your speech's main idea and supporting details?	1	2	3	4	5	6
How effective were your visual aids?	1	2	3	4	5	6
How useful were your notes on group members' speeches?	1	2	3	4	5	6
How fruitful was the discussion of all the speeches' main ideas?	1	2	3	4	5	6
How fruitful was the discussion of how well the speeches' visual aids supported their main ideas?	1	2	3	4	5	6
How insightful was the analysis of how visuals helped speakers relate their points?	1	2	3	4	5	6
How productively did you share your opinions regarding how key details support the message?	1	2	3	4	5	6
How relevant were your responses to others' questions and comments?	1	2	3	4	5	6

Name _______________ Date _______________ Assignment _______________

Performance Task 17a

Informational Text 8 Trace and evaluate the argument and specific claims in a text, assessing whether the reasoning is sound and the evidence is relevant and sufficient to support the claims.*

Task: Assess the Claims in a Persuasive Essay

Write an essay in which you assess the quality of the claims in a persuasive essay.

Tips for Success

Write an essay in which you evaluate the argument and claims in a persuasive essay you have read. In your essay, include these elements:

- ✓ a description of the essay's argument and claims
- ✓ an analysis of which evidence to support claims is relevant and which is not
- ✓ an analysis of whether there is enough evidence for each claim
- ✓ an evaluation of which claims are persuasive, based on the relevance and quantity of their evidence
- ✓ language that is formal, precise, and follows the rules of standard English

Rubric for Self-Assessment

Criteria for Success	not very					very
How clearly do you describe the essay's argument and claims?	1	2	3	4	5	6
How effectively have you analyzed which evidence supporting claims is relevant and which is not?	1	2	3	4	5	6
How effectively have you analyzed whether there is enough evidence for each claim?	1	2	3	4	5	6
How thoroughly do you evaluate which claims are persuasive?	1	2	3	4	5	6
How successfully do you use standard English?	1	2	3	4	5	6
How successfully do you use a formal style and appropriate tone for your audience?	1	2	3	4	5	6

* Other standards covered include Writing 4, 9b; Speaking 4; Language 1, 3.

Name ____________________ Date ______________ Assignment ______________

Performance Task 17b

Speaking and Listening 3 Delineate a speaker's argument and specific claims, evaluating the soundness of the reasoning and the relevance and sufficiency of the evidence.

Task: Evaluate the Claims of a Politician

With a partner, take turns role-playing a politician trying to persuade the city council to take some action. Then summarize your partner's argument and specific claims, evaluating how well each claim is supported.

Tips for Success

Take turns delivering a political speech and evaluating your partner's speech. As part of your participation, include these elements:

- ✓ provide strong evidence for the claims in your speech
- ✓ take notes on your partner's argument and specific claims
- ✓ analyze how sound the reasoning supporting your partner's argument is
- ✓ identify which evidence supporting claims is relevant
- ✓ identify which claims do not have enough evidence and which evidence could be verified
- ✓ evaluate which evidence logically supports your partner's conclusions

Rubric for Self-Assessment

Criteria for Discussion	not very					very
How strong was the evidence for the claims in your speech?	1	2	3	4	5	6
How useful were your notes on your partner's speech?	1	2	3	4	5	6
How effectively did you analyze the soundness of the reasoning supporting your partner's argument?	1	2	3	4	5	6
How accurately did you identify which evidence was relevant and supported your partner's claims?	1	2	3	4	5	6
How accurately did you identify which claims did not have enough evidence and which evidence could be verified?	1	2	3	4	5	6
How convincing was your evaluation of which evidence logically supports your partner's conclusions?	1	2	3	4	5	6

Name ______________________ Date ____________ Assignment ______________

Performance Task 18a

Informational Text 9 Analyze how two or more authors writing about the same topic shape their presentations of key information by emphasizing different evidence or advancing different interpretations of facts.*

Task: Analyze How Authors Shape the Same Information Differently

Write an essay in which you analyze how two authors writing editorials about the same topic shape different presentations of key information.

Tips for Success

In your essay, include these elements:

- ✓ summaries of both authors' arguments and claims
- ✓ an analysis of similar facts with different interpretations
- ✓ an analysis of where the editorials focus on different facts and why
- ✓ an analysis of whether two editorials present conflicting information and, if so, which is stronger
- ✓ evidence from both texts that supports your findings
- ✓ language that is formal, precise, and follows the rules of standard English

Rubric for Self-Assessment

Criteria for Success	not very					very
How clearly do you summarize both authors' arguments and claims?	1	2	3	4	5	6
How insightful is your analysis of places where the two editorials cite similar facts but interpret them differently?	1	2	3	4	5	6
How insightful is your analysis of places where the two editorials cite different facts and why?	1	2	3	4	5	6
How insightful is your analysis of whether the two editorials present conflicting information, and if so, which is stronger?	1	2	3	4	5	6
How well do you support your analysis with details from both editorials?	1	2	3	4	5	6
How successfully do you use standard English?	1	2	3	4	5	6
How well do you use a formal style and appropriate tone?	1	2	3	4	5	6

* Other standards covered include Writing 4, 9b; Language 1, 2, 3.

Name ______________________ Date ____________ Assignment ______________

Performance Task 18b

Speaking and Listening 4 Present claims and findings, emphasizing salient points in a focused, coherent manner with pertinent descriptions, facts, details, and examples; use appropriate eye contact, adequate volume, and clear pronunciation.

Task: Present Claims Comparing Two Editorials

Give a presentation about the similarities and differences between two editorials on the same topic.

Tips for Success

As part of your presentation, include these elements:

- ✓ logically sequenced summaries of both editorials' arguments and claims
- ✓ an analysis of similar facts with different interpretations
- ✓ an analysis of any conflicting information in the two editorials
- ✓ descriptions, facts, and details that support your ideas
- ✓ adequate volume, good pacing, and clear pronunciation
- ✓ appropriate eye contact and varied body language
- ✓ polite, informative responses to questions from your listeners

Rubric for Self-Assessment

Criteria for Discussion	not very					very
How clearly and logically did you summarize the editorials' arguments and claims?	1	2	3	4	5	6
How clearly and logically did you analyze similar facts the two editorials interpret differently?	1	2	3	4	5	6
How clearly and logically did you analyze any conflicting information in the two editorials?	1	2	3	4	5	6
How effectively did you present descriptions, facts, and details to support your ideas?	1	2	3	4	5	6
How well did you achieve adequate volume, good pacing, and clear pronunciation in your talk?	1	2	3	4	5	6
How effectively did you use eye contact and body language?	1	2	3	4	5	6
How polite and informative were your responses to questions?	1	2	3	4	5	6

Name ______________________ Date ______________ Assignment ______________

Performance Task 19a

Informational Text 10 By the end of the year, read and comprehend literary nonfiction in the grades 6-8 text complexity band proficiently, with scaffolding as needed at the high end of the range.*

Task: Read and Contrast Two History Books

Read two books about the same historical event or period and analyze how the authors emphasize different evidence or advance different interpretations of facts.

Tips for Success

In your essay, include these elements:

- ✓ summaries of both authors' versions of an event
- ✓ an analysis of how the two books focus on different facts
- ✓ an analysis of the two books' different interpretations of similar facts
- ✓ an analysis of any conflicting information in the two books
- ✓ an evaluation of which book's version is more convincing
- ✓ evidence from both books that supports your findings
- ✓ language that is formal, precise, and follows the rules of standard English

Rubric for Self-Assessment

Criteria for Success	not very					very
How clearly do you summarize both authors' versions of an event?	1	2	3	4	5	6
How insightful is your analysis of the way the two books focused on different facts?	1	2	3	4	5	6
How insightful is your analysis of the books' different interpretations of similar facts?	1	2	3	4	5	6
How insightful is your analysis of any conflicting information in the two books?	1	2	3	4	5	6
How helpful is your evaluation of which book's version of the event is more convincing?	1	2	3	4	5	6
How well do you support your analysis with details from both books?	1	2	3	4	5	6
How successfully do you use standard English?	1	2	3	4	5	6

* Other standards covered include Writing 4, 9b; Speaking 4; Language 1, 2, 3.

Name ______________________ Date ____________ Assignment ______________

Performance Task 19b

Speaking and Listening 5 Include multimedia components and visual displays in presentations to clarify claims and findings and emphasize salient points.

Task: Use Multimedia Components in a Presentation

Use multimedia components in a presentation about two history books in which you analyze how the authors emphasize different evidence, advance different interpretations of facts, or present conflicting facts.

Tips for Success

Make a multimedia presentation about two history books you have read. As part of your presentation, include these elements:

✓ photos or art from the books showing the event you are analyzing

✓ video clips of the event, if possible

✓ a talk in which you read aloud a passage from each book that presents the same event differently

✓ an analysis of the two books' focus on different facts, different interpretations of similar facts, and conflicting facts

✓ key statements from both books, blown up to large type, on poster board or banners

✓ music that evokes the same emotions as the event

Rubric for Self-Assessment

Criteria for Discussion	not very					very
How well did the images represent the event?	1	2	3	4	5	6
How effectively did the video clips bring the event to life?	1	2	3	4	5	6
How effectively did you read the two passages aloud?	1	2	3	4	5	6
How informative was your analysis of how differently the books treated the event?	1	2	3	4	5	6
How much did the enlarged statements from the books add to your presentation?	1	2	3	4	5	6
How well did the music reflect the emotions of the event being discussed?	1	2	3	4	5	6